DO I NEED TO??
IN LOVE

DO I NEED TO?? IN LOVE

V. Raghupathy

KALPAZ

ISBN: 978-81-7835-995-3
Price: ₹ 299

First Published 2013

Published by

Kalpaz Publications
C-30, Satyawati Nagar,
Delhi - 110052
E-mail: kalpaz@hotmail.com Ph.: 9212142040

Laser Typesetting : Rajender Vashist, Delhi
Printed at: G. Print Process, Delhi

Cataloging in Publication Data--DK
Courtesy: D.K. Agencies (P) Ltd. <docinfo@dkagencies.com>

Raghupathy, V.
Do I need to?? in love / V. Raghupathy.
p. cm.
Novel.
ISBN 9788178359953

1. Indic fiction (English). I. Title.

DDC 823.92 23

Contents

Contents

Acknowledgements

The vague ideas made a regular visit to my head, but the trigger to capture the ideas and bring them in a literary work, called "Do I need to?? In Love" is attributable to a world of ordinary yet great people. The greatness which I sensed is not even known to them. Hereby, my innate self takes this opportunity to thank them.

I thank my brother, Ravi Chandran who has unknowingly passed on his sense of humour through the days we grew up.

I thank my wife Ayushi, who has not only given me strength and drive to find time and write incessantly after office hours, but has also lent her creativity by giving life to the book through her sketches and cover page design.

This work would not have been possible without the guidance of my publishers, Kalpaz Publications, the team of editors and production manager.

I also thank my friends who have guided me from time to time by being absolutely critical about the book. To name a few, Ruby Ritolia, Roopa Kubasad, Kuriachen Pathrose, Dhaval Jagad, Vishwanath Kubasad, Tarun Kapoor, Rakesh Makkar, Rahul Koundal, Induja Rajagopalan, Subhashish Bhattacharya, Debashish Bhattacharya, Raghavendra Kukatla, Aman Gupta, Govind Shanbogue, Suresh Warrier, Ankit Dave, Puneet Arora, Devesh Jerath, Neera Gadgill, Vipin Sharda, Aishwarya Gupta, Mario Fernandes, Ishaan Gaunker, Amol Lanke, Dr Dayanand Rao. They all have contributed in one way or the other, be it big or small; the contributions have been as defining as they could be.

A special thanks to my sister in law, Lakshmi.She has not only encouraged me, but handled my family as well, who stood with me while I wrote.Thank you Amma and Appa!

Acknowledgements

There are many who fail in love.....

More are those who are failed...........

In a world that is ruled predominantly by forces of power, lust, money, ambitions and changing colours, is a boy who wants to cut through all of them and live by an ideology of his own. The idea of living life on his terms gets hit severely when he finds love in the girl whose ideology dissects that of the guy, which unleashes a series of passion, drama, sex, betrayal, chaos and cry but with the ultimate victory of "THE RIGHT." The two players in any relationship have to be like the matching blocks of a puzzle fitting naturally, any effort to tamper them to match or mismatch leaves behind a catastrophe that can dent the following future. The guy is Rama and the girl is Smitha!

The story of Rama and Smitha begins with the most awkward way, when a drunken Rama, who is far away from class and sophistication, takes his entire class of MBA by surprise by solving a complex numerical on the board. That manages to arouse Smitha's interest in the guy, whom she otherwise thought to be of zero use.

The zero use ideology gets transformed into a CEO outlook, which forces Rama towards his downfall ravishingly. However, have you ever seen a CEO working like a peon? If no, then please pad up to witness the fate of a hapless CEO who has a lady boss (Smitha). Once the lady boss ensures that CEO is reduced to a peon with no alternative, he is made to swear that the lady would always remain the apple of his eye, he would tolerate all her tantrums and would never complain, and if ever he did so, he would be reprimanded for a fortnight to harm himself and the result, not surprisingly would be a defamed mark sheet.

Now, this peon hero falsely dreams that his love for Smitha is tremendously strong that no force will ever be able to do them apart. But does it happen that way? There is no love without hiccups, and if you thought it was, either you were never in love or you were a stamped idiot!

Hiccups; Love is only the romance of the employed, forget about loving a girl, an unemployed man will attract heavy duties, taxes and penalties for even looking at the girl, but our hero has a narrow escape from such headaches as he manages to land into a job after his mind weakening struggle. And did a job seal everything for them? Get ready to be introduced to the variables which can be pivotal to break or make your marriage. But Rama's case was the neither of the two, he believed in hanging in the middle.

Hang why? Because, he hit Smitha. Hit Smitha why? Because, Smitha spoke shit about his mother? Spoke shit why? Because, Rama questioned Smitha's character? Question why? Because, he was simply a proven idiot. But does that legalize stepping on Rama's breathing pipe?

In fact, Mr. Idiot had sworn by his head that how so ever he is hanged; he would continue to hang instead of snapping the rope. They dumped Christianity on him, and he was fine. They commanded separation from his parents, he was fine. They squeezed him to save 50 thousand every month, he was fine and before they coerced him further, he said fine for everything, put down an undertaking and said, "Now get us married at least."

Defeating all the shackles, clearing all the hindrances and winning every condition, Rama manages to convince his family and Smitha's family to strike a day of engagement, but, for all the ruthlessness god unleashed on the lovely couple, everything comes to a deadlock thus leaving the engagement cancelled, leaving both the lovers thirsty for each other's blood!

The failed engagement and subsequent abandoning by his family and Smitha marks the downfall of an already proven idiot boy, who was born to fly for the efforts he had put throughout his life to reach where he was. Albeit, he was labelled as a pure alcoholic, found himself in a neck deep debt and in the middle of a drug abuse which finally makes him land in a hospital for the case of excessive alcoholism.

The stint with the hospital acts as an eye opener for Rama, as his pitiful condition manages to melt his family who own him again. The reunion with the family reignites the old fizzled fire in Rama, who struggles to find his lost touch and glory by trying to bring his best out at work, accepting the challenges and eventually getting rewarded!

And just when Rama discovers himself to be completely out of Smitha's enigma, to his surprise, Smitha mends her way back into his life. The re-entry of Smitha will leave you awed as she showcases a different approach and attitude towards Rama; she even manages to convince her Mama to let her marry Rama. To summarize, it is all about human to human respect.

This brings a twist to the tale as one begins to question that what is so irresistible about the boy which draws the girl back to him. Is that his death like true commitment? Is that his god loved loyalty? Or is that Smitha's courage to break the hypocritical barriers developed by her Mama?

Read on to discover the bitter facts of love and hate affairs, the vultures those keep an eye on the prosperous lovers and what it takes to make and break a relationship in a country that boasts of a secular society where most of the people find themselves to be literate and not educated.

1
How it All Started

"Will you get converted?"..... Booom.... That was it; I did not know what to say as all I could feel was Smitha slipping out of my life. "Yes, I love her. Anything for her!! Take my word, I stand by her thick and thin", said a troubled me. Illogicality had struck me and I did not know what I had agreed for would change my life forever.

Mama (Smitha's mother) was happy and so was Smitha because she was going to spend her life with someone whom she had loved for almost a year now. "Eat *beta* eat", Mama said decisively as I just enjoyed the tunes I was dancing to. She served me some more mutton. I had told Smitha zillion times that I am not a born non-vegetarian, I can't eat rubber like meat, I was fine with chicken and I was sure her mother would have known this fact, but still, she made a deliberate attempt to cook mutton. Her serving and royal treatment continued.

I thought, "Is it a test I am undergoing to prove that I am a real Christian and I am absolutely comfortable in eating what all was available in my class nine biology book." I felt I was being treated like Sunny Deol by Amrish Puri in *Gadar* when he is being asked to shout *Hindustan Murdabad*. The only difference was that I could not react the way Sunny did. He could do that because he was already married to someone he loved and the stage was set. I was neither Sunny Deol, nor Smitha's home had a hand pump stationed which I could uproot to vent out my frustration.

All was fine with me because I loved Smitha like Smitha loved her Mama. She could do anything for her parents and I could do anything to keep Smitha happy. I suddenly became Mama's darling; hence, she did everything she could to make my stay as pleasant as possible. She asked Ranjan, Smitha's younger brother, to leave his king size bed for me to sleep.

"It is really cold in Delhi during winters, here is your quilt", pampered Mama. "Has she forgotten the fact that I stayed in Delhi for twenty two years", I thought. "Thank you Mama, good night." "Good night *beta*", she kissed my forehead. I looked for Smitha, because I wanted to give a return kiss to her. She was invisible as she was busy preparing Mama's bed. Mama left and I switched off the lights to sleep.

It was actually colder than what I found Delhi was during my twenty two years there. I was satisfied over the fact that I was able to win Mama's confidence which would make Smitha mine and no force would ever be able to wound the relationship. I felt proud of myself that I could take such a drastic step of getting converted (My name is Rama Chandran Iyer, I come from a Tamil Brahmin family) for someone I loved. I could not have given a better token of love to Smitha. I smiled at my future and my accepted wisdom said, "Sleep now".

My phone rang and I thought it was Smitha, who had sneaked out of her Mama's clutches and was standing at the door to give me a good night kiss. I looked at the phone to see "Amma calling" flashing on its screen. Amma is my mother and she is a jumbled "Mama."

"Hello, yeah tell me", I spoke half asleep even when I had not slept. Those were my Diwali vacations and I was supposedly going home but I chose to come to Delhi to meet Smitha's mother. I lied at home that we had just a day off at college and every day counted because of my short attendance due to all the time I had spent on interviews during placements.

"How are you doing? Why did you not call up the entire day? Why was your phone switched off? Why are you sleeping so early, its only eleven, you sleep by one right? Aren't you feeling well?" Amma had asked me five questions in one go and I was wondering which one to answer. "I am not feeling ok. Have a slight fever." I answered the first and the last. "I have taken Crocin, and was sleeping, is it ok if I call you up in the morning?" Amma was worried and said "Yeah sleep properly and take care. Poor you, could not even enjoy your Diwali." She hung up.

I felt irritated that I was on a lying spree. I had eaten mutton, not Crocin, I was not sleeping and I had no plans to call up Amma in the morning. "Why am I lying to Amma? I am not doing anything wrong. I love Smitha and if I have guts to come and face her Mama, then why not my parents?" I quizzed myself. "Fuck you", I said to myself and switched on the lights, all to rewind that what all has happened which was making me anti-parents.

It all started on June 2nd, 2006, the first lecture of my MBA first Semester. "Smitha Suzanne Swaminathan", called Mr. Saloria, the quantitative techniques professor. "Present sir", came a timid voice from the desk right in front of me. Everyone wanted to catch a glimpse of someone who had such a secular name. She was sitting with Piyush Bhardwaj, my batch mate from graduation who happened to be my batch mate at Post Graduation now. He was a typical character who had this habit of cracking sad jokes in front of his female friends which obviously girls found really funny and broke into laughter, he was a self proclaimed singer who would sing anything but romantic numbers, also, he knew a bit to play guitar, and he was studious as well. So, that bugger had all the qualities to have a huge female fan base.

"Are you a Tamilian?" I asked Smitha. "Yes", she said affirmatively. "Do you speak Tamil?" I asked. "No", she answered as if Tamil was the most backward language of modern era.

I had this habit of asking Tamilians whether they were Tamilians despite I was least interested in them.

I ignored her thinking that she was snooty. "Dude, you were trying to hit upon her and she ignored you" commented Om, my first friend in MBA, while lighting up my cigarette. "She is a bitch and there is nothing great about her. Hardly 50 kgs with a chest like a runway and the mother fucker Piyush would have degraded me a lot before I said hello to her" I said defending my self-esteem, after all Om was not so close yet to question me. Om nodded in agreement.

This conversation reminded me of something great about guys. If a girl speaks to a guy freely, without much discomfort at the first go, we call her a slut and if she does not, we call her snooty.

"There is she, 3S, your chick", said Om pointing towards her as she was taking a stroll with Piyush after the dinner. She stopped and gave him a stern look. "Probably she heard what you said" I warned Om, "All Delhi girls are like that, they think every guy around them is discussing them", his pitch was higher this time, probably he wanted her to listen to what he had just commented about the capital girls. "Screw her", he added and passed on the smoke to me. I gave him a dirty glare and thought that if I continued to stay with him, none of the girls would even think of saying a hello to me. "Why isn't he arrested for eve teasing?" I thought.

Friends like Om are really dangerous to the budding relationships. So, keep watching of him.

2

First Impression is the Last Impression

"Do you have some water in your room?" I barged into Om's Room. "Yeah, but it is already mixed with Vodka!" replied Om. That is Om for you, he always had a bottle of Shark Tooth in his room, and he ensured that he depleted that by some amount every day.

It was Thursday and we had relatively lesser lectures, one in the morning at 9.15, one in the afternoon at 3.15. So, I realised that we still had three hours for the lecture to start and it would not be a bad idea to help Om in depleting the contents of Shark Tooth.

"Hang on, I'll get cigarettes from my room." I said. We had run short of cigarettes during our booze session, "But I have only a small Gold Flake. That is ok right?" I confirmed with Om as I had always seen him puffing Classic Milds. Om was a free man under the influence of alcohol, "Get beedi as well if you have." said Om. Confirmation taken and contentment showed on my face because I had made friends with one of the most down to earth guys I had ever known in my life.

"Here it is ." I lit two cigarettes at one shot and handed one of those to Om. "Its 2 lets catch some sleep and we will leave by 3 for the lecture." I proposed an idea which was turned down by Om, "Screw you, there is only this much left in the bottle, why to leave this?" Om showed the bottle to me. I found it a better proposition and we decided to do with the last pegs of Vodka.

"We are late and we are drunk dude." I said breaking the silence. "How about the problems Subbiah had given on time value of money? Did you solve them?"

Subbiah was our financial management professor and was one of the biggest losers I had come across. He had a very simple method of judging students. Those who sat on the first two rows were very good students, the next three rows degraded from good to average, and the last two rows were meant for the gone cases. And sadly, I and Om were part of the last row as we were always late for the class and we had no intentions of flaunting our incomplete knowledge by sitting on the first row.

"He will surely ask us whether we have solved the problems or not." said a tensed Om, "Dude, he might even ask us to come and solve it on the board" he added.

"We can't even hold the marker, how will we write? And what if he comes to know that we are drunk?" I asked.

"Let's skip the lecture" proposed Om. "No we can't, these are the initial days and the first impression is the last impression, lets rush, its only 3, we will wash our faces on the way to the lecture hall and we will sit in one of the first two rows. Hurry up." I gave a brilliant idea. "Yes, fast and he will not ask us questions either!" said a delighted Om appreciating the idea.

We left the room at 3.05 and briskly walked towards the lecture hall. We were walking all over the place and the Shark Tooth made us feel that we were flying. "I think we are acting funny, lets be normal. People are staring at us." I said. "Yeah, keep walking straight." added Om. We saw the crowd gathered in front of the lecture hall 2 and we realized that we were late. "Let's run", I said as I started gaining speed.

It is true that a person with high alcohol content in the blood does not understand that distance is equal to speed multiplied by time. I gained more speed to cover less distance and forgot to slow down and bumped into the crowd gathered in front of the hall. I crashed into Piyush and tipped over to push Smitha onto the ground. Suddenly, there was a pin drop silence as if 9/11 got repeated. I saw Om slowing down at the correct time to avoid embarrassment. I helped Smitha to get up and said, "I am sorry, burp." Everyone, in the radius of at least three feet could smell something nasty; they started waving their hands against their face, which looked as if they had constipation.

"You are drunk? Disgusting! Jesus Christ!" shouted Smitha and cleared all the doubt of the foul smell which others had.

"Doesn't your father booze?" I lost cool and wanted to slap her. Om chipped in to control the situation and dragged me inside the lecture hall while saying "Remember, first impression is the last impression." I did not understand that why he said that. He probably believed that I was hitting upon Smitha.

We reached for the first two seats of the first row right under the nose of Subbiah. Smitha and Piyush sat next to Om and both of them could smell Vodka from him as well. I was happy that I was not the only convict which people thought. By then, Piyush and Smitha knew that even Om was drunk and this would also spread like wild fire because even if Smitha kept quiet about it, Piyush had a heart of a female, he would for sure spread the news. I was content that I had a partner in the crime and if expulsion happened, I would not be alone.

"Do you have extra pens? Can you give two ? One for me and one for Rama!", Om asked Smitha. Amidst all the rush, we forgot to carry our notepads and pens. She gave a pen and a pencil to Om along with the same stern look which she had given the other night when Om called her 3S. Om kept the pen with him and gave the pencil to me.

"Piyush has two pens in his shirt pocket. Why didn't he give one to us?" I whispered in Om's ears, Om was indifferent. "And see he has made his chick sit next to guys loaded with alcohol, and still these girls think that guys like Piyush are decent and chivalrous" I spoke without much idea and sense.

"Delhi girls!" Om reminded me. "I will knock his bloody head off one day." I said decisively to Om. "I hate him…" I added. "Chill dude!" said Om, sounding more serious than ever.

"Nobody likes you either, you drunkard!" said Smitha just to make me realize that I was loud all the while and she heard whatever I spoke. "Hey Pussy (That is how I addressed Piyush), ask her to keep quiet." I bypassed Smitha to speak to Piyush. He ignored me. I did not expect anything else from the spine less idiot.

"Shut up and make sure both of you return the pen and the pencil after the lecture!" intervened Smitha. I threw the pencil back to her and said, "Keep this with you and go back to nursery. One doesn't need a pen and a paper here. A B-school runs in your mind." I made a strong statement which closed the argument but left me with no pen and paper and the probability of me being questioned by Subbiah was nearly 100%. Om was enjoying every bit of it; I could see that on his fishy smile.

Then stepped in Subbiah, a villain straight from Telugu films; 6ft, thick moustache, white shirt, white pants and brown shoes. He had his cell phone placed on his belt and he deliberately took it out from his phone holder every day, looked for something in it and kept it back again while making some clicking sound of those buttons with magnetic effect. His appearance always made me doubtful of weather he really was a CA, LLb and CFA. That is why I call him a loser; why to work as a professor when you are already a consultant to big MNCs in Hyderabad, a practicing CA and a lawyer. That is because they don't want to forego any of the avenues of money, as a B-School fetches you around 5K per lecture for doing nothing.

"Is this the first semester?" he asked with MTI (Mother Tongue Influence). "God he does not even know whom is he teaching, how does he know what to teach? Will he remember the problems on Time Value?" I asked myself. "Yes sir." came a unified answer from the class.

My hobby of observing people took over me under the booze effect. I lost track of what was happening around and continued to observe three demons at that point of time, Smitha, Piyush and Subbiah. Om was intelligent enough to keep his head down and pretend that he was taking down notes and enlightenment which third demon was giving to us. Probably he had attended lectures after Vodka earlier as well. It was first time for me though.

Subbiah wrote Annuities in **BOLD** on board and he started deriving the present value formula using geometric progression without telling students what he was planning to do. Everyone in the hall was blank. Smitha was busy copying down the solutions on time value from Piyush without knowing whether he had solved them correctly or not.

"Why does she want to study finance this way if she can't solve problems on her own?" I thought. And Piyush used to exploit this plight of women to his benefit.

"I am sure even Piyush has copied it from Sri." I said while leaning against Om. "At least he did that!" Om reminded me that we had not solved the problems.

"You!" Subbiah said pointing towards me.

"Me? Sir?" I confirmed pointing towards me.

"Yes you. What are you up to?" asked Subbiah.

"You are dead dude", Om mumbled while continuing his act of taking notes.

I looked at Smitha and Piyush, both of them were giggling away to glory. I looked at Om in vain. "What can Om do? Even I should have used some of my acting skills to take down notes. Why did I have the hobby of observing people, I should have loved acting, it would have taken over me and helped me take notes?" I thought fast and cursed myself.

"You don't have a pen and a notepad. Why do you join a B-School and waste your parents' money?" Subbiah took off.

I wanted to tell him that I had taken an education loan and my parents were not under any pressure, so he better meant business instead of making personal remarks. But I chose to keep quiet.

I looked at Smitha, it seemed that she wanted Subbiah to discover that I was drunk and there was no place for students like me there. The embarrassment level set higher records when Subbiah said, "Don't you have courtesy to stand up when your professor is talking to you?"

"Who will tell sir that he can't stand today and is born to fall?" commented Smitha in Piyush's ears loud enough for me to hear. The love birds continued to giggle. I struggled to stand up pretending that the arrangement of desks was congested and the leg space was not enough. Om gave a push and patted my back gesturing "Relax, I am there."

"I am sure that you have not solved the assignment and you have no interest in finance," commented Subbiah on helpless me.

"No sir, I mean yes sir. I have done the assignment but forgot to get it while rushing for the class. I am sorry." I begged for mercy.

"Ok, Can you come and explain what I have done on the board to the class?" he threw an open challenge and I had no option but to accept it.

I looked at Om; he gave me a hopeless look. I looked at Piyush; he was telling Smitha that I had been a pathetic performer since graduation days. I gave him a "Fuck you" look. "Who will tell Smitha I scored 72% in B.Com (Hons) in DU and this asshole got 57%?" I wondered. I decided to ignore the "Love Birds" and went towards the board with my heart beating faster than ever.

Subbiah handed over the marker to me. I was absolutely alert and did not want to reveal by any manner that I was drunk and ignorant about the proceedings on the board. I was careful that I maintained distance from Subbiah because I did not want him to smell what rest of the class had already done. I started, "Sir, You have applied the concept of geometric progression and if the annuity is for n number of years, the sum of n numbers in a geometric progression is $a(1\text{-}r^n)/(1\text{-}r)$. Since r here is 1/(1+i) because in annuity even the interest what we earn on the money is re-invested, so money multiplies by (1+i), hence r has been replaced by 1/(1+i). 1/(1+i) is lesser than 1, that is the reason we have considered this formula of Geometric Progression." I derived the formula once again and took the whole class by surprise who had underestimated my abilities, especially Smitha.

Subbiah was not yet convinced about my caliber, he shot one more trick at me, "Can you solve the fifth problem of the assignment? I have got calls from a few students that they could not solve it. You have solved the assignment right? So will you mind solving it for the class?" he handed over the assignment to me.

I looked at Om and he looked surprised as well that who were the bastards who had started apple polishing the professors. I was skeptical to accept this challenge because I had not even looked at the assignment, forget the fifth problem. But once again, I had no option but to accept it. Om had closed his eyes in horror; he did not want to see his friend getting royally raped.

"I need a calculator sir." I said meekly.

"Why did you come to the class, no pen, notepad, no calculator?" Subbiah criticized me "Go take it from your friend" he pointed towards Om.

I wanted to laugh at the situation; Om did not have a calculator either! Before anyone realized that, Om acted swiftly to pick Smitha's calculator and gave it to me as if it was his. I winked at Smitha. She gave the same stern look. I wondered if the stern look was a part of her personality.

I read the problem. I learnt that day why a numerical is called a "Problem." It was not a question; it was a five line paragraph. Vodka interrupted my attempt to comprehend it. I had to read it again while popping my eyes out. I looked up to see that everyone was silent and contemplating what was next. They reminded me of the edgy thrillers; all they needed was popcorn and a Pepsi to add to the excitement. I did not know what made me look specifically at Smitha. I charged up myself and got all my logic and senses at one place and told myself, "You are the dude! What if you have not done it earlier, annuities is your strongest area, go ahead and rip them apart, if not for you, at least you need to prove what you are to Smitha and Piyush! Go for it dude." I closed my eyes, then opened it and went towards the board.

There was a trick in the numerical, it required an effective rate of interest to be calculated as money changed different hands from A to B to C and then from C to B to A during maturity.

I erased whatever Subbiah and I had written earlier on the board without bothering that the crowd had taken it down or not. I started writing on the board without caring if I was maintaining any distance from Subbiah. I wrote from left to right and was on a full swing, wrote certain self-derived formulae which never got discussed in the class, did some calculations on my own and suddenly surprised Piyush by saying, "Can you do these calculations simultaneously which are written here. It will save time." I pointed towards the board. I wanted to show Smitha that it was Piyush who was a loser and not me.

I had already spent close to 20 minutes doing circus in front of the class, 5 minutes in explaining the geometric progression and 15 minutes in the numerical, but, I was sure that I had the solution right there, it was just a matter of few more minutes and the entire class could take down the correct solution. I had entered an equation in the calculator and waited for it to give a result; I kept my eyes fixed at the calculator.

The answer popped up, I turned around and with oodles of confidence, I wrote on the board, circled the answer, put the cap on the marker and tapped it on the dais and said, "Sir, here it is. I think I have done it correctly, what do you say?"

He looked at the board for a second. He went from left to right and then right to left. He stopped at one of my self-derived formulae and asked, "How do you know this?" I smiled and answered, "Annuity is my favorite area, so I don't use tables' book, and instead, I work out my own calculations." He said "Well done...." and paused which meant that he wanted to know my name. I said with pride and victory, "Rama Chandran Iyer Sir" while looking sideways at Smitha. "Well done Rama!" Subbiah completed.

I came back to the desk and did a high five with Om who felt honored; after all, he was acquainted with the "Man of the Day." I returned the calculator to Smitha and said "I'll give you the copy of correct solution, copy from that. What you are copying down blindly is not correct!" She stopped copying and Om patted my back and said "Chill dude!"

The lecture finally got over and we walked out of the class for tea and smoke. "Everyone is talking about you dude, you rocked!" said a joyful Om while putting his arms around me and shaking me wildly.

I reminded him, "Dude, did you return the pen to 3S?"

"Oh yeah..." He turned around to go back to the class just to find that Smitha was standing right behind us. "Oh yeah, thanks, here is your pen. Anyhow, did not need it much. It was a marker which ruled today. Anyways, thanks!" said Om; indicating to my cameo.

"My name is Smitha and not 3S. Do you get that?" said Smitha firmly.

I did not respond. I said, "Let's go Om." She spoke again and this time catching my attention, "When can I get the correct solution for the assignment?"

"Am I not disgusting now and am I not born to fall?" I threw sarcasm at her.

"Sorry Rama, but you were damn impressive, A for sure in FM." said Smitha (A meant A grade and FM meant Financial Management). "Yeah let's see." I said casually. "You will get the solutions during the dinner. See you in the Mess at 9.30. Bye." I added. "Bye." she responded.

Om had to intervene; he could not keep mum for long. He said, "Dude, first impression is the last impression." he stretched "dude" infinitely in his statement while shaking me wildly again.

3
Stop Acting Smart

It was 9 by the watch and I said, "Let's have dinner."

Om said, "But you told Smitha you will meet her at 9.30. What about that?"

I looked at Om with a straight face and said, "I was supposed to meet her to give a correct copy of the assignment, not for anything else. Where is the assignment? We have been celebrating since evening. So, there is no point meeting her. So, let's go."

After my class performance that day, I was assured that Subbiah had developed tremendous confidence in me and it would be very unfortunate of me if he asked me any question from there on, so, we thought of giving up the assignment and continued our booze session, this time Bagpiper which I got from the city the other day. Om raised his shoulder in despair, wore his tracks and said "Let's go but stop acting smart."

"Hey Rama! Wait, where are you going?" called Sri from behind. Sri Shanbhag was unarguably, the best student of our batch, he was marvelous in accounting and finance, he learnt flute and table and he spoke on any topic without any hassles and most importantly, whatever he spoke, had content and meant something. So, his curiousity about where I was going raised Om's eyebrows and he said, "Why is this nerd talking to us?"

"Don't know, but he is a nice guy" I corrected Om but still, I liked to stay away from the sensible ones as they get you into unfavorable situations at times.

"You guys headed for dinner?" asked Sri.

"If you knew, why did you stop us to ask where we were going?" replied a rude me. Om was astonished to see my transformation from the "nice guy" logic to rude in a second.

"I thought that I'll join you guys" spoke Sri without reacting to my rude response. That is a perfect MBA in the making, absolutely unmoved emotionally. "Hi Om" said Sri while extending his hand towards Om. Om smiled and shook hands with Sri and all three of us started walking towards the mess.

"You guys are still drunk?" asked Sri.

"Yes, we continued after the class." said Om confirming the fact that we were drunk during the lecture as well. Om used to get moved immediately by "Nice guys" and especially by those who were the first to extend a hand to him for friendship. I was still not able to digest the reason for Sri talking to us; it could not have been just like that.

"Can you tell me how do you manage to solve problems without using tables?" Sri came to the point. Om looked at me and gave me the same fishy smile. I did not respond to Sri's query because I did not like guys who got acquainted with somebody for some reason. Look at me and Om, we struck chord the very first day without caring for anything.

"I asked you something" Sri reiterated his point.

"It just comes naturally, there is no clear logic behind it, I do it because I don't like going to tables because it wastes time and we have been provided with scientific calculators, still you need tables, it is a real shame." I spoke as if Isaac Newton was my forefather. Sri nodded in appreciation. I looked at Om and he showed his middle finger to Sri without making Sri aware of his gestures.

We reached mess and joined the queue. Everyone created mess about the mess food saying that college did not serve according to the money we paid, but I always thought that food was god's gift and it should not be compared with money. Think about those who don't even get to eat and with philanthropic logic, I filled my plate with rice, sambhar and curd. Om and I stood for some time looking for a place to sit while Sri continued to serve himself. I spotted a place for two at the corner of the mess. I signaled to Om that we had a place there.

Om said, "We are three but there is only a place for two."

I got irritated and said "Have you come with me or him? You can go and join him if you want to, I am going there and Sri will obviously go and find solace with someone whom he can discuss something more meaningful like Indian Economy and books like *Argumentative Indian*. We are drunk and it might not be great for his image to join drunkards for dinner, didn't you notice that he stopped speaking to us once we entered the mess?" I started walking and Om followed suit thinking that I made perfect sense.

I and Om did not use spoons (another reason why I found Om down to earth), we ate with hands which made people stare at us. The chirpy gang which was freewheeling post dinner with dried plates on the table which I and Om chose decided to leave because they did not like the sight of rice balls going into our mouth through our hands. "Delhi gang!" commented Om.

"Their forefathers came from Britain." I added. It was a table with eight chairs and it was only two of us occupying that table then.

Sri and Piyush joined us on that table. Blood started rushing into my head whenever I saw Piyush and I thought, "If Piyush is here, Smitha must be in the vicinity." Smitha emerged from the crowd immediately as if she knew what I was thinking. I and Om stopped discussing whatever we did then and I said, "Hey Pussy, don't you have any other place to sit, or have you gone blind to see that I am sitting here?" I went hard on Piyush for no reason.

Smitha intervened, "What do you think of yourself? What did he say that you are being rude? And is this table your property?"

Blood which had got into my head started oozing out, "Did I speak to you? Just stay out of it! I can't understand that why a guy who did not even say hello to me during grads and always bitched about me wants to share the same table with me!" The alcohol made me speak naturally without caring who felt bad and who did not.

Om kept his hand on my shoulder and said, "Bro!"

"I am in no mood to discuss that how I solve annuities without using tables, so, you guys please stop following me because I really don't like people who are around only for a reason. I have two years to spend here and I better make friends with those who are actually friends." I continued my rampage while putting stress on Friends every time.

"Hey, don't be weird man." spoke Sri to calm me down with the same smile and unmoved emotionally.

"We just thought…." He continued but I cut him short by saying, "We? It will be better if you speak on your own behalf Sri. Can you tell me one valid reason that made you speak to me and Om and then join us for the dinner? We know that we don't have the best of the reputes in the college and till this evening, none of you would have ever thought of us. Thought?" I stressed on "Thought" this time.

"Now why are you representing Om, can't you just talk on your behalf?" spoke Smitha with sarcasm.

I stopped eating and left the table, kept my plate on the trolley meant for soiled plates. Om did not follow me this time because he thought that I made zero sense. He continued eating and I left the mess and went to the library to read newspaper.

I kept on flipping the pages of the newspaper without stopping at one article or topic to read. I had a very short temper and did not know any way of keeping my point in a parliamentary way, I thought, "I should have given zero attention to Piyush and why do I behave this way, probably yes, Smitha was right that table was not my property, anyone and everyone had the right to sit wherever they wanted to, but why did they come to speak to me and Om was still unanswered."

My phone rang and it was Om who called up. I went out of the library to answer his call, "Yeah Om, where are you?"

"Where am I? Where are you?" Om cross questioned me.

"At the library. Why what happened?" I asked.

"Come down, I am at the stage, I don't have cigarettes." commanded Om.

"Yeah I'll be there in a minute", I said and disconnected.

I reached the stage and found that Om and Sri were sharing a joke. I stood at a distance disbelieving what I was seeing then. I went towards Om, gave him the cigarettes and said, "Sorry Sri, I lost temper for no reason." I was consistent in getting into arguments with people unnecessarily and then cut a sorry face. "I have no problems with you but I can't stand Piyush" I cleared any doubts which Sri might have developed.

"Man, it is ok, you have to be what you are, I appreciate that you aren't plastic like others. But we should always understand that we are not living in isolation, world is not perfect and you are a part of it. We will always come across different kinds of people during our life and they might be of different characteristics, it need not be a compulsion that everyone is to your liking. There is also a chance that people might not like you, but still they accept you as a part of society. So, always be open and think broad. I know I am talking philosophy but just to tell you simply, I liked the fact that you and Om had guts to come to the class after getting high and I was noticing you all the while when you solved that problem on the board. Believe me, you might not have noticed that, even Subbiah could make out that you had not done the problem earlier and you were reading it for the first time, but the way you accepted it, read the problem, closed your eyes, murmured something was evident to the whole class and then you solving it in a flash defined your personality. You are good, try to be better!" Sri elaborated my weaknesses and strengths. I was zapped and looked at Om. Om was mesmerized. But still I wondered that why was he giving me so much of *gyaan*, it was tough to accept that someone with no reason cared so much for me.

Om started clapping and said, “Subbiah raped you and Sri did the post mortem of the rape victim.” All of us burst into laughter.

“Jokes apart, Will you be a part of the marketing group?” asked Sri. I and Om never thought somebody would want both of us to be in their group; we thought that once all the students formed their groups, we would go to the professor and ask him to put us in any group which was short of two people. But this was real bonanza, working with Sri and Om would be great.

“I am game, but who all are there?” I asked.

Sri was hesitant in answering this and left it to Om to answer who said, “You, me, Sri, Smitha and…” “And Piyush right?” I completed what Om had started. I gave a dejected look to Sri who said, “Your colleague in your office might not gel with you, but still the company needs both of you because you both are valuable to the company...”

Before Sri could get into another round of philosophical torture, I said “Fine, its ok, but I need to go now.” I got up and started walking, took a few steps and stopped, “Do you have Smitha’s number?” I inquired.

“No I don’t.” replied Om, “Shut up you ass, you won’t have your girlfriend’s number, forget about somebody else’s. Yeah Sri, do you have her number?” I asked again.

Sri broke into laughter and took out his phone, gave the number and asked, “But whose girlfriend is she?”

“Piyush” I answered if it was obvious. Sri smiled and said, “Come on, she is not his girlfriend, but where are you going now?”

“I promised Smitha that I’ll give her the correct solution for the fifth problem, I am going to the room to solve it. That is my style of being apologetic; I misbehaved with her as well. See you guys in the room.” I said as I started walking. “Go to the library, she is there.” shouted Sri from behind.

I reached the lobby of the library and called up Smitha. “Hello!” came a timid voice from the other side.

“Yeah hi, Rama here” I spoke hesitantly. “Hi, what is it? How did you get my number?” asked Smitha.

"Sri. Can you come out for a minute? I am in the lobby." I requested her.

"Yeah coming", she obliged.

She came out and before she spoke anything, I said, "Are you carrying the assignment now? I wanted to solve it for you." I spoke as if I was giving a life time opportunity to her. "Yeah I do, but its ok, I'll manage" said an egoistic Smitha.

Now, girls always make you think. Literally, she meant that she had the assignment with her but she did not need my help. The other way to interpret it was that she had the assignment but wanted me to apologize further and then help her solve the assignment because if she actually did not need my help, why would she reveal the fact that she was carrying the assignment and when she said that she would manage, it meant that she won't be able to manage and wanted me to help her out.

I decided to interpret it the other way and said, "Look I am really sorry, let me make up for that by doing this tiny job for you. Please."

She smiled and said, "Its ok but I don't have a calculator!" imitating me when I made the same statement to Subbiah.

"We will take it from somebody. Let's go to the reading room" I said. As we walked towards the reading room, she said, "Rama, a sincere request, please stop acting smart unnecessarily. It isn't good." I accepted the first in the list of conditions imposed.

4

YOU ARE THE CEO MATERIAL

Once the marketing group was designed by the "Nice Guy", we entered into a serious discussion to decide who would be the Group Leader. As per the conventional definition, a group leader is the one who shoulders the responsibility of commanding his forces in a way that the task for which the group is formed is accomplished given the constraints and the available resources, however, as per the definition in my college, a group leader was the one who had the maximum chance of interacting with the professors as our Profs did not like to be crowded in their cabins when they were busy watching porn or accessed Share Khan. In short, a group leader had the maximum advantage of scoring the best grade by breeding on the jobs done by his forces.

Om could not become a leader due to his attitude towards everything, he was easy going and was sure not fit to control and plan his life, forget about planning the strategy for the group. Piyush could not become a group leader because he had two votes against him. I did not have a chance either because I did not want to spend time with professors in explaining how tough doing the project was given the resources I had. Forget Smitha, she was a little slow in picking up things and would always need Piyush, who would virtually control everything and become the navigator of our group defining his moves through Smitha, the Prime Minister. So, we had no one but "Nice Guy" to be declared as leader. No one had any issues with Sri because, as mentioned earlier, he was unarguably the best of our batch, I did not mind even if he ate into our grades, because, I did not know, I developed a respect towards him and sensed that he would not backstab any of us.

"So, guys, GK has assigned 'Post Aurangzeb Era and Marketing Concepts' for our group", Sri informed us after the meeting of group leaders and GK (G Krishna, the marketing prof). Shocked to hear the theme, everyone looked at each other. I looked at Piyush, who looked at Sri as if the first nail in Piyush's coffin had been put by Sri, "Could you not argue to get a better topic for the project?" Piyush condemned Sri as if Sri was the union leader and he could not convince the management for our demands. Smitha joined Piyush and said "Yeah, Sri, please get it changed. Is it a compulsion to work only on the projects assigned to us, can't we choose to do something on our own?" Sri remained silent, another trait of a perfect MBA, as he would have known before hand the first reaction from the group. His philosophical side let the group vent out its frustration, it would make the team feel better and bring the best out of them.

Sri asked me, "Don't you have anything to say?" I smiled because I liked the fact that my say was valuable to the group. Before I said anything, Om said, "Damn good Sri, this sounds interesting!" Piyush and Smitha nodded their heads in disagreement. Countering this gesture, I said "Come on guys, we declared Sri as our group leader and we should trust him. You guys are talking as if history is his most sought after field and Aurangzeb is his favorite super hero. GK is not Sri's uncle to accept whatever he says, just because he is representing us does not mean that he lost his brains and is depending purely on us. He is wise enough to have accepted it and if anyone of you thinks that you can do it better, please go ahead to speak to GK. I am ok with the topic Sri." No one said a word and it was presumed that the topic had been finalized.

"How do we relate marketing concepts to the post Aurangzeb Era? What nonsense?" cribbed Piyush, we met at the dome of our college post dinner as that place was far away from the usual noisy structures and it had enough plug points for our laptops to get charged. "We will work something out, relax, every group has a bizarre topic, they must be trying to find a way out, if it was not possible, GK would not have thought of this at the first place." said Sri settling the turmoil in Piyush's empty brain. Smitha looked on without contributing much and waited for some sort of guidance from Sri. Om was listening silently to what Sri said hinting that he had developed enough confidence in Sri as a leader which Sri had in GK as a professor.

"Lets do one thing guys, we break for five minutes, do some brainstorming and return with the points jotted down to discuss." said Sri exhibiting his leadership qualities. The word "break" always lit up our eyes, as a break would mean "smoke." I stopped typing on my laptop, closed it and went to the stage with Om for a quick fire smoke.

"Where do you think this is headed to?" asked Om and took a long drag. I watched him anticipating that he would pass on the smoke. Not bothered about what he asked, I raised my middle and index fingers making a "V" sign indicating that it was my turn to take a much longer drag. Om passed the smoke and realised his mistake, "Sorry, I forgot that we have lit only one." and he asked again, "Where are we headed to with this? I don't think Piyush has any interest in this, we are actually five minus one, four in the group!" I realised in no time that what I and Om discussed would not be called "Brainstorming" in any part of the world, but I decided to pacify him down by saying, "Take it easy bro, we know that we are not relying on Piyush, we are doing it for us and not for anybody else. And if you think, he does not contribute and acts smart, he can't escape, we will get it done by force." showing my fist to Om. Om grinned and said, "Yeah, you have sworn that you will knock his bloody head off one day, this might give you a good reason to do so."

"This is all we have jotted down", said Smitha, holding an A4 sheet against us which had something scribbled on it. Om tried hard to read from a distance, gave up and asked, "We? You mean you and Piyush?" Smitha got disturbed at the remark and said, "No me and my mother! Happy?" Om was amused and replied, "I knew he was girly, but did not know he was a mother of 20 odd something girl!"

I fell down laughing and said, "We don't have magnifying lenses in our eyes; please care to read it out for us!" Smitha read out the outcome of the "Brainstorming" of the slowest pair of brains I knew. What she read out was reasonable enough but not strong enough to move our thinking cells.

Om shrunk his nose and said that, "Its ok but there is nothing different in it. We took you in our group because we thought you would prove to be a real asset as you are a BBA in marketing." He looked at me and winked. I gave the fishy smile which Om sported all the while and thought that he was in no mood to do the project, he was more inclined towards public speaking as he got the first opportunity when people had surrounded him for discussing anything, so, he wanted to derive best out of it by speaking whatever came to his mind. Smitha was disgusted and responded as if this was the most ghastly act of the history, which included Aurangzeb.

"May I know what you discussed and let us see what you have to share." Sri exhibited another quality of a leader by trying to tone down the situation by giving a new direction to the discussion. Piyush and Smitha were least interested in what Om was about to speak.

Om said, "See we should divide the topic in two parts. We should provide a different picture when we are submitting the report and shall come out with an entirely different point when we are presenting it which is scheduled after a month." Sri liked his point and even Piyush and Smitha were stunned. I was not sure whether what Om said was what he really thought, but, as they say in cricket "it does not matter how runs come as long as they come." We eventually had an amazing thought which came from none other than Om. Om sat down as if his job was over and it was left for the others to convert the spark into the fire.

"Yes, he is actually right", I gave some oxygen to the spark and continued, "Guys, we have actually got into silo thinking. The term 'Post Aurangzeb Era' is worthy to note; it need not necessarily mean history which everyone has been cribbing out. It actually signifies the time after Aurangzeb's sad demise." I smiled at my own poor sense of humor, realized no one smiled and then continued, "That means we can discuss whatever has happened in the marketing history till date... Do you get that, we have time from 1707 to 2006, that is fucking three hundred years and there is so much we can cover." stressing on "fucking three hundred years".

Om and Sri put their thumbs up and Smitha showed first signs of interest by coming and sitting right next to me, listening carefully to each word I spoke. "But, wait wait wait wait" Smitha stopped me. "I am not running anywhere" I said because of four waits.

She smiled and asked, "Why did you precisely say 1707?" I bowed down my head slightly, acknowledging her listening skills and answered her, "Great listening abilities, I must say that, well, I am not as bad in history as you guys are, Aurangzeb died in 1707, so his era came to an end in….?" I left that for Smitha to complete and she said, "1707" happily as if that was the final question of KBC and she got it right.

I liked the childish behavior of hers, the smile, the sparkling eyes and the enthusiasm which she displayed even in the smallest of things. I regained my consciousness and said, "Well, I have done a bit of research on how Aurangzeb ruled and what were the loopholes he left and what happened after he died which left a long decline for Mughals", I turned my laptop towards everyone. Sri Picked up the laptop and started browsing what I had done and Om joined him. Smitha was more interested in listening and I spoke sense that night catching everybody's attention.

"As Om said, we will have two themes to be presented; one in the report and one in the presentation. We will have two plots set in two different centuries; we have had greatest of marketing heroes during this time. So, we will present their thoughts." I was going all guns blazing. Sri responded, "Fantastic, we have so many of them, Kotler, Keller, rise of Unilever, Virgin, Richard Branson, BCG Matrix, Porter's Model. All we need is to zero in upon one of these or combination of them." Sri patted my back and said "Great job Rama." Sri spoke as if he did not want to be left out and allow people to consider him to be the weakest link in the group because; surprisingly he had not contributed much till then apart from giving everyone a chance to speak. I thought, "He will do well in GDs."

"No dude, we are not going to present anything from the heroes you named." I got up negating Sri's only point till then. Smitha got up as well and asked me, "Then what do we do?"

I had done my groundwork really well that day and that was one of those rarest days when ideas leak just to fall in place. I said, "I did some research on what happened after Aurangzeb died, let us not be conventional and present what everyone is going to otherwise. We will use the concepts of Kotler, Porter and BCG and then place them in the plots we plan to pick. We will do the same thing differently."

Piyush started showing interest for the first time. I could not make out if the interest was due to what I proposed or was it due to Smitha's increasing interest in me. Adding to Piyush's woes, Smitha wax lyrically said, "Oh Wow! Too good!"

"We will present British as a marketer in our report and then we will use Gandhi as a protagonist in the second plot for our presentation." I took the discussion to an entirely new level. Om lit up a cigarette and said, "Guys sorry, I need smoke to comprehend this murder mystery." Everyone ignored him but I knew that Om understood every remark I made much better than anybody else and it was just a damn excuse to smoke. I reached to him and snatched the smoke from him and took a drag. Om commented on me, "My lord, will you mind enlightening the downtrodden us with your established wisdom that how are we going to use British and Gandhi to speak for us?" I laughed hysterically and said, "Screw you."

Smitha said, "Please tell us how we will do that. Have you thought about it?"

I was enjoying the attention and especially from the only lady in the group. It was like conquering a fort for a guy to garner attention of a lady in a group which had three other guys, one of them a prospective boyfriend. I said "British had to establish East India Company and they had to sell an idea that they were just traders and Gandhi had to subsequently stand up as competitor to down turn British and sold the idea of freedom and independence."

Everyone started pondering over what I said except Smitha who was more interested in listening. I stepped into the shoes of Sri and before Sri could realize that, I said, "Ladies and Gentlemen, it is almost 2 now, we should wind up for the day, girls have to reach hostels by 2.30." Smitha showed her listening abilities once again and said, "Day?

Lets wind up for the night and by the way, you said ladies and gentlemen, but its only me, so you should have said lady and gentlemen." Smitha started giggling on her own gag bag, while everyone wondered that what was there to laugh about. However, I and Om would never let go any chance of screwing up Piyush. I said, "No, it should be ladies and gentlemen, as we have two ladies here, one you and the mother of twenty odd something Piyush." Smitha did not realize whether the joke was cracked on her or Piyush (As mentioned earlier, she would need two runways to take off). She made a semi-smile, "semi" because she did not want to hurt Piyush and smile because she wanted to get along with the other intelligent lot.

"Yeah, lets wrap up, I told you guys that there is always a light at the end of the tunnel, I knew that we would somehow find a way out with such brilliant guys in the group." Sri made a wrap up speech while not letting go off his "leadership" stature.

Om stepped in to correct Sri, "Brilliant Guys?" asked Om and put stress on Guys. "Let us not take any credit from Rama and try to share, we are anyhow going to share the results of this one man show in reports and presentation, Brilliant Guy Sri! not guys." Om spoke with emotions. Sri remained silent and did not want to comment because his brilliance was being challenged as well in open by Om.

I thought the other way, "Poor Sri wants to play diplomatically and does not want to please one of us and he is appreciating the entire group and putting my efforts collectively as a team effort, hence, he said brilliant guys, so as to avoid any claims of partiality or rifts." I maintained in my inner self while considering it as another leadership quality.

I packed my laptop and started walking, Om joined me and handed over his laptop to me, Om never carried his laptop bag and the charger which I found really irritating, the college had provided us with laptop, laptop bag and a charger, but Om behaved as if the admin guy gave him a laptop but retained the charger and the bag with himself as a part of his commission. I stared at Om, but the moment I saw that he was going to light up a cigarette, I was more than happy to help.

Sri, Piyush and Smitha followed us. Smitha called from behind and asked me where I was going. "White House for tea!" I revealed the secret of where I was headed to. (White House was a small canteen right in the middle of the college lawn which boasted of some amazing tea, samosas, puffs and Maggi. Since the establishment was painted white and we got cigarettes through the owner, we named it prestigiously as White House) "Would you like to join us? I swear we are not going for booze there!" Om made an irrevocable offer to Smitha which was instantly accepted and the first clause of the agreement was rolled out by Om. Keep reading, you will understand the agreement.

"The tea is really nice here, I thought you got only smokes here" said Smitha. "Yes, we come here every night before we sleep" I said and thought, "Why would she say that? She has to have this much of sense to understand that no sane guy would run such a stall only for smokes and she must have visited this place with Piyush before as well since this was one of the favorite hangouts of love birds after the reading room of our college."

I smelled that she wanted to kick off some discussion and she was not finding the way to do it, I either created an uncomfortable zone around me or she was finding Om's presence as a hindrance to start the conversation. I agreed with the latter and said, "Dude, you go to the room, I'll accompany Smitha to the hostel and return, we need to speed up, its 2.25. Come on Smitha, finish your tea while we walk." I picked up Smitha's bag because I thought that a fifty kg girl would not be able to carry her bag while having tea, which Smitha found as a great sign of chivalry. Chivalry my foot, things like chivalry was meant for guys like Piyush. Om reacted quickly as if I was his master and his sole duty was to obey my orders, his behavior once again reminded me that he had developed a self-belief that I was hitting upon Smitha.

I was not really comfortable accompanying Smitha to the hostel, in fact, there was no need of doing it, because nobody was going to abduct Smitha and rape her inside the campus because there were lot of girls going back to the hostel after their share of cuchikoo with their respective and prospective boyfriends. However, something drew me towards her and I was just following it blindly without realizing that this walk towards the girls' hostel would be a regular affair in days to come.

Smitha was different, she was one of the "no non sense" and "touch me not" types, and so, there was absolutely no benefit for me for being chivalrous. Chivalry, according to a girl's dictionary is exhibited, when somebody picks up her baggage, from purse to her king size suit case; by this theory, every coolie was the cousin of Prince Charles when it came to chivalry and sophistication.

"A for sure in MM as well", said Smitha while we walked towards the girls hostel (MM meant marketing management). "I don't know, all depends on how well we present it." I replied.

"Oh come on, you are being modest. The way you were keeping your points and making every one believe that what you said was actually possible was like selling ice to an Eskimo." Smitha praised me, "The way you are going, I am sure you will do well in the presentations as well." added Smitha.

"But it all depends on the questions handling after the presentation and as a rule, the leader has to answer them, which is Sri in our case and we should be supporting him with our points, so, the chances that I will get to show my mettle gets minimized, and if I get A, I guess everyone in the group would get A. What do you say?" I got into a discussion mode and wondered if this was what she wanted to discuss with me.

"Yeah, but I guess since the entire thing is your brainchild, I think you will be the best person to handle it", Smitha spoke in appreciation, "How come these kinds of ideas did not come to me? As Om said, I am Bachelors in marketing." she spoke like a kid with a disheartened face.

Someone, from, somewhere came and left a thought in my mind, 'Dude, you can't see her sad. Just cheer her up.' I said, "Oh chill sweetie, its nothing great which I had done tonight, we had a task in our hand and we had to do it, I just thought hard about it, did some permutations and combinations, and when Om said, we will present two reports, it clicked to me. I am not sure what you call it, but I call it teamwork. All of us need to get A and I am the one who is putting in efforts today, I am sure, you would be key in the next assignment. And I am there with you right, I will make you learn the art of generating ideas. Just keep your eyes and ears open, that is it." I made a terrible commitment by saying that I was there with her and I would help her during her MBA, I never appreciated guys teaching girls, because, girls studied seriously and guys would be busy looking and thinking something else with a chick around, and eventually, girls would outshine guys. I did not want to be stupid of at least this order and hoped that she did not listen to my commitment carefully.

I forgot that she had great listening abilities, and my advice to keep her ears and eyes open strengthened this ability of hers, she was quick to respond, "A for everyone, including Piyush?", she exposed my inner hatred for Piyush, I said, "Yeah, why should he be left out? Personal issues are different than the professional ones, we can't mix them." I gave the same crap which Sri gave to me.

"And are you sure you would help me with my studies here?" asked Smitha, she was taking a promise from me and hang on, I just told her that I'll help her in generating ideas and she was feeding words into my mouth by saying "Studies" which was a wider term than "Idea Generation" and I was falling prey to this trap.

I thought, 'If I join Smitha for combined studies, then apart from her bag, I will have to carry her books as well because I can't see people from Somalia carrying huge cans of water, we have to help them, fuck! How will I get out of this? Chuck it, I'll ignore her from tomorrow.'

"Yeah, sure sure, no issues, anytime, just give me a call whenever you need any help. Here is your hostel, see you then, good night." I said and thought I would avoid her from then on apart from group meetings, but she said something which left me wanting more of her.

"You are the CEO material dude!" said Smitha and the way she said it made me feel that I was actually ranked with Tatas. I had got this compliment earlier as well, but I never got carried away, but, hers was captivating and she made me accept this compliment as truth. I was moved to death and said "Thanks and yes, we will start tomorrow, sharp at 6 near lecture hall 2." I made a commitment, looked at my watch and started walking towards my hostel with a sense of pride ignorant of the fact that my downfall had just begun.

5

Agony of Scoring Less Than 7

I promised Smitha the other night that I would be helping her out with the subjects she was weak at. Since I made an open offer without mentioning the subjects, it turned out that I was helping her in any subject one could think of; my conscience cried out that the only subject she would have been good at was English; no surprises as every girl of her generation from the top school of Delhi would be zero at anything but English.

We were battling eight subjects in the first semester including soft skills (I expected some help from her at least here, but she was used to accepting favors and did not believe in any barter system).

"What is that? Are you so fed up that you have packed your bags?" I asked Smitha while pointing at her huge bag which I never saw when she roamed around with Piyush. "Shut up, it has books... Ok teacher" she said and smiled. I was confused at the contradictory statement (never heard a student who is getting free tuitions asking the philanthropically great tutor to shut up) and amazed that it did not ignite my angry hormones.

The dimensions of the bag raised doubts that it carried holy bible of all sizes and not books. Scaring me further, I thought, if it had books, then what all books she carried. I gathered courage and asked my scholar student, "Why such a huge bag? What are the books you are carrying? There is no point in carrying so much weight; we will go one by one!"

She replied, "Well you are good at fin, I know that, then obviously, you will be good at quants as well, marketing no words and I thought it would be good to discuss human behavior, so I got that as well and accounts too." She covered her hopeless talent by appreciating me.

I thought with a flat face, "What did she do all her life? She was supposedly a science student in Class twelve and I was a commerce student, and she expects me to teach her quants? Or probably she is one amongst those who forget in class ten what they studied in class nine . She must have for sure mugged up math during school."

I concluded without any hitch that she was absolutely dumb, and if she was not, why would she chose to be friends with Piyush. "So what do you want to start with? I think accounts must be tough for you! Let's start with that." I proposed and thought that judging her first in what I was good at would be perfect and then would plan further. There wasn't absolute conviction in my approach and willingness to teach her, yet I decided to continue because I had committed and every time I thought of not to teach her, her CEO comment reiterated its importance to me.

"Its up to you that how we proceed, please ensure that you don't disturb your schedule while you teach me!" Smitha said politely. She spoke as if I was the privileged one to have forty eight hours allocated in a day, out of which I should find time to teach her without disturbing my schedule. I looked up to god and requested him to strike it to her that my schedule was already disturbed and with her acumen level, it will get distorted further.

"Fine then, do you have any clue of what accountancy is? Has Piyush taught you anything, he is also a commerce grad?" I asked two questions which had no link either with each other or with my decision to help her out. However, this was a part of my personality where I discussed something out of thin air which gave me utmost pleasure and in this case, Piyush's accounting abilities.

"No, I really don't understand why Dr is called debit and not doctor and…" She replied to my first question and before she continued her atrocities, I raised my palm facing towards her signaling that I understood that she understood nothing about accounts.

"Well, accounts is the subject where you will need my help the most because this is the subject I have dealt with for five years, Fin is still new to me, so, you might have to help yourself in that while I continue to support you." I suggested. She frowned and did not praise the suggestion, but chose to keep quiet. This is a general phenomenon in every relationship that the male partner speaks during the initial days and as he climbs up the relationship curve, he looses the freedom of speech and then eventually the liberty of thought; The words freedom and liberty eventually find place only in the female dictionary and become extinct in men's.

I settled to ignore her reaction and continued, "Please give me a pen and a notepad, I'll tell you why Dr is called debit and not doctor!" Unpleased, it was written on her face as she thought that I was giving sarcasm to her and was making an effort to flaunt my superiority at that point of my time. She was accustomed to a princess like treatment, and could not accept if people (even those helping her) dictated their terms. But everyone has a teaching style and so did I, I overlooked everything when it came to imparting knowledge; I was least affected by what people thought about themselves, what they felt, what they thought about me; they have to go the hard way if they have to learn it, and a harder way when they took my way.

Smitha gave the pen and a notepad to me, but, her mind, somewhere else, was still fighting out the misery of getting tamed by a fellow student. I started writing on the notepad and was explaining everything to her so slowly that even an archaemedilo would have successfully completed chartered accountancy after that tutorial session. I finished writing and found that I had done a great job first up and it was left to Smitha's good judgment to comprehend what I explained.

I looked up and asked her, "So, did you understand the three basic rules? You shall be able to comprehend accounting entries now I suppose!" Smitha reacted as if I shook her from her slumber and asked her something in ancient Pali. As I mentioned, she was still fighting out the misery of getting tamed by me, my question broke her illusion where she must have tamed me and put a leash around my neck and left me in the rain smelling like a wet dog. She nodded her head sideways and looked absolutely disinterested. I regained my patience and started explaining it again but she was still thinking something else.

I balanced my emotions, closed my eyes and asked her that what was wrong with her. It was not usual of me to keep cool and let my patience be tested, especially when it came to serious issues like time and academics.

She asked me something totally irrelevant, "Why don't we study in the reading room?"

Looked astonished, I replied "You mean that club, where everyone pretends to study but no one does, that is nothing but just one lovers' club, soon it will be a make out arena."

She looked more astonished at my reply and asked me, "Why do you speak so bitter?" I said, "Truth is always bitter." Smitha had nothing to say then. She advised herself to concentrate again on French and Greek which I taught her.

Once I wrote the entire accounting stuff again, I found that Smitha was busy scribbling something on her notepad. Girls generally have this tendency of doing something totally disconnected and behave as if they are living in a different world where reality is thousand light years away from existence. I could not take that non sense any longer. It was not that she had paid me for running tutorials that she would do anything she wanted while wasting my time in whichever way she wanted. I had to study as well in the twenty four hours I had, which Smitha thought to be forty eight hours (For her slow brain, she took twice the time than everyone else did to comprehend things). I had to get decent grades; else the same girls like Smitha would not even add me on Facebook.

I decided to ignore her and started doing my own stuff. I picked up my calculator and financial management book and started doing my own numerical not bothered about what she wanted to study or what she did not. It was clearly evident that she was aware of my move but wanted to act indifferent of what was happening. As mentioned earlier, she was a pampered girl who could not take anything against her self-proclaimed majesty. I raised my middle finger in my mind to her and decided to do with my numerical.

The theory "Ignore the girl to get her attention" held true as Smitha spoke after a gap of five minutes, "What happened? Why are you not teaching me accounts?" she asked me in the sweetest of voice she could throw, pretending that she was really innocent. I liked girls who were innocent, but hated those who pretended to be when they were not. One of my biggest weaknesses was that I did not know how to pretend. I was dry and blunt.

"Speak normally, why you are acting like a child. It is better that you carry on with what you have been doing all this while, that is, roaming around with Piyush and allow me to do what I have been doing. I can't waste my time this way; I have to study hard to get decent grades unlike you who will settle with one of the IIMites later on, you don't have an education loan either. Forgive me, you go your way, I go mine." I spoke bluntly without being aware of the fact that within a year's time, all my ways will be blocked and It will be Smitha all the way.

"Thanks a lot for all the help, the time and the efforts you had put in to make me understand whatever subject you were teaching. Really sorry to have wasted your time, go ahead, and get yourself a 10, if possible, get 10+. Bye and thanks, all the best." she replied with her voice going bleak and it was the most discouraging "All the best."

She stood up swiftly like Jonty Rhodes used to from the ground, packed her bags in the vengeance and left the scene as if she had a stomach trouble. I had actually disturbed her delicate internal balance, but it was not my problem, I thought, "I had come here to study and not for social service, there is nothing called free lunch in this world, she was not so close that I went out of the way to help her out."

CONFUSION

The term "confusion" was equal to the number of red blood cells in my body. At times, it became difficult for me to judge myself, the uncertainty in my behavior hanged like an axe on my head, which would fall anytime to chop me off. For instance, I had promised Smitha that I would help her after getting swept away by her CEO comment, and today, I opined that there was nothing called as free lunch in this world. I found myself to be a selfless guy forever and a day, but my behavior that day depicted all signs of selfishness, but they say that there is always a thin line of difference between being selfish and being genuine, I was confused and finally decided to place myself in the genuine category, thus acting truly self-defensive against myself. Does this choice mean being selfish or not is for you to decide, I can't decide as my confusion just gets multiplied exponentially and radically.

As the time went by, I honed my skills of booze and smoke with Om being my coach. Slowly and gradually, we turned out to be the biggest drunkards of our batch, as the needle of our fuel tank was always on the extreme right every night. This was again contradictory of the thought which I carried that I was there only to study. For fleeting moments, I thought, wasting time with Smitha would have been a much better job than to survive on corex, and super strong beers and shark tooth dug deep into our souls.

Our first lecture used to be at 9.15 every day which I and Om always missed, because it took time to recover from the hangover. We used to get up at 10 and then rush to the next lecture by 10.15. The walk to Subbiah's class under the influence of Vodka had made us really proficient in carrying our alcoholic body really well, but late. It had become a normal phenomenon that whenever I and Om rushed towards the class, Piyush and Smitha would come down from the library staircase and Smitha, will pass on "I care a damn" look. It clearly showed that both Piyush and Smitha were putting their maximum efforts in filing the assignments and thesis on time, their class performance perfect as they had track of what was being taught in class because they attended the lectures regularly unlike Jack and Daniel (I and OM).

However, it always remained a mystery how I ended up scoring amongst the toppers in all class tests. I also participated in the class discussions without much idea of what had happened in the previous lecture, but still, my baritone carried off the nonsense I spoke really well, thereby impressing the lecturers.

Sri, who was spending more time with Piyush and Smitha, wanted to unwind the mystery of my cake walk and scoring almost what they scored with not even one third of the effort each one of them was putting in. I was soon becoming a threat to his supremacy and my gaining popularity amongst the students was rival to that of Sri's.

"May I come in", asked someone, who sounded like some leader. I and Om had switched off the lights and were rolling joints under the torch light so that everyone thought we had slept. "Sounds like Sri. Shall we open the door?" whispered Om in my ears. This was the most stupid thing which Om could ask me. "Do you want the entire college to know that we dope?" I replied.

Sri was sharper than we thought him to be. "Guys it is only 8, I know you have not slept, open the door, and let me join you guys for booze." I kicked Om because it was his idea to switch off lights while we rolled joints, I agreed as well, without realising that lights off at 8 in the evening would create more serious doubts amongst people.

I opened the door slightly and Sri sneaked in. We felt that we were running an unlicenced brothel in an open market place where people sneaked in without much hush and noise. Sri took a sip of vodka kept there and came to the point straight away. It seemed Vodka gave him the courage he required. I and Om were looking with our tongues wagging because we had assumed that Sri did not even know how to spell soda, forget alcohol.

"With all the non-sense you guys do, how do you manage to study?" Sri asked bluntly calling our day to day activities as non-sense.

We decided not to respond and Om asked, "Joint?" as he offered the rolled work to Sri for lighting it up.

"What are you guys up to?" asked a surprised Sri as if we asked him to get hold of a live cobra. "Is this grass?" asked Sri revealing his innocence.

"Yeah" replied Om with pride as if he was the one to introduce grass to the mankind. "Heaven" Om added another adjective in the appreciation of grass. I looked on and enjoyed Om's single letter conversation and Sri's baffled responses.

I snatched the joint from Om, lit up and answered Sri's long due question, "This buggar does not have any inclination towards studies, he dozes off after the booze session. I study from 11 to 4, then sleep." Sri confirmed, "11 in the night to 4 in the morning?" "Hmmm" I replied while throwing the dark smoke out. "Wow that sounds amazing" said a delighted Sri. "How do you manage?" Sri interrogated. I showed him Joint and cigarettes indicating that I survived on them for five hours when my concentration level was deep. "Both of us generally don't go to the reading room or library, we prefer to study in our rooms from 5 to 7 in the evening, we discuss topics, newspaper articles, magazines, anything and everything." I revealed the secret while Sri listened cautiously. "We keep this 5 to 7 slot for theory subjects like marketing and all, when we read the topics and related case studies and then discuss it between ourselves thus staying up to date", I continued. "We then go to buy booze and have dinner. At around 8, we are back and you can see what we do at 8. From 8 to 10, we try to make it to heaven, and then study again from 11 to 4." I revealed the secret time table. "Did you see how organized we are and how particular we are about the timings?" Om cracked a joke. "Yeah, very particular but not particular when it comes to class timings" Sri continued with the joke. I nodded my head sideways.

"Will you mind if I join you for studies Rama?" asked Sri revealing his CID intentions of finding out the secret behind my consistent performance despite my involvement into illegal activities and contacts with drug peddlers of Hyderabad. Studying with Sri was always beneficial for me and Om because, he would for sure not erode value if not add anything. "Yeah, pleasure my dear friend!" I exhibited sophistication under the grip of joint.

Our first semester exams were exactly twenty one days away when Sri came to my room for the first time with the bag exactly of the size which Smitha carried. I thought he was not as stupid as Smitha, then why was he carrying such a bag. I ignored because I was not taking any additional effort of teaching Sri. "Hi, sit man sit", I spoke and I made some space for Sri on my bed. "Why such a huge bag?" I asked and pointed at Sri's container size bag.

Before anyone of us could utter a word further, I saw Piyush standing at the door step like a dog wagging its tail. I looked at Sri ferociously, Sri could realize that I was about to throw him and his bag out, he used management skills to tame me down before I did anything. "Relax man; Piyush wants to join us as well. He is well read and will be handy in covering the syllabus and for healthy discussions. Look at it professionally, he needs you and for sure, we will have benefits from him as well", said Sri. Had Sri said he needs you and you need him, I would have continued my ferocious act because I in no way needed Piyush, but Sri's verbal skills saved him as he said that we would have benefits from him. It all meant the same but it was about taming people down. I bought Sri's point.

There was no doubt that the subjects involving practical applications and numericals would be done by each one of us separately and that forum would be used to discuss the issues we faced with practical subjects and the theoretical subjects which needed discussions so that we had numerous examples and logic in place to cover the boring stuff like HR and marketing which needed a lot of reading.

Every time Sri and Piyush came, I thought about Smitha, that what she would be indulging at. Would she be teaming up with girls who smoked up to study like Sri and Piyush joined me and Om? Or will she be scribbling her note books to glory while travelling to and fro from reality and dreams? Will she be struggling alone to understand the difference between dr and doctor, *beta*, cost of capital, PE, EPS and other words which were Greek and French for her? I thought Sri could be spared but I felt like crushing Piyush's empty head for what he had done to Smitha. That is why I call him an asshole, a bastard; he used Smitha all the while for making assignments, thesis, reports, presentations and for hanging out, but when it came to the real test of character, when she needed her supposedly best friend the most, he left her in the middle of nothing and came to join hands with those he had nothing to do with. Anyhow, it was none of my business, "That is being professional" I recalled Sri's remark and then recalled mine, "No free lunches".

I, Sri, Om and Piyush continued our methodical approach and all four of us were set to keep the scoring tables under our belt with each one of us targeting 9+ and Sri learning new skills of vodka and smoke. During those days of combined studies, the group Sri, Piyush and Smitha broke and I saw Smitha coming and leaving the class alone. It was a clear indication that all was not well between Smitha and Piyush; good, reality had struck her and I thought that she would appreciate the fact why I hated Piyush then. Whom she argued for and whom she banked upon to score good grades and whom she considered to be the best friend was now not giving a short lived glimpse, it was bound to break her heart. I thought of approaching Smitha couple of times, but always dropped the idea thinking that her egoistic nature and fury on Piyush would result in an unpleasant behavior. But, I could feel the pain she was undertaking to pick up things jumbled after Piyush's planned exit from her life. I could commiserate with her but I had no plans of queering the pitch I developed with Sri and Piyush.

"Fuck Man, six days, and no sleep. Let's booze tonight like crazy and hit the hay!" said Om. We had eight papers on six days on a trot with two days witnessing us answering two papers in a day. And everything had gone smoothly. "Sure, left with only five hundred bucks, got to reach home as well." I said while I checked my wallet.

We boozed to the hilt that night and rushed to catch our trains next morning to go home. I met Smitha at the station; she was all alone and sported an extremely dejected look. It was evident of the fact that her first semester at MBA had got screwed up magnificently, all credit to herself for being friends with Piyush and then myself because I did not keep up to my promise of helping her. Om had already left as his train was before mine, Sri was catching a flight. I was alone as well and thought of going to Smitha and accompany her.

"Hi, so how were the gruesome six days of marathon with no sleep?" I kicked off the conversation almost after two months we spoke last.

"Hi", this is all she said and looked somewhere else. "Some coffee?" I asked another question to which she smiled which meant yes. I got up, came back in five minutes with a hot steaming coffee and some sandwich for myself. Smitha thought that both sandwich and coffee were for her and accepted them with both hands. I was perplexed and thought for a while that I should go and get another sandwich, but decided against it as that would have embarrassed Smitha.

I noticed her body language closely, her fingers were trembling, her lips murmured something which only she could understand in her subconscious state, and she twisted her ankle in all possible angles available for humans. All these signs demonstrated one thing, that she was excessively tensed about something which was eating into her endangered brain cells. I thought of saving her from slipping into coma and asked, "What happened? Why are you so calm? Its ok, what happened between us is a thing of past. You don't have to show such a dejected look just because I am around." I smiled while making the atmosphere light; however, my attempt was futile as Smitha continued her intense thinking.

I kept mum after that and thought it was of no use to try anything different to make her smile. "Have you ever felt that you have been used and then treated like a door mat?" she asked. I continued my mum posture and thought, "Has she slept with Piyush who impregnated her and left her when she revealed the news of her pregnancy to Piyush which generally happens in most of the Bollywood capers."

"Hey I am talking to you" Smitha emphasized on her presence and question.

"I am sorry, where does this come from?" asked a puzzled me. Her next statement was absolutely different from what she had asked first, "You guys will for sure score 9 + and Rama you will hit a perfect ten." I realized quickly that she referred to Piyush's exit from her life and his association with us for combined studies.

I gave a semi smile because I found myself in a situation like the one when you are blessed with a baby boy and your neighbor lost his father. "Yeah let's see. But how about you, your papers went well right?" I asked her a question for which I knew what the answer was.

"No, not so good, I am banking totally on internals, they will help me scrape through." She said.

"Its ok, anything above 8 is good and helps you to get shortlisted easily for interviews", I said.

"No, 8 seems like a distant reality. I don't think I'll be able to cross seven!" said Smitha as the first drop of tears tickled down her face.

"Oh relax lad!! It is absolutely ok if you score 7, you have got three more semesters left, interns, and then the final research project. You have got all the opportunity to pull it off as desired. Chill! Don't blow it out of proportions. Everyone cannot score 9 and plus, it is not a crime to have scored less."

"It is god damn easy for you to say this, because you have never tasted the agony of scoring less than 7. I feel I am finished and don't know if I'll be able to recover what I have lost", she said and boarded the train while I helped her with the luggage.

6

I Don't See Any Reason to Say No

The break after the first semester was very short and we had to report for the second semester in two weeks' time. Our college was a ragging free zone but it was highly surprising that college authorities themselves had arranged for our mass ragging by announcing the results on the day we reported.

I was sure that I was crossing 9 but how much above 9 was the point of anxiety for me. Om came to my room and asked, "May I come in Professor?" "Shut up and come in" I replied.

"What shut up? You will score 9 for sure and soon you will be in the league of extraordinary gentlemen like Sri. You will stop coming to my room and won't smoke up any longer. You will become one of those assholes which are flashy but stink", Om was speaking pointlessly; this is the behavior of those whose blood pressure crossed all levels under the pressure of exam results.

I ignored his remarks and said, "Screw you. Shut up and let's go." I got up and dragged Om out of the room and locked it, while Om said, "What shut up? Won't you score 9? But where is Sri, he did not come, I went to his room, he wasn't there, tried reaching on his phone, but he did not pick up."

I noticed that Om made three points about Sri, all of them were negative and said, "That is being professional, you are with someone for some reason, somewhat like joint ventures, he does not mean business with us any longer, he will probably wait for the results and see who scored how much and will make friends on that basis and why the fuck did you go to his room to lick his ass?"

"No, actually I was, you know, hmmm, let's see!" Om searched for words to cover his stupidity when Sri emerged from the gloomy result oriented atmosphere.

"Where are you guys going?" Sri asked a baseless question. It was like asking somebody that why he was carrying an umbrella when it was raining. Om looked at me with his nostrils swelling as I had developed wrong thoughts about Sri. I smiled and pointed towards the academic block indicating that the result was on our minds.

"Oh! Ok. I checked mine on the students' domain on intranet, I have got 8.62. One can view only his or her result, yours was not available to me, you need not walk all the way to academic block." Sri said while lighting up a cigarette, "I was expecting 9, shit!" he added disappointment. Om was mighty pleased to see Sri's transformation from the nice guy to those who dared to smoke on the corridors; he took a cigarette from Sri's packet without hesitating when Sri offered. I pulled one as well from Sri's packet and we came back to my room.

"You check yours first!" I asked Om while logging in using his ID and gave the laptop to him. Om checked while Sri looked from behind and said, "Congrats man, 7.4 is good enough. Good job." Om looked up with a face which was somewhat like a semi smile status; 7.4 was less for the efforts he had put in, probably class performances pulled him down. But I would like to highlight a point about people like Sri here. For the amount of efforts he had put in, he scored 8.6 for which he cribbed, but, if the same efforts from Om got 7.4, he advised Om to cheer up and said the score was good enough; the guys like Sri bestowed themselves with demi god status where they decided themselves who deserved how much, CRAP.

Om lit up a smoke which looked like a sign of disappointment, Sri also lit up a smoke which looked like a sign of satisfaction. "You check yours. All the best", Om said as he handed over the laptop back to me.

"How much?" asked Sri, it looked that Sri was more interested in my results than me. I did not even check by then, but thought of saying 10 which would have made Sri either faint or jump out of the window. "9.6!" I said while taking a long drag, which Sri misheard as 5.6. He did not look surprised, rather digested the rubbish fact. He nodded his head and consoled me, "Its ok! You have three more semesters and final research.." This is the *gyaan* which everyone gave to each other in the event of scoring less. I declined him further freedom to speak and said, "Bugger, not 5.6, 9.6!" Om got up and hugged me. It seemed that he wanted to answer Sri somehow for his cheesy act, and he thought that My outdoing Sri was the day of the millennium. Om was happy for me.

Om said, "Let's go down. Let's see how much others have got. You are there amongst the top three for sure!" Om wanted to flaunt my results to everyone and show to people that this Jack and Daniel pair was no less by any means.

"How much did Piyush get and Smitha?" I stumbled and my tone had a touch of concern when I said Smitha; for I couid recall the tears that soaked her soft face.

"No clue." said Sri, with a sense of grief that I scored more than him. It looked as if it was the end of world for Sri, he looked totally down. However, I and Om did not want to indulge ourselves in giving *gyaan* to people that it was ok to score less.

None of the students whom we met on the way to academic block scored more than me, thus making me a potential topper; however, a final confirmation on the notice board was quite mandatory before we called the shots. However, the agony of scoring less than seven lurked in my mind and for that moment it seemed very important for me to know that how much Smitha scored!

Almost after two weeks of her agony statement, I was not able to figure out why did it come to my confused mind once again. What was making it so important for me? She was no competition for me, I had come to academic block to see whether I was amongst the top three or not, the ecstasy of being a heavy scorer was being outclassed by the worry for Smitha's score. Bright morning was laden with foreboding all of a sudden; could feel the trouble in my knees, a glimpse of Smitha's maudlin face flashed in front of my eyes. I stopped and took out my phone to call up Smitha while Om kept on walking dreaming of the booze rain that night which he would take bath in if I was amongst the top three.

"Hi Rama, congrats!" came a voice which sounded entrancing for the first time to me.

"Hi! How much have you got?" I replied ignoring her "Congratulations"!

"As if you don't know! Why do you always find ways of embarrassing me? It's there on the notice board, entire college can see that, why did you take the trouble of calling up and asking me personally?" said Smitha.

I realized that I should have used my brains to check her results on the notice board; my behavior suggested that I was trying to show off my result by asking her score. My honest intentions got accused of an unenthusiastic act. I tried to clear the murky labyrinth which was trying to make way and said, "Listen Smitha, I am not like others, I understand the difference between issues which are serious and non-serious. I know how important it is for you to score well, in fact, it is important for each one of us to score well. I did not call up to embarrass you or something.

Just that what you said before you left at the station bothered me; I called you up out of concern and by no means, wanted to show you down. It is absolutely perfect if you don't want to share your results, but lets catch up, I wanted to see you, your sad face affected me badly, I somehow feel that I can't see you crying, you have to smile and that is what you are born for!" and before I continued my emotional drama, Smitha said, "Excuse me!" She jolted me nicely and brought me to reality because had I continued for some more time, I would have proposed to her while flowing with emotions. "Yeah, tell me." I said.

"Ok, fine I'll come down in five minutes. Where are you? Would you mind coming to the girls' hostel gate? I don't want to come towards the academic block." Smitha made a mandatory request which I followed and went towards the girls' hostel.

"Hi! Real congratulations man! I told you right, you were absolutely fantastic!" said Smitha while shaking hands with me. For the first time, I realized her hands were so soft, I felt like kissing them. I picked up my senses and said, "Thanks a ton! But I have to check if I am there amongst the top three or not!"

Smitha was shocked and asked, "Are you sure you don't know who the toppers are?"

"Yes! I just checked my result, don't know about others!" I answered.

"Do you have any idea or any clue that how much have you scored? It is mighty 9.65 dude!" Smitha spoke excitedly while stretching words like "any clue", "any idea" and "mighty 9.65".

"Yeah but!" I started speaking but was interrupted by her, "What yeah but yeah? You are the topper dude and you have no clue about it. Shit man, look at your face, it seems that you knew that you would top. Great attitude man!"

Assault number 2 had taken place; the first one was the CEO comment and the second one about my attitude. I was blown away to pieces and was high like a kite. The compliments and the wishes could not get any better. Despite a decent circle of friends who would have known by that time who the topper was, I did not get any call or message from anyone. That is world for you, excessively mean, you plot a normal distribution curve for them, and they will be all at the center, so mean. The girl, whom I ditched, was the first one to wish me; attesting how wrong I was about her.

My fate was sealed with cracking 9+ in the first semester. Even if I scored a mediocre 8 in the second semester, I would have been through because I would be still averaging well above 8.5 to qualify for the top payers by the third semester. So, it was unquestionable why I did not help Smitha then, because it was not a problem even if she wasted my time as aforesaid. Built on such a thought, I challenged Smitha's ego and said, "Do you really mind if I help you in this semester? I promise that I won't leave you in the middle unlike others!"

"Unlike others" was an unnecessary suffix and Smitha understood everything including "Unlike others" and said, "Please let us not discuss about Piyush. He did what he wanted to, but I am ok with that and as far as your help is concerned, thank you, I don't need favors. Thanks, really thanks, sweet of you but its ok."

Smitha's ego mashed answer drove me into a frenzy and I said, "What do you think of yourself? Why do you want to keep your ego high unnecessarily and score lesser in the second semester? Keep it aside for some time, you will need it in days to come. Just understand one thing that never stand on your ego when your house is on fire. You need help and there is nothing wrong about it. Relax, you take it or not, I will be there for you throughout this semester and if things permit, throughout MBA."

Smitha and I started studying together to discover that Smitha was not as slow as she seemed to be during the only evening we studied together during the first semester. Or probably, I was magical enough to transform a snail into a leopard. As a matter of fact, Smitha was largely responsible for her improvement, her attitude to strive for the better, and if not for her attitude, then she would have lost it by a big margin and her dream to crack one of the big investment banks would have gone to drains; so, indeed, she put her heart and soul into each and every session of our combined studies.

Smitha's growing interest in the studies and her improving abilities to challenge my points helped me to thrive. We struck chord and it became unusual for us if we did not meet every day. Our sections were shuffled and we had a different time table and a set of assignments to follow, however, we made it a point that we met, if not for anything, then at least for dinner. The group now ranged from people like Om to me to Sri to Smitha. Smitha was getting more allocation of my time than anybody else including Om and I could sense that *Om was not pleased with that happening and sooner or later, Om was to prove that association with guys like him was dangerous to budding relationships.*

We chose one of the Saturdays to go around the old city of Hyderabad. Om and Sri were supposed to join us, but because of the heavy booze session the previous night, Om could not match up with the time, by this time, Sri had taken my role and was the regular booze partner with Om, so, he could not match up either. I tried only once to get both of them even when I did not want them to join. Who would spoil the chance of dating a girl who was becoming my way of life?

I left hostel without informing the two sleeping beauties and met Smitha at the college gate when she asked, "Where are the other two?" I felt like going back and covering the faces of sleeping beauties with pillows to death.

"No they don't want to come", I lied; I could not say that three of us boozed crazily. I was not bothered about them; I wanted to save my ass. Smitha looked at me suspiciously, it appeared that she was thinking that I had done away with Sri and Om purposefully and wanted to convert the normal city tour into a date. I did not respond to her reaction, and quickly said, "Lets go, the bus is here!" and boarded the bus without giving her any chance to speak.

I did what I had never done before in the first semester, booze almost a liter of vodka every week, and then, I was again doing what I had never done before in the second semester, I was carrying bags which contained all the equipments covered under the head "Shopping." The city tour which was to cover Char Minar and some Hyderabadi delicacies was covering only the by lanes around Char Minar where we bought pearls, some small, some big, some shining, some old, some new, on bangles, on chains. Finally, Smitha could realize that I was not really pleased with this way of city tour and said, "Hey Ramcy!" (Yes, this is the way Smitha started addressing me because Ramcy, sounded more western) "Let's watch a movie before we take the bus back to campus!" The relief made a signature on my face and I said, "Yes, sure!" and said, "*Central chalo*" to the auto driver.

Lagey Raho Munnabhai was my choice and Hrithik was Smitha's choice. We settled for Dhoom-2, the comic action movie. She advocated for Dhoom-2 as if Hrithik was to jump out of the screen and strip for her and finally have sex with her. I chose to make way for her romantic fantasies towards Hrithik and said, "Dhoom is ok with me as well." I felt like getting into the screen and scuffle Hrithik to death as well. The movie was absolutely a bore, or you could say that I was interested more in Smitha. I was sleeping on Smitha's shoulder in no time because the movie never took off. Smitha shook me, I got up and was shocked to see my head on her shoulders. I felt that I had been there for ages and all I could remember was strange beards and flowery shirts. I apologized to Smitha and she said, "Its ok! I know you do not like the movie, you can catch some sleep!" I did not take it as any kind of signal from Smitha and then shifted to rest my head on the guy on the other side.

Once the movie got over, Smitha woke me up and said, "Let's go, I know you are tired of carrying bags, its good that you got to sleep!" Wow! What a justification to make someone watch utter crap. My financial acumen wanted to say that I had paid for the movie as well, then why didn't we watch a movie of my choice. But its ok, I was managing to impress Smitha through my cute nature. It was Smitha only who found my nature of mood swings cute.

At Hyderabad House, one of the best restaurants for authentic Hyderabadi Food, a man in a white shirt and black pants, supposedly called waiter ordered us to order food. Things did not change since morning; Smitha decided it was worthless to ask me what I wanted to eat and went ahead with Mutton biryani and Mutton kebabs which the waiter scribbled down on his writing pad. Smitha being half Tamil and half Brahmin, I expected her to at least ask me if I was ok with meat. I had never eaten mutton in my life and told Smitha, "Can we order chicken? I can't eat Mutton! I have actually just tried it once, it is like dead rubber." "Oh! Is it?" she giggled and said, "Eat it, it is really good. Tastes yummy." Smitha dismissed my application and decided the food for me.

Girls never give obvious hints, but one should be smart enough to pick those subtle hints, like the one Smitha threw at me by ordering the food for me without asking me. Girls call this caring for you and you have to accept it, else screw yourself as there are lots of others to pick those subtle hints and accept them.

I was eating only the rice component of the mutton biryani and said, "Its actually yummy." Smitha just nodded her head and dived back into the plate to wear and tear the poor dead lamb. She must have thought, "Who the fuck is bothered if he likes the food or not, as long as he is listening to me, I am cool, and if he does not, he is a fool." I digested the thought, the rice component and small chunks of meat to impress Smitha. I could see her face illuminating when she saw me gulping down pieces of Mutton. I swear I did not like any part of it, but thought it was ok.

I had unknowingly taken care of Smitha's likes and dislikes very well till then. It was absolutely necessary for me to smoke after the food, which I apparently did. Girls always look for free washrooms, and they make full use of it; Smitha spotted one at the restaurant and asked me to wait. I waited downstairs while catching up a super quick smoke. However, Smitha was quicker than the usual, probably, the entire washroom was soiled. She saw me smoking, came up to me, snatched the fag and threw it and stubbed it with her feet as if it was the only mosquito in the world which had been spreading dengue.

Now, girls call this exercising rights and the bloody excuse is that the rights are exercised only on those who are blessed with the love of the girl who is actually flexing her rights on you. I did not utter a word and was quite happy about the proceedings. I was falling for her, if not; I would have slapped her for throwing the cigarette.

It was 9 when we left the restaurant, and we took the college bus at 9.15. Since you must have realized by now that how stupid I was, I will tell you something which will profound your thoughts about me. December nights, in any part of India are cold, and "close the window if you can" kind of buses are teasing in such nights. I could see Smitha shivering and rubbing her arms. The wind was hitting her face, her hair was getting disturbed whenever she adjusted them against the wind, I enjoyed the nice little contest between the wind and her hair. I recalled another form of chivalry and took off my jacket and gave it to her. Smitha took the jacket and she must have said thousand "thank you" for that. The stage was set, I was falling for her; I was helping her with the studies, I had almost dated her, I exhibited chivalry by donating my jacket temporarily, I watched crap for her, I carried her bags, I ate mutton, she exercised her rights, she cared for me, she was also giving me subtle hints!

I said, "I love you!" It seemed that the time had frozen, I had never proposed to anybody, Smitha looked at me as if I proposed a fuck buddies concept, stopped rubbing her arms and made austere expressions. We spoke nothing for another five minutes; I asked her again, "Did you hear what I said?" "Yes" she acknowledged, "But I need some time to think." she continued.

Girls always want to think even if they are sure about it, it is still unanswered that didn't she think when she was giving me those subtle hints and carefully exercised her rights on me. I wanted to ask her this, but chose to keep quiet.

We got down at the college gate and asked her again. She said, "Lets go to my hostel first, we will discuss this at the hostel gate if you are ok."

I thought quickly, "What is the logic behind discussing at the hostel gate? Is she scared that if she says no, then I'll drop her bags here and she might have to carry all this till hostel?"

"Yeah it is ok" I said. As we started walking, someone held me from my shoulder. It was Om, and he was drunk, and I had ditched him, because I promised him that we would booze together and I was late. Smitha distanced herself from us and started walking briskly. "Where the fuck were you ?" asked Om, with red eyes. Smitha could hear that, I looked at her and said, "Language Om."

"Fuck the language and what is this you are carrying?" Om asked while pointing at the bags I carried. "Nothing we just went shopping", I replied.

"Oh! Shopping and all, you motherfucker, then why the hell did you ditch us in the morning and left without telling us, do you think we would have stopped you from shopping, I would have helped you carry this burden of bags", Om said. His statement sent Smitha fuming, she thought that everything was set up nicely and I lied to her that Om and Sri did not want to come.

"Tell us bugger, you just went shopping or you went fucking her? We would have helped you carry that burden as well, had you taken us along", said Om, while showing his palm to me for high five. I looked at Smitha, she was frozen. I knew Om was blunt, but did not expect him to fall down to such levels. I dropped whatever I carried and slapped Om. He was half my size and his alcohol ridden body could not stand the impact of my slap; he fell down.

He was super high and started hurling bad words, "You mother fucker, son of a bitch, you stabbed at my back, you slapped me for this slut who roamed with another mother fucker earlier, she is a Delhi g remember! She stinks, you stink as well. Get lost". He kicked me when I gave him a hand to get up. Om broke into tears when he said "get lost."

I had choices then, either to move ahead with Smitha and leave Om lying there or help Om to get to his room and then meet Smitha for the discussion. I decided to go ahead with the first as I trusted Om, I knew he would be fine and accept me again as his friend next day, he was probably a little too drunk, but Smitha had to discuss something which looked absolutely important to me.

I and Smitha did not speak till we reached the hostel gate. I kind of did not want to discuss it either because what I had done with Om kept on tormenting me. I gave the bags to Smitha and said, "Bye!" and started walking. "Wait" she said. She took off the jacket and gave it back to me, and said, "Sit here! Don't be sad, I am not really bothered about whatever has happened now!" I knew she was lying but I felt that this entire Om's episode was working to my advantage. "And you wanted to know what I feel about your proposal to me, right?" she asked me thus creating more suspense. I felt like being amongst the top two for the Miss Universe crown. "Please! Stop this murder mystery." I pleaded.

"I don't have a reason to say no" she said and suffixed it with "Sweetheart" after a little pause. I almost got it, but even the obvious hints didn't work for me then. I confirmed, "I don't understand all this, is it yes or no?" "Shut up; take your jacket and go! See you at the mess sweetie at 8", she said and left and also left me wondering that how and why the fuck shall I get up at 8 on a Sunday morning after the booze session to please Om.

7

Days of Separation

Enrolment no	*Name*	*Gender*	*GPA*	*CGPA*	*Result*
06BS2736	Smitha Suzanne Swaminathan	F	8.48	7.8	Pass
06BS3773	Ramachandran Iyer	M	8.00	8.78	Pass

The above scoreboard marked the end of an eventful second semester and it was time to move to do the internships. Smitha craved for her mother and therefore, her influential dad fixed her up with a German MNC in Delhi, and since my family was not influential, I had to crack one of the companies which came to college to pick students for internships. And fortunately, I landed up in Bangalore, my home! And that meant that Smitha and I were going to be distanced for more than one hundred and twenty days! It did hurt.

Smitha did not believe in spending much and I did not have options to do so as the stipend was limited; hence, the most convenient way to communicate was to chat than to call as it turned out to be cheaper. During one of the evenings when I returned late from office, I waited looking at the screen for the machine to pop up "Smitha is online"

The wait did not bring Smitha online, albeit a message popped up on my phone, it read, "Mama around, I mite not be able to come online baby, will try in the nite. Luv", it was just about coming online, yet it left me disappointed. Small things made me happy in life. However, the wait bought me something which I longed for during grads.

Pooja, a sultry chick, a super sexy female, a bombshell and the hottest I knew in life was online. She was my batch mate from grads, and she was the dream chick of every dick in the college. She hardly spoke to guys, and I was one amongst the fortunate for being good with studies. She was probably bored to death that evening, else, why would she choose to speak to someone so useless like me?

"Hi Rama" she messaged. I looked at my screen once again before believing that she was the first one to begin the conversation, such things happened only once in a millennium, I took time to respond but I did.

"Hi Pooja. How are you?" I replied and I did not expect a reply.

"I am good, so Piyush told me that you guys are in Hyderabad, studying in the same college" She said

"Yeah, you in touch with him?" I asked, stupid enough because Piyush remained in touch with all the hot chicks.

"Sorry, he is in touch with me, not the other way" she had airs about herself, and she was vocal about that. Fair enough!

"Cool. So, what are you up to these days?" I asked

"Nothing much, I am busy shopping these days. My friend's brother is getting married. Lot of *masti*. Just wondering which sari to wear, I have already shortlisted one, you know 20k, but I want to wear a costlier one". Pooja proved that she was typical Delhi, and a Punjabi as well. Only girls can get orgasms thinking about somebody else's brother's marriage, and Delhi girls got twice of that; I mean who shops for 20k sari for some XYZ's wedding who is not even related to you. There you go, I thought that she was stupid enough to waste resources, but you don't say those stuffs to hot chicks, you agree with their stupidity, even if it costs a fortune.

"Oh, that is great" I said.

"You wanna check the *Sangeet* pics?" Pooja *ji* offered an invitation to her calendar. Who would say no? I thought, "Am I cheating on Smitha?" and my other side told me, "Are you an idiot? It is just about seeing the pics? Its ok."

I obeyed my other side and said, "Yes, sure, who would say no to such a pretty girl like you?" I actually wanted to say hot and not pretty!

She shared her pictures in a flash, one following the other without allowing me to stop at one, and this is when girls act stupid; Who shares pictures, and that too Pooja type pictures with some random guy on internet? I could have used them to my advantage. But I think that she thought, "I was not that type of a guy".

Ladies, please understand that all guys are like that only, there are no varieties or species! I stopped at one of the pictures which had Pooja draped in a white sari which had silk work at the borders, her blouse was noodle strap which went round her shoulder to her neck to somewhere at the back not visible, overall, the picture confused me, but it had something more to concentrate on, the neck deep blouse had exposed her world famous cleavage line! Getting flirty, I sent the picture back to her, and said, "this one is the best… : P"

And she said, "Naughty you! Every male friend of mine likes this pic only".

"Ok, so you have shared this with others as well. Great, anyways, bye!" I discontinued the conversation, as something began to torment me for getting flirtatious with some other lady.

"Why? What happened? Hey, I am sorry, I was kidding!" Imagine, Pooja type girl apologizing to me, and asking me to stay back to chat. Yet, I logged off!

The next morning, when I cut across the city of gardens to spend time in office, I sent an SMS to Smitha, "Hi baby, Good morning" I got a prompt response generally, but something went wrong that day!

I threw myself to slumber in an hour's drive to office, and then got up to check my phone, Smitha had not replied till then, more than unusual. If things permitted, she would fix a transmitter in my mind to track my movements. I messaged her again, "Hello! What happened? Where are you?"

"Its all over . There is nothing left between us. Stop messaging me now!" Smitha sent something which was unable for me to understand, but the source of that message was still a mystery!

I lost all the concentration on the work which I hardly did, I sent a flurry of messages to Smitha expecting her to spill the beans for the sudden heart attack. I did not eat that day, and kept my eyes fixed at the time on the computer screen, and the moment it hit 4.00 pm, I punched out of office and rushed back home, logged in and saw if Smitha was online as she had switched off her phone!

My mailbox had a message from Smitha, sent at 12:59 am. Did that mean Smitha came online the previous night? Then why didn't she message me? I would have woken up from the death to chat with her. I could not decipher anything and I read the mail.

You all are same, you cannot be loyal. That is about it, I can't tolerate infidelity. Anyhow, it was nice being with you! Take care. Bye

Smitha...

"You" meant "All Men" and Infidelity was some crap, I was soon to find out. I continued to call her while being glued to my laptop and neither of the two worked. I had dinner just for the sake of it as Amma continued to pressurize, as the thought of losing Smitha hammered me.

But the patience paid off, as Smitha came online. I unleashed a series of "Sorry" and "Love you" for which she remained unbothered to reply! I gave up at one point of time and changed the gears, "Will you mind telling me the reason?" and Smitha did not mind! She told me something which left my mouth wide open.

"I am sure you were dating Pooja in your college and you were acting coy with her last night! You could not wait to see her nude pics!" Excuse me? Was Smitha keeping a check on my chat box? How did she crack my password? I guess I leaked it out some day and wearing sexy clothes does not make one nude; Smitha was acting out fashioned. But I had to get this confirmed!

"Are you checking my chats?" I asked instantly.

"Yes, And I think I was right in doing that. Don't ever speak to me again, its all over" and she logged off. Smitha was not to be blamed; her cousin was treated to domestic violence and infidelity!

But all that was fine, I had to get Smitha back at any cost, therefore, I unleashed a series of mails, messages and whatever form of communication available at my disposal. My efforts were good enough only to irk her up who blasted me into pieces when I dragged her into one of the chat sessions by threatening her of suicides and other idiotic stuff! And trust me; I had never apologized to anyone like that. But what was I apologizing for? It happens!

"Will you stop irritating me now? I don't want any sort of communication with someone who is dishonest, and not at all loyal. Please stop this madness, you are insulting me by trying to speak to me again and again" Smitha blasted me.

"But what have I done?" I pleaded mercy.

"Aren't you ashamed of asking this?" Smitha insulted me further.

"Anything for you baby!" I was losing temper, but I maintained my cool!

"What baby? You dare call me that! I feel shit to have got associated with you. You are almost like a dog, tail wagging and tongue hanging! Get lost". Smitha used everything to test my patience, which was demolished by then, and I responded, much to her shiver!

"What the hell? First of all you don't trust me, I feel ashamed that you have been keeping a check on my chats. And you did not find anything vulgar or something, it was just someone from my college. And had you seen the chat properly, it was Pooja who said hi. I did not initiate the conversation and it was she who wanted to show me the pictures. So, get your facts right before accusing me. Do you get that?" the first round of defense was through.

"And the moment she showed her pictures, you began to flirt with her, you cannot be trusted. I am sure you must have had many more affairs which you had hidden from me like you always lied about booze. All you men are the same". Smitha was getting unbearable.

"Oh shut up. Affairs me? I don't understand what the fuck makes you say that?" and then I said something uncalled for, which was an issue with me. Speak and then regret!

"And you have been talking nonsense about men right? Your dad is also a man! When did I hide about booze? You always knew that I boozed. And tell me one thing, have you ever checked what your Dad does abroad? He had lived in Germany for so many years, do you know what temperature does Berlin record? One can't survive without boozing there, he must have been lying to your mom and you have believed him blindly. And plus, he has seen your mother only once in a year for the last eighteen years, and how are you sure that he has never dated anyone there? Every man does two timing, so does your dad do that as well? So, just think twice before you make any baseless remarks. The drama you are doing is absolutely unjustified. Fuck off!" And I disconnected!

It did not take me long to discover that I had done the blunder by dragging her father into it and expecting her to be with me anymore was sheer stupidity, hence, all I had in my hand was to do a repair job! But nothing was going to work, so, I decided to abandon everything till the college reopened. However, I dropped in a smiley and a sorry every day on Smitha's phone!

. *

I looked up to the sky and thanked my fate, because it took less than what I thought for Smitha to reciprocate to my regretful messages. She called me up within a week and said, "Hi Rama."

"I am really sorry" I found an apology!

"That is ok! I think I also went overboard. I should have trusted you". Smitha turned the tables. She was serving me food!

"Thank you. I am sorry; I should not have spoken like that. I get irritated when I am being put under the scanner unnecessarily" I said candidly.

"That is ok" Smitha sounded cheerful! "Fine, so, how is your interns going? Mine is going rubbish, I have no clue what's going on!" Smitha answered about her internship without getting to know about mine!

And I did not want to answer about mine, because I had to act that I was highly bothered about hers, "Oh my god! What happened? Do you need me to do something?"

"No that is fine, I'll manage" she said.

"Oh come on! I want to compensate for the wrong I did. We will do one thing, we will do your project in the evening from now on. Online at 7! Ok?" I said!

Smitha turned obedient on that one, and ensured that she remained online sharp at 7, I logged in and before I connected the mouse, Smitha pinged, "Hi, so how are you? You know what, we just have one and a half months left and I have no clue about my project."

My case was far better than hers, yet I kept it secret, and said, "That is really sad, so what is that you are doing?"

"I have been asked to work on the calculations around sales force productivity and incentives. Sameer has been helping off late." Smitha said, leaving me to concentrate on the last portion of her statement!

Who was Sameer and why was he into social service? I could not allow anyone to help her out, thus replacing me, therefore, I pushed for the top gear to complete her project, and in that process forgot that I had a project in hand as well.

"Ok, relax you get me all the data", I said.

"What all do you need?" Smitha said.

"The total markets, the workforce of each market, the fixed salaries they get and the sales they have generated in the last 3 years. I work with a few IIM guys, I'll speak to them and they will for sure give some suggestion. We can probably establish a trend line and work towards it." I gave instructions to Smitha, assuming those to be better than what Sameer would have told her.

I discussed the data with the people in office; they gave some brilliant suggestions, trying to figure out if that was my project. And with proper directions available, mixed with my degrading acumen levels, I got back to Smitha. The next few weeks of punctual chat sessions saw Smitha bombarding me with the details which I asked for and which she wanted to dump me with.

I used the details to process them into meaningful graphs, charts and excel models with repeated simulations of different business scenarios. I thought that I was drawing Smitha closer to me by selflessly taking up her project and working on it, staying up late at times while seeing her off to sleep. It was only love and nothing else which made me do which otherwise was a distant reality.

The internship days were going to end soon and Smitha's project was well built, however, my project was in doldrums as my entire thought process and energy was channelised into manufacturing hers! I thought to mention this to Smitha in one of the chat sessions, "Baby, your entire project is through. You just have to make the presentation. Can you do that on your own? I have to complete my project as well, can I do that?"

Smitha inferred what I did not intend, and said, "Fine, why don't you say that I have been disturbing you? Thanks a lot, I will manage on my own, and I will not even use your excel work! I will see what I can do" and she logged off! Smitha's trick did not work this time, as I ignored her tantrums with full determination!

However, her logging off dropped a log on the concentration needed to complete my project in three days, as compared to three weeks for her project, I managed to make something creepy which was to be termed as "Misrepresentation" and not presentation as I cooked up the data, fudged them to fit into the scenario which I had dreamt of and finally goofed up on the presentation day.

I was fuming over Smitha, as she stole the focus, and did not call her up! And when I speculated on the presentation evening that how well I screwed up, Smitha called up. It was important for sure, as Smitha never called as she chose chat for communication purposes!

I answered her call, down and low, "Hi. How are you?"

Smitha was bubbling with energy and she caught for her breath to say, "Yay, yay. My presentation was terrific. Thank you baby, your excel sheets, graphs and data were excellent, they did not ask any questions. They even said that they don't have any questions as the graphs and calculations answered whatever questions they had. Brilliant. I got an A!"

As Smitha exhibited her happiness, I hindered the same, "I had my presentation too".

"Oh, yes. How did that go?" Smitha bothered to ask.

"It should have been great, there is no doubt about it" she answered herself. I thought, "What the fuck? How could it be great with just three days effort? You have to make sense at least once! And how the hell did you use the sheets prepared by me after bragging about not using it!"

Rather I said, "I don't know how did it go, but I can tell you the grade, it is C." and I disconnected!

8

Love in the Granite

"Here is your 6k", said Smitha while returning the money for the flight tickets which my brother booked for her to Hyderabad from Delhi, sadly, her dad's card was not working on that day! The money which should have been routed to my brother (as that is what it was meant for) faced the obstacle in the form of my crooked mind. I knew my brother, his quintessential kind; in fact careless nature would have never expected that money to kiss his kitty, therefore, I decided of gulping down that money and fund my dates with Smitha for the semester.

Smitha then went to Mumbai to attend her cousin's engagement. She was there for a couple of days, and trust me, these Indian family get together ideas leave you with constipation, tension, goose bumps, especially when your girl, who is supposedly next in the queue for the institution of marriage is a part of it, because, all the females, who have crossed their forties, have this unusual yet a common hobby of match making; and females of this category were plenty in Smitha's family.

Yet, Smitha escaped all the attacks called "Proposals" and headed to college unbeaten. The opportunity to use that stolen money did not keep me waiting for long. Smitha was reaching college on a Sunday morning, so, I planned to pick her up from the station, go to some nearby place, stay overnight and then join college on Monday! "But what do I tell my caretakers, Sri and Om" kept creeping in my head. I could not tell them that I was going out with Smitha, and staying overnight!

Brilliance, when dishonest, never betrayed me; the placement season was about to start and passport was indispensable. Yes, the idea aroused, "Guys, I am off to Bangalore, got to go through passport verification!" I said to Om and Sri. I went straight to the station.

I gulped down almost fifty cups of bitter hot water, called "coffee" on Indian stations, repeatedly bought platform tickets after every two hours, the idea was to spend the entire night at the station and receive Smitha absolutely fresh. The train arrived early morning; I hugged Smitha, "Let's go to Nagarjuna Sagar baby!" I said while patting my butt, a traditional way of signaling that one had cash!

"No, not so far!" she said.

"Why? Then where?" I said.

"Baby, all we need is to spend some quality time together, only you and me!" she said.

I hoped that she knew what quality time means, and prayed hard that she actually meant it the way she said it. I asked the auto driver to drive us into one of the good hotels; he drove us straight to Hotel

Granite. Smitha's slower brain had engulfed her and it took some time for her to realize that *Granite* was the same construction where she had stayed with her mother when she had come for admission.

"Rama Chandran Iyer" I wrote this name on the register and provided my Delhi address, dishonest brilliance told me that since I was born and brought up in Delhi, my driving license served as a proof that this Rama Chandran Iyer was from Delhi and not from Bangalore! Smitha's name was changed to Kritika Iyer as well. As I filled details like place I was coming from, address, religion, nationality, I felt that I was not a complete liar as this form filling session was no less than passport verification.

This entire exercise had started taking its toll on Smitha; the uncontrollable nervousness made her speak, "What are we doing?" she asked. I glanced sideways to ask her to keep mum for a while. She obeyed my gaze. Actually, it struck me that since Smitha used this place as a base camp during her mission admission, there could have been others as well from Delhi who would have used the same place for the similar purpose. So, there was a serious probability that those people along with their respective partners chose the same Granite for making out like I and Smitha did. Therefore, if anyone of them, while checking in checked the register, it was highly unlikely that they came to know that the people from the same college were making out in the adjacent rooms.

Smitha was disquiet about the proceedings, something played cheeky in her head, and there you go, she asked me something irrelevant again, "How do you know all these manipulations? You and Pooja have done it before right?" the only way of avoiding an answer to Smitha's query was to jump into the lift. Smitha had to follow me because I was carrying her bag.

"All men are like that!" she said furiously. I wanted to ask her two questions; "All men are like what?" (She was probably suffering from "All Men" syndrome) and "What was the fuss about?" but chose to keep quiet because I did not want her to get different from her "spending quality time together" thought!

As we entered the room, to lighten her mood, I said, "I am a year younger than you, if you are a girl, then I am still a boy, and today I will be man!" Smitha mused over it, but was not amused. She did not know what lust was! I accepted her innocence.

Smitha decided to rest her ass on the chair in the room, while I decided to take a power nap as I did not sleep the entire night and kept myself at bay with the railway dogs of all species, colors, and diseases.

And most importantly, I did not live like an owl the night before just to experience Smitha's unnecessary tantrums! The best way to end an argument was to keep quiet.

"Ignore the girl to get her attention" theory proved right again! Approximately, after an hour, I felt my head shaking. Scared, I opened my eyes to see that Smitha tried her best to put my head on her lap without waking me up, but she failed. Addendum to lust, she did not know what romance was!

Smitha was never so close to my body, I could sense the waves percolating through my ears, she smelled great, I held her thigh with one hand, the other hand around her waist, turned around to put my face between her knees, but sleep had conquered my body! I dozed off again.

Since Smitha was ignorant of both lust and romance, she was not furious of my stupid gesture. However, girls are self-learners; it was unfair to expect Smitha to not react on my stupid act of keeping my head between her laps and sleep. And the way the past three months had been, Smitha had been having an issue with everything. And who wants to lose an opportunity of spending quality time together. "So, better make love buddy", I said to myself and pounced on the situation.

Since Smitha was feather light, the animal inside me got up from sleep and dragged Smitha down with her thigh, I got her underneath me, denied her any movement. I looked straight into her eyes, they were fixed, did not move. I looked at her lips, she knew what was coming. I kissed her tight, hard, and made all the love in my body to travel into her body through the opening called mouth. For a few seconds, Smitha did not reciprocate, but she did not stay away from action, soon, I felt her tongue entangling with mine and we kept our lips locked.

Hostel was a breeding ground for porn, I had seen plenty of them; decided to copy some of the moves from some of the porn I could recall then. I unlocked the lips, slid down my body to get my face right on her breasts. Smitha had been watching porn as well, I reckoned, as she stopped me getting any more close to her breasts. I removed her hand, locked them with my hand, and unbuttoned her shirt with my teeth.

"No let us not do this, lets limit ourselves to kisses only." said Smitha as she panted. "Who told her that I would listen to her?" I asked myself. Also, the way she said it, I felt all the more encouraged to unbutton her shirt and bite her breasts and the animal Rama did that in a flash. Both her breasts, in a second, were in my hands. I played with them like clay, sucked them like hot chocolates.

We toiled and played with each others body, incessantly lying over each other, then, I did something which left Smitha's mouth and eyes wide open; I slid my hands into her underwear, and felt her right down there. She kept on saying "no no" while my fingers did the job, however, my experience with the porn reminded me that porn actresses always said, "Yes baby Yes, yeah, right there, ooh, oh my gawd!"; they are never so negative. I should have understood that those are the dialogues which are meant to be said in the movie, that goes with the script and that is what they are paid for, who would buy porn then? Yet, the stupid and the caring side of me received Smitha's no very seriously and I stopped there, took my hand out, hugged and kissed her forehead and eyes!

A drop of a tear ran down her cheeks, she smiled and said, "I love you for this!" She confused me; I nodded without being aware of what she loved me for! Did she love me for picking her up from the station? Did she love me for doing her interns project? Did she love me for locking my lips with her? Did she love the animal in me? Did she love me for eating her breast? Did she love me for feeling her down under? I fought with my own thought system, got routed and asked her, "What? What do you love me for?"

Making out is just making out for guys, but girls always have a third eye view to it, rub your ass, you will never be able to develop the angle with which they view such delicate things, "If you wanted, you could have gone further, and I think I would have hardly made an attempt to stop you baby, but that is you, my baby, my love, you realized that I was in pain, and was getting uncomfortable! My first time right! (Right, I had been doing it every night with Sri and Om), as far as I know about guys, no one wants to leave an opportunity, you had it and you denied it! You love me, no doubt." said Smitha.

"But do you love me?" I invited another round of philosophy. "Of course I do! You doubt? You know what? (No, I don't, even if I do, will that make any difference to you? you will not give up your explanation any way) Be it any kind of a girl, if she is giving her body to any guy, that means a lot to her, the girl places her life on him, and today, I gave you my body, I felt protected, I felt appreciated, I trust you!" That was an excessive way of defining making out, I wonder if all girls thought this way, I am sure Pooja, who flaunted her breasts every now and then would have ever thought on such lines!

Amidst all those thoughts, the four walls of the room which had just one paint now looked painted in red and blue, topless Smitha in my arms did not provoke lust any more in me, love planted deep within me cultivated itself into a big grown tree, the tree which thrived only on Smitha's smile now. She was my world now; assault number 3 had taken place, she trusted me, I did not ask for anything else, in fact, I did not want anything. All I demanded from life was Smitha; and delight I demanded for Smitha!

Speechless with a peaceful mind, in a quiet room, with glowing Smitha in my arms was questioned, "Baby say something!"

"Nothing, I love you!" I said and dragged myself again to sleep on Smitha's laps.

9

All because of the Leopard

Essential for the minds to meet when bodies have already met, the relationship got into a different trajectory after we made love. My opinion that Smitha spoke philosophy because she got carried away at that specific moment was condemned by Smitha's changed, yet a better behavior.

Affection, Smitha's way of behavior with me was getting thick with every new day, she loved me the new way every day, the feeling that every day was better than the previous one was getting profound in me. I could not see any abnormality, which everyone else did, in meeting Smitha at 6 every day in the morning.

The schedule was as follows, get up at 5, a hardship after sleeping at 1, then ensure that even Smitha woke up, get ready quickly, pack everything I needed for the day, leave hostel gates before 6, a five minutes' walk to the girls hostel, then straight to the reading room, prepare for the lectures till 8, back to mess for the breakfast, and then we would part ways till lunch for our respective lectures, lunch together, then again head for our respective lectures, and once the lectures got over, I and Smitha would spend the entire evening together, at times studying, chit chatting or anything else which ensured our togetherness till 12 mid night.

***

"How do you put an equation in the calculator baby? I never get it" asked Smitha.

"A leopard can't change his spots!" I murmured and said, "It is so easy baby! Here, pass on the calci!"

Smitha said, "I am not here to judge your proficiency with idioms, I heard it!" she began to pack her bag and got ready to leave when I said, "Baby, just that I have taught this equation thing earlier as well and how many times? You forgetting is not good at all, will I be there during the exams to help you recall how to do it?" An attempt to hold Smitha back to normalcy was rendered futile, as she would not budge, she continued to do what she was best at, that is get angry for stupid reasons, and within a count of hundred, she vanished from the reading room.

An unwarranted halt was put to my concentration, which disallowed me to complete my numerical, numerical is called a problem as well, and dude, I had a new problem in my hand to solve, and that was to convince Smitha and get her back smiling. But this was not my usual self. If it was Om, I would have kicked his ass and asked him to get lost, but it was ironical to provide a long list of justification about your feelings to someone whom you have committed yourself to. Eat the shit, if you don't want more!

My long strides covered the distance quickly, I stopped Smitha before she left the academia, but let me tell you, I still believe that Smitha deliberately walked slowly, so that I could catch her and get into a round of apologies and divert away from something of greater importance.

"Please sweetie, why do you get me wrong?"

"No, I don't want to listen to anything, I am not here to be at your mercy" she said ferociously.

"Don't create a scene here" something I wanted to say aloud, instead I pleaded, "Baby, just that I was concentrating hard on that numerical, and it was broken all of a sudden, that was a tricky one and I was right in the middle of finding a solution to it, but your equation thing disturbed me and I lost track, please don't misunderstand me."

"So, its ok, you better don't waste your time in banging your head with someone who is not up to your levels, I can manage on my own. So, Please!" said Smitha while putting all her energy on "please." This was absolutely unwanted after corrupting my CGPA in second semester and then handing me a "C" in interns.

This bond with Smitha had transformed me into an eloquent personality, I said, "Baby, that is what you call love. If I were to be slow with calculations and other such things, and you were helping me out, would you ever think that you were doing a favor on me, or you were helping me, no right? So, don't abuse my sincerity towards you by calling my gesture of love as a favor and a help."

For the first time in my life, I was weighing my words before I threw them out, still, my stars had decided to fuck me that day, Smitha said, "Ok, so you really think that I am slow? And when did I say that you were helping me, it is you who has said that, I get it my dear friend, I got it, I can see what you think of me."

Smitha sounded decisive. In fact, she said that I should not be banging my head with someone who is not up to my levels, Oh god, would you mind providing me with the supernatural powers of interpreting what Smitha said exactly and the way she wanted it to be interpreted. God is still following the research done in Chinese Labs. And when you are being addressed as "My dear friend", then the onslaught has been launched, and you have no option but to defend.

At times, it becomes very important not to pester anybody, especially when they are fuming; so I had put off my nozzle which was throwing anti fire extinguisher, and allowed the fumes to fizzle out themselves.

Smitha turned briskly like a leopard, and whizzed towards the girls' hostel. Calling her leopard was a sin I had committed that day. And she did not expect my long strides this time around. My eyes followed her till the turn for her hostel. I was pissed off as well, but to add to my agony, I saw Om confronting Smitha and saying something to her, a little pause and Smitha walked again. And Om walked towards me, I ignored Om thinking that he will pull my leg, and I did not want that when my angry cells were on. I guess Om did not see me, my cell rang and it was Om.

"Yes? What is it?" I asked in straight tone.

"Loverboy is alone today, so, thought if you would join for a smoke, lecture in fifteen minutes, *tera hai kya*?"

"Hmmmm. No."

"What no? Lecture no or smoke no?

"Both." I said and disconnected.

Since I could see Om, I followed him and tapped him on his back when he was about to light up.

"Here, I knew you would join!" said Om while sliding one cigarette out from his pack. I dragged it and lit up the cigarette with Om in unison. I took a puff and asked, "How did you know I was alone? You are a magician or what?"

"Big deal, I met 3S on the way, that meant that either you were in a lecture or in the room. I was coming from the hostel and you were not in the room, so I called you, and you picked up, that meant you were not in lecture either. So, you not in the lecture, and Smitha not with you, it means that there is trouble, and what could be the better way of getting out of it, SMOKE!" Om said and took a long puff with his head high as if he had found out that where was Osama hiding which Americans found difficult to do!

Smitha decided that it was useless to keep any form of communication with me. I kept trying the "Ignore the girl…" theory, but this theory is not useful when you have graduated from a friend to a boyfriend! I gave up my entire ego and called Smitha in the evening, but she would not pick up the call.

Whenever, Smitha's delicate internal balance was shaken, she would find sleep as the best remedy; I assumed that she was asleep, so she did not pick up the call. Reason? Over confidence that Smitha can't keep herself away from me long! Fool I was.

"Let my baby sleep" I thought, and decided not to disturb her. I swear, this is what I thought and there were no other hidden intentions. I went to Om's room for a smoke, I was getting a chance to smoke freely after a long time, else, all my evenings would be occupied with my love. Ambience of Om's room had not undergone any change in the last thirteen months; the contents of Shark Tooth which were still getting depleted every day (courtesy Om and Sri) lured me to get loaded with them.

"Hey Sri, Come to my room. We have a unique guest of honor today" Om told Sri over a call, and made some space for me to sit. "You asshole! Unique guest? Who me? Screw you!" I said. Sri came in and said, "Yes you are!" while patting me.

I lit up a cigarette and said, "Lets booze guys today!" I faintly remember what made me suggest that, I was probably out of mind. Om immediately took out three steel tumblers, which he flicked from the canteen obviously, quickly made three super large vodka shots and somewhere from his chaotic bed, he dragged out a bottle of warm Sprite, mixed it with vodka, and handed over the drinks to me and Sri.

"Bottoms up!" said Sri, and without caring for anybody else's approval, he took off. Banking on my booze capabilities of the yore, I joined him, but could not complete. Om gulped down the entire content as well in one go. I coughed and said, "Dude, you trained him like hell!" Om laughed while pointing at Sri.

"Just a smoke" meet turned out to be a high budget booze session, where Om, Sri and I siphoned off one and a half bottle of Shark Tooth. And since my luck was having sex with Rahu, Kethu and all such demons one could think of, my cell phone rang and it was Smitha.

I jumped from the bed, gained all my senses and said, "Hello!' The most planned and the conscious "Hello" of all times.

"What Hello? It is me".

"Yeah babieee, This is Rama hear."

"Oh shut up! Dinner?"

"Noooo, don't feel like this thing of coming down!"

"What the fuck? What has gone wrong with your English man? And why are you stretching words'?' Smitha made me realize that in an effort to sound normal, I was sounding more than abnormal. Sri and Om were laughing while shaking their legs and holding their stomachs. I realized that I was digging my own grave, and before Smith could put a nail in the coffin, my brain cells laden with white spirit did some random calculations and forced me to speak the truth, "Baby, burp, I am drunk!"

"What?" she asked.

"Nothing, had a couple of vodka shots." I said.

Om and Sri shouted in the background, "And each shot was at least two hundred ml." and they started laughing again between themselves. I kicked them, and Smitha said, "Cool, so you are partying! And you are least bothered about what I am feeling. Bull shit!"

"What? Who is partying? And I called you up so many times. You did not respond, I thought you had slept"

"Yes, I was sleeping, but that did not give you the licence to booze. Fine, you can celebrate. Bye!" And Smitha disconnected the call. I called her up repeatedly, but she kept on disconnecting before switching off her phone.

Message for all the females reading this, "Never hurt a male ego when it is loaded with alcohol, the results are extreme but uncertain, so, it is advisable not to take risks with your relationships. Love them when they are drunk, for the embarrassment might force them not to repeat what they did"

Smitha had never read the above message, she hurt my ego, and that too in front of my friends, I decided not to call her up. Plus I got to hear two statements from the two wise men around.

Om said, "What the fuck? Be a man. Tell her that she has to accept you the way you are. Look at you; you are not the same Rama we knew. She does not love the Rama we know, and you are not what she loves. Why are you trying to be what she loves? You are not that Rama, you are this Rama." Om tried this "*Dil Chahta Hai*" trick on me; he succeeded in only confusing me with this Rama and that Rama. For that moment, I felt that I suffered with "Multiple Personality Disorder".

Sri's philosophical skills had got eroded with Om, but the form is temporary, and the class is permanent, Sri said, "Listen Dude, you are drunk right now. She is fuming. Whatever you try to say to convince her, she will not like it purely because of the fact that you are drunk. Chuck it till morning, she is not going anywhere. Speak to her tomorrow. Could be a chance that you know, you are high and you might speak rubbish if she probably, continues to rebuke you" Sri made great sense.

After some fifteen to twenty minutes when Shark Tooth was made toothless, Om said, "Come on guys. Lets go for dinner. Today we have chicken". Sri popped out of the bed, and slipped his feet into slippers and got ready to go. I decided to back off, as vodka, which kept me going during Subbiah's classes, pulled me back. I locked Om's room, threw the key to him, headed to my room and dozed off.

"Zurrrr Zurrrrr" along with "Sweetie Calling" hammered my sleep. And all hell broke loose. Any other guy would have needed ear muffs to tolerate Smitha's voice levels.

"What? Why the hell are you shouting?" I asked while trying to fight the hangover.

"NOTHING. DUDE WHAT THE FUCK! I MEAN WHAT THE FUCK YOU THINK OF YOURSELF?"

Smitha thought that repeating fuck would fuck me, and it actually did, because Smitha's lingo never got degraded to these levels. So, yes, it was serious.

Protecting the relationship from withering off due to its fragility was a tougher fight than fighting the hangover. I deployed all my forces on the job in hand; the job to figure out what went wrong which was transforming a ten watt pocket radio into a loud speaker.

"Listen sweetie, whats wrong? Why are you shouting? Calm down first"

"SHUT UP. YOU LISTEN TO ME FIRST. YOU THINK THAT YOU CAN BE SMART AND GET AWAY. AND YOU THINK THAT I AM A FOOL."

"Where did this come from?"

"IT CAME FROM NOBODY BUT YOU. YOU. DO YOU UNDERSTAND THAT?"

I lost temper and my voice began to rise, "Would you mind making it CLEAR NOW? DON'T BEAT AROUND THE BUSH, TELL ME WHAT IS IT?"

All of a sudden Smitha's voice levels dropped, and she sounded really sensible, but her entire shouting spree had tickled my angry bones. This is the trick women play, knowingly or unknowingly, they create situations when you are pushed to behave immaturely, and then the lady in the toned down voice would tell you that you are immature and don't understand her! Smitha did the same with me.

"Listen, I have been noticing for a few days that while we study, you seem to get irritated when I interrupt you for doubts" Smitha said.

"YEAH. IS THAT WRONG? EXAMS HARDLY 10 DAYS AWAY. SO WE NEED TO GO QUICK RIGHT. WE CAN'T JUST BE SLOW. EVEN IF I GET IRRITATED, HAVE I EVER DENIED YOUR DOUBTS APART FROM TODAY, AND Just BECAUSE I DID THAT, I HAVE BEEN PAYING FOR IT SINCE THEN, I HAVE HARDLY PROCEEDED WITH ANYTHING!"

"Yeah, but your uneasiness could have come from you than anybody else"

"What uneasiness, I never wanted to complain, and who told you this?"

"Om. I met him when I left the library in the afternoon"

"Om? And what did he tell you?"

"He said that your friends should also be allowed to exploit your talent, and he squandered it off by laughing. I did not take that seriously, in fact, I don't take him seriously."

"Ok, if you don't take him seriously, then why are you being serious about what he said, and then arguing with me?"

"But why did you lie to me that you were drunk? If you did not want to waste time with me, you could have said that straight to me."

"How do I react to this?" I thought, "Is it wrong that I boozed or is it wrong that I lied, but when did I lie, however, as long as she thinks that I did not booze, its good for me" I decided.

"But what? Where are you coming from? What are you talking?"

"I had dinner with Om and Sri only. Om was telling that I was getting hyper unnecessarily, because you had not boozed at all. You were in fact busy studying in the room. So, thats what, why the hell did you lie to me that you were drunk and did not want to come down and all. The fact is that you wanted to study alone, the bigger fact is that I am a disturbing element in your life. I can't pick up to match up to your speed, in fact you think that I am pulling you down. Also, get this straight into your friends' head that nobody is exploiting you, you are not a kid, it is your call to be with me" Smitha clarified.

To counter these allegations, I thought it was better to convince Smitha that I did booze, because it was impossible to win her again after making her feel that she had been using me and wasting my time and eroding my acumen.

I said, "Listen, couldn't you smell alcohol from those buggers? If I was with them, then it is logical that I boozed as well? And why would I lie to you on such things? And why wouldn't I want to study with you?"

"Exam ten days away, simple! It is ok to think about yourself. There is no charity, why would you just waste your time just because you love me, you have all the rights to think about yourself, just that you could have made this clear to me" said Smitha sarcastically.

Enough was enough then, it became habitual for Smitha to suspect false intentions in me; she would relentlessly question my attitude and feelings towards her. "Drastic, carefree of the consequences, irrevocable", a step had to be taken which had above three features in it. But what could that be?

Guys, guys, guys, don't even think that I could leave Smitha; such an idea never entered my mind. I had to do something which developed Smitha's confidence in me immensely. It was not even Smitha's fault to doubt men!

There was turmoil in my head; Smitha's response combined with the alcohol effect drove me mad. In a rage, I called Smitha, and no prizes for guessing that she disconnected. I recalled Sri's nice words that she would not listen to me purely because of the fact that I was drunk, but Smitha thought that I was not drunk. I quickly realized that I had to catch hold of the person who threw me into this mess. I got up from my bed like a ***leopard***, and left the room in my boxer itself to confront Om.

"You sonovabitch, open the door" I shouted as I banged my fist on Om's door. Sri opened the door and said, "Dude I am sorry on his behalf. Come in first" Sri's calm and matured face cooled me down quickly, and I said, "But why the fuck did he do that?" and I pointed with my opened palm towards Om. I reached to catch hold of Om's collar. Sri interfered and said, "Just talk, don't be physical, he is not equipped to fight you out, we know that. No point socking him, he says he had a point to prove to you. Listen to him."

"What will this brainless asshole prove? What the fuck does he have to prove" I said vigorously. "And why didn't you go to law school you bugger?" I asked Om specifically, "You could have got a chance to prove many things there." I continued.

"Does she love you?" Om shot it back at me. Om possessed a terrific quality of shooting one liners which made you think (Remember that Aurangzeb and marketing concepts). I was zapped, for a moment, I forgot all the languages, looked at Sri hopelessly and probably after a pause of ten seconds, I said "Yes, but does it really matter to you?" and "Is this what this bastard wants to prove?" I asked Sri.

"No, I was just wondering what sort of relationship you guys are into. I just said one thing to her, and zero is the trust she has in you, she just accepted without considering the fact that what sort of character are you. How much time have we spent together dude? I can blindly trust you, I can say that, you, the brainless asshole will never back stab anybody. And, she who has been spending twenty five hours of the day with you, lost trust just in a second, just when someone said something to her. Bull shit, this is bull shit Rama, why the fuck you don't understand that she does not love you? I, even Sri does not like this fact. I am least bothered in proving this to you, but just that it came up now, I thought let me just clean any air which would have developed. Do you get that? What you guys call love is merely an association of two opposite genders of different acumen levels, where one is a parasite. That is it, rest is up to your fucked up mind. Still, you wanna beat me up? Do that, you have already slapped me when there was nothing between you guys, I won't be surprised if you knock me down now!" Om spoke with lot of emotions before going to his balcony and lighting up a cigarette.

Sri looked scandalized for the fact if that was an end to our association as friends. I looked at Sri, confused, in fact, Om made a valid point, I did not have anything to say. I could not lose Smitha, I could not hurt Om. I had to find a solution to the issue, could not expect Om or Smitha to understand.

Om was still a friend, ending the association was entirely my call, Smitha was love, but I was not in the middle of any choices.

"A year ago, I believed that I was here only for a scintillating GPA and a brilliant job at any cost. Though this still remains a priority, but that any cost does not include Smitha" I thought, and then I thought something big, "Let me stop studying. Let me stay behind this time. Let me score less deliberately. And let's see if that helps Smitha to trust me, trust me the way Om said. Blindly!"

Sept 2007, the first T20 World Cup was underway, so, if I was not studying, the best alternative was to spend the entire day in the TV room. Smitha was least hesitant in avoiding my calls; I did not meet her for next ten days after she left the reading room that afternoon. Om's and Sri's efforts to convince me to pick up a book and get into the groove were rendered futile. In a space of two days, entire boys' hostel was aware that something was wrong, even the most hopeless guys were seen with books. Some tried enquiring, some joined me in matches, some came for doubts clarification, and I entertained everything but the idea of picking up a book and studying.

***

"Dude, does she know what you are up to?" asked Om.

"No, I don't want her to know this" I replied taking a drag.

"Then what is the point in doing this if she is not aware of it?" interrogated Sri.

I looked at both of them, "I don't believe this. You are crazy. Please, hardly a day left, you can still give it a shot. Please study, the one whom you are doing it for must be studying for sure, she must be least bothered about what you are doing!" persuaded Om.

"He is not doing it for anybody, it is not going to help him, and I don't know how will this help in Smitha to score more." Sri made a point.

"I know this is not going to help anybody, she thinks that I am a selfish pig, which I am not. I just want to prove this to her." I said and left the TV room.

It was India-Australia semifinal at the World Cup; everyone had finished studying prior to the match. The TV room which could accommodate two hundred guys, was filled more than its capacity; people thronged at the windows, the lighter guys found place on the laps of heavier guys, in a nut shell, TV room looked like a cruel prison of Second World War which sheltered prisoners of war in the worst conditions.

The atmosphere was electric, I was leaning on the wall, and Om was leaning against me; he was light, I was heavy. Moment, Sreesanth knocked out Hayden, my phone started ringing, the crowd and the noise did not make me realize that. Om, who was sitting on my lap, felt the vibrations from my pocket and said, "Dude, your phone is ringing, it is Smitha, and pick up the phone." and he made some space for me to get the phone out, and I said, "Yes, it is Smitha, how do you know?" Om just shrugged his shoulder and made more space for me to get away from crazy TV room, which erupted like a stadium.

"Yeah, hi!" I said while covering the phone with my left palm so as to avoid any form of noise disturbing the conversation. "Hi, may I ask you what you are up to?" asked Smitha.

"Yeah, what happened?" I asked speculating that she knew what I was up to.

"Why aren't you studying at all?" she inquired.

"You called me selfish, you thought I was a selfish pig, I wanted to get rid of this tag, I wanted you to trust me blindly, that is it, I love you, but who told you about this strike I was holding?" I answered and asked a question.

"Om, he called me some time back and told me that you are bullshitting with yourself!"

"I love you." I said and there was a stunned silence.

"I love you too baby, I did not know that you love me so much. Love you sweetheart. Would you mind studying now?" said Smitha.

"Baby, there is no point I study now, and match is getting interesting. Please, can we talk later? I'll call you in an hour or so?" I said.

"Yeah baby, but!" Smitha was about to say something, and I realized that she might be stuck with some doubt and said, "Baby, you have some doubts to be clarified, you want me to come?"

"Yeah, kind of but you carry on with your match." Smitha tried diplomacy unnecessarily. "No baby, please avoid these things with me. Just give orders, I'll be there. Matches keep on happening. See you at girls' hostel gate in five minutes" I said, went to the room, packed my bag and rushed out of the hostel.

Smitha was there at the gate, and I said, "Hi." Smitha hugged me tightly, with zero space between us and whispered in my ears, "You are my love baby, I am proud of you, proud of this relationship; I can't get better than this. I am really sorry." she tightened her arms on me further before releasing it and said," You are right there, right there in my life." she saluted in the air indicating the height.

10
Placement

Horrendous six days of mugging and then puking got over on 30th Sept, and then were the days to begin which would seal our fate. Yes, something which everyone waited for, the *tamasha*, the nasty placement week.

My CGPA still hovered well above 8.5 even after two continuous debacles in the second semester and interns. My stars were nice to me that the results of third semester were not out yet, and with my acumen which was declining of course, I should be able to crack any of the big paymasters.

Getting shortlisted for all the seven companies on Day Zero was nothing short of an achievement; and with all seven of them ready to shower you with money you never dreamt of, it was indeed more than an achievement for someone in early twenties like me. Even Sri, who was a CA, had not got shortlisted in all of them.

"Deloitte, KPMG, UBS, GE Capital, JPMC, DE Shaw, and Karvy" I said.

"Hmm, Impressive baby!" said Smitha.

"I am only in two of them" she said as she showed her two fingers like a kid. I kissed her index finger, to which she smiled.

"But how will you manage to attend all of them?" asked a curious Smitha.

"Hmmm, let's see; have spoken to placement officers to schedule it in such a way. Let me clear GDs first, interviews are secondary." I said nervously.

"Oh baby! You are my hero, remember CEO material" Smitha said vivaciously and we kissed, we were at the Adda. Adda was the place in college where nobody came, I and Smitha found Adda as the safest place to kiss and make love with our clothes on.

"White shirt, black trousers and black tie baby." said Smitha as I left her at the hostel gates, reminding me of what I looked best at.

All the women can dream of their men in the best get up, even when their men cannot afford a handkerchief. I could not afford anything then, but Smitha knew what I looked good at. Yes, I looked terrific, high on confidence, confidence that I would not fail in all seven. And I'll be soon pocketing at least twenty lakhs every year, and first level will be crossed. Young boy loaded with money, intelligent, capable, a perfect one for Smitha to introduce at her home. I smiled at happiness around the corner.

Om had not got shortlisted in any of them; still, he was unmoved about it. He did a high five, polished my shoes, and punched his fist against mine, and wished me luck. "You will have to rock" said Om. I and Sri left the hostel, met Smitha at the acads. She was appearing for De Shaw and Karvy. And Sri was appearing in all five other than JPMC and Karvy. It was disheartening to see ourselves getting through without Om, but I knew it was Om's personal choice to not appear in any of the Investment banks and brokerage houses, he waited for Corporate Finance.

You are not an MBA if you have not been getting minimum of two newspapers, especially *Economic Times* and *Business Standard*, without caring for the fact that the news is same in both of them; moreover, who cares even if you read it or not; subscription is the most important thing. And flipping pages of *Business World*, *Outlook* and *Harvard Business Review* is also significant, not because you gain anything, but, you send shivers with the other lot, who, presume you to be god of everything and sea of knowledge.

I did only few of the things mentioned above; hence I was slightly low on confidence, when I faced GDs. DE Shaw was the first to begin the proceedings, which I, Sri and Smitha attended. However, three of us made sure that we don't land up in the same group, thereby cannibalizing each other's chances.

"Why Delhi should not be the Capital of India?" was the topic for my group to discuss. Calling my group a "group" was a sin because it was an association of twelve speakers with no listeners. Moderators call it "Fish Markets", it was for the first time I realized that nobody was a friend, people were interfering in each other's' point of views, none of them were willing to agree with each other, everyone thought that he or she was right in his or her own perspective, there were few of them who would not mind if anybody was listening to them, but they spoke continuously, there were parallel discussions, there were diagonal discussions, there were debates, there were guys from the same gang making cartels and allowing no one to speak, some got up from their chairs while speaking, some got angry because Delhi was their hometown, I felt like slapping a few of them, but I chose to keep quiet and observed the entire group screwing up Delhi and other metros. Everyone ran out of points in seven to eight minutes, and it was last two to three minutes, when there was a pause of close to five to six seconds, as everyone gathered their thoughts once again.

Yes, that was the chance, I jumped on to the fruit, and said, "I think Goa should be capital of India" and paused, expecting some emotions to generate, and as I expected, the idiot lot did react.

"I beg to differ." said one, "You may." I said.

"I am sorry." said another, "Don't be." I said.

"You must be joking", said a lady with the shirt which she wore last in her school; her boobs were tearing the buttons to come out, "You must be exposing, your boyfriend is a lucky bastard!" I thought.

"May I know why?" asked another.

"Exactly!" I said, with a smile, as I waited for this question to come up, "The way the points have been put forth by the esteemed members of this team, and more importantly, the viewpoints which everyone had, I felt that there is no place which is better than Goa. In fact, each one of us should understand the features or qualities of a particular district which distinct it from other cities to be declared as a capital of the nation."

"Infrastructure" said an over enthusiastic candidate.

"Yes and?" I said. Suddenly, the group realized that I was making sense and it was a chance for them to give points in the last two minutes, they started giving out different qualities of a capital.

It came one by one; the group became a disciplined lot.

"Economy, Employment, History, Geographical Advantage, Assembly seats, Achievements"

"Fantastic, let's see if Delhi possesses all these qualities or not." I said.

They thought for a second and said, "Yes" together.

"That is it; then Delhi deserves to be capital of India. Why do you want to disturb the balance which is rare in our nation?" I concluded.

"That's it." moderator called off the GD and we left.

And then were the flurry of GDs I participated in; all of them as chaotic as De Shaw. I was worried for Smitha; the monsters in the group would not let her speak, the Delhi girl was thrashed in both the GDs and was shown the door in the first round itself.

Surprise, surprise! Against all my expectations, Smitha was candid to co-ordinate the operations for me, managing the juggling which I would have faced alone, running from one GD to another, and then one interview to the other; My love took a personal commitment to communicate with the placement officers, and managed my files, which had copies of CV and certificates.

It was surprise to the power of 2 because, the lady, who would bring a house down if she scored less than 7, was not reluctant to get over with her dismal performance and promote me as the front runner in the relationship. I came out of the fish market organized by UBS, it was a splendid act by me; and I was shortlisted.

Smitha, who had collected all the results till then, came up to me and planted a kiss on my cheek and updated me, "Baby, you are there in the interview of all the seven." she showed seven of her fingers like a kid again. "I told you baba, you are my hero. You rock." Smitha exhilarated.

CONFUSION STRIKES AGAIN

For me, 1+2 is always equal to 3, *yet you find the quintessential types, for whom, it is 12. Smitha placed herself in that category by behaving the way which was unexpected of her. No one would have got a remote of my attention if I were to be a holder of the result of 2 debacles. Was Smitha making a conscious effort to be normal, so that I was not demoralized? Was Smitha aware of her failures before hand? Was Smitha eying something big? Was Smitha trying to be the ideal girl who would support her man till the last moment to see him succeed? Was she the one for me? Do I leave everything and hold Smitha's hand, and give her the support which she gave then? Should I plant a kiss on her cheek as well and say thanks? Is she doing it in return of the support she enjoyed during our study days? Did she think that I deserved and should get seven of them? Should I smile because everything was going my way, or be upset as everything was not going our way?*

I said, "Baby, but you are not shortlisted in any of them, I am feeling so bad, it would have been really good had both of us got placed today and together."

Smitha came closer, adjusted my tie and said, "Coffee? You have half an hour break before your interviews start."

"Sure" I said and went towards the small canteen at the academic block, but Smitha said, "Wait here my baby, I'll get coffee for both of us, relax and recollect whatever you want to before the interviews."

She came back with the coffee and said, "Baby, just one thing, I want you get placed first, so that I can tell about us at home. I want you to get all seven of them. Go for it. I'll wait here till you are done with your interviews" and she saw me off to the den, den which had established financial wizards pulling up their handcuffs, chewing gums, and waiting to rip young aspiring financial wizards, and I was one amongst them.

Smitha had got the placement officers convinced to keep my interviews back to back so that I could go and push something into my tummy which had not welcomed anything apart from a coffee full of love; after all, I was running around for all seven of them since morning. It was a record of sorts, so, I could see other candidates accommodating my request of back to back interviews. The monsters had a sporting nature as well.

I started with UBS; Sri had qualified for the interview as well. The interviewer, I thought, did not like my face, he however, found it easy to read my face, he had probably fixed CCTV at all the places I visited in the last one year, he asked me everything I did not know, he raped me at his will, he exactly knew what were my weaknesses, and he continued to hit me there, and I kept on giving up, and I knew the grit and determination was withering off and I was sweating. To give that mother fucker who was drunk with UBS, another reason for not selecting me, I left sweat marks from my shirt on the chair, which clearly showed my confidence levels.

The UBS man, I guess, had plotted a conspiracy against me, because, all the interviewers were as ruthless as UBS guys were, if not more; for the footages he recorded from CCTV, were probably shared with all other interviewers. All the interviews were the replica of UBS interview. I was blank in all of them, the questions they asked were inscrutable, they made me speak two things, which were contradictory, leaving me absolutely dejected.

JPMC was different, because, they discussed more of general topics in the interview. It was by no means an "Interview", the only question I was asked was, "Your colleague is continuously bullied by your boss, however, your boss is nice with you. How will you react to this situation, when you know that your colleague does not deserve the ill-treatment?"

"I will ask him couple of times that what is wrong between him and boss, if he is willing to share, then, I'll probably give him a suggestion or advice, if not, that will be the last time I'll discuss the topic with him, and let it go the way it is going. I'll mean business with my job and profile." I said.

"But someone witness to murder is a culprit as well." Interviewer shot back at me.

"I beg to differ sir, whats happening here is not murder, it is suicide, if my colleague wants to commit it, I am not a culprit then." I confirmed and the discussion was over. I felt I had done relatively well in JPMC.

However, the best was GE Capital. I was asked what my favorite area was, and I was quick to reply, "Annuities" and they tried their best not to select me; they asked me to write down all the formulae involved in annuities and derive at least two of them. I recalled Subbiah's lecture under booze effect. After three hours of flop performance, GE cap was the first company where I got the chance to turn the tide in my favor; I pulled my chair, took out a pen from my pocket, wrote all the formulae in five minutes, derived two of them in next five minutes, closed the pen, tapped it on the table and handed over the sheets to the interviewer, who did not ask anything else, but smiled and said, "Good show Rama, I think there is nothing else I want to ask." he sort of confirmed my appointment with GE Cap.

I was sure that I would get selected in either JPMC or GE Cap, however, I did not tell Smitha about my flop performances in other interviews, because of the confidence and expectations she had. I allowed results to spill the beans!

The results of all seven were put at different notice boards in the evening. Since UBS was paying maximum at forty six lakhs, Smitha wanted to check its results first, and she was shocked, but I was not. Then the act of getting shocked continued for some more time, with I getting screwed up in all five of them. Then was JPMC, where I hoped some positivity, but my name was not a part of JPMC list either; JPMC guys took some pain to inform the placement officer that I lacked the X factor which managers have. I looked at the list again, trust me, none of the assholes, who got selected had any factor in them.

Smitha was devastated, it seemed as if that was the end of the world for her, fear of losing Smitha was profound in me for the first time, but not more than the confidence of getting through GE Cap. Smitha decided to stay away from looking at the results of GE Cap and asked me to go alone and have a look at the result, she said, "Baby, I'll wait at the dome, I am scared, you go alone please!" She held my palm with her right hand and patted it with her left hand giving me courage to face the brutality god had let loose on me.

"What?" asked Smitha. Silent me picked up the bag and started walking towards the adda, she could not understand what was happening and followed me, "I have an attitude problem, I get carried away." I told Smitha at adda, hugged her and cried madly, "I am not there in GE as well" I said as I cried.

Impossible had struck us; getting shortlisted in all seven , making it to final rounds of all seven and getting rejected in all of them, there was something seriously wrong. "I will not be able to marry you as I will not have great job to impress your parents" I continued to cry. Smitha decided to stay calm, providing me the due support.

Day zero saw the cream of the batch getting placed, Sri was through with UBS. My score of zero out of seven made me the hero of "Day zero." Every Tom, Dick and Harry who praised me before the Day started was giving me false words of consolation. I was talk of the town, yet there were few who came up to me and asked me about the results, trying to rub salt on my wounds, I yelled back at them. I walked through the pavement towards the hostel, and felt that every eye was fixed at me, every mouth cracking jokes about me, I looked for a place to hide my face, and there was not a bigger loser than me. I reached hostel and thought, "Do I thank god for giving me so many opportunities or do I abuse god because he embarrassed me?" Unable to find an answer, I slept.

Then began a week stamped with anguish for both of us. Smitha was not getting shortlisted, even if she did, the monsters did not allow her to speak in GDs, and she was slipping into a shell. For me, getting raped in final interviews became almost a routine; such was an effect that I appeared in the interviews with dropped shoulders; my endangered self-confidence was soon going to become extinct. Even Sri's words of philosophy and encouragement did not make us better. The list of shame had more laurels; HSBC, ICICI, Adventity, HDFC, Duestche, Citibank, Motilal Oswal, SBI, Infosys, McKenzie, Religare, Standard Chartered, Reliance Money.

After an agonizing week with seventeen companies showing me the door, I was shortlisted with Donne for corporate finance which was Om's choice, but he was not their choice. There was a new ray of hope with Donne, they were paying well enough for me to stand up and ask for Smitha's hand. Letting off this opportunity was no short of a punishable offence for me, I told myself, "Don't drop your shoulders, tear them apart, they have come to pick two, and come what may, one is reserved for you. You have to do it, else jump from the top floor tonight."

"Fish market" conducted by Donne was the most sensible GD, they gave us a case study to discuss, the essence of which was poverty. I belted the GD right in my favor, screwing up those who spoke non sense, declining those who gave non proven statistics and steering it right till the end with a proper conclusion in the time prescribed.

Getting in to the final rounds was never an issue, however, there was jinx attached to the final rounds. They gave us a break of an hour to have lunch, but I decided against it, and stayed there. Smitha said, "Baby lunch?"

"No" I said, "You go and have it, I'll stay here. I'll eat and drink only if I crack it", I continued, pushing Smitha lightly. "No, I'll stay with you", said Smitha encouragingly and clutched to my sleeves. I was fourth to face the interview.

The ability to differentiate the faces of interviewers had vanished in me by then, but, I concentrated hard, fighting hunger and thirst, for the hunger and thirst to get the job was more intense. There were three of them, two sitting, with their loose ties, and one of them was standing, without tie and folded sleeves, and sported a casual look.

The "Casual Look" man started off, "So, you look tired, whats wrong? Didn't have your lunch?"

"No, nothing of that sort. I am fine sir." I said.

Since interviews were conducted in a glass chamber, one of the "Sitting" men saw me outside all the while, and said, "No, I don't think he went for lunch, I have seen him standing outside."

All of them looked astonished at this madness, and the "Casual Look" man opened a water bottle and passed it on to me. To my embarrassment, I forgot to pour the water into the glass, and started gulping it down from the bottle itself, quickly realizing that I have done a blunder and closed my eyes in horror. Realizing what my state of mind was, the second "Sitting" man said, "Its ok, you might be really thirsty" leaving me to judge if it was mockery or not. I smiled like an idiot.

But they made me comfortable, the "Casual Look" man was after my physical attributes; first, he found me tired, and then he asked, "Why are your eyes red?", and I said, "Sir you are right, I guess I am tired, so red eyes" and smiled again. All of them laughed at my sense of humor.

"Sitting" men got serious and said, "So, Rama, tell us something about yourself which we don't know."

"Yes sir, first I would like to know what do you know about me, then I can tell you things which you don't know about me." I said.

"Casual Look" man interfered "We know that you have got rejected in seventeen companies. But, we don't know why? Have you thought about it?"

I was crestfallen to anticipate the dismissal once again, and became my natural self, outspoken, "Yes, I know the reasons sir, but what does really matter to you? The reasons of rejection or the fact that I have done the analysis to understand my weaknesses?" I cross questioned without giving them any chance of humiliating me. "We will come back to it." said "Casual Look" man.

The "Sitting" men gave me a balance sheet to be analyzed, asked me to calculate certain ratios and interpret how healthy the company was with its operations. I had mastered in this act of analyzing stupid balance sheets, so that was easy as well, but I did not allow my emotions to flow the way they did in GE and JPMC. So, I was proven technically sound.

The "Casual Look" man, as he said, went back to the old question, "What was the reason of you getting rejected?"

"I have a poor attitude, and I get carried away", I said in the flattest of tone.

"Oh! Is it? We don't think so" said the "Casual Look" man.

I looked up in surprise and said, "Thank you sir for deciphering me so nicely and giving me my lost confidence back."

"So, you have stayed in Delhi through out your life! Lets see how good is your Hindi" said the "Casual Look" man.

I shifted gears to Hindi and said, "*Poochiye, kya poochna chahte hain aap Hindi mein*?"

"Dearness allowance *ko hindi mein kya kehte hain*?" asked the "Casual Look" man.

Slightly puzzled, and I said, "*Mehngai Bhatta.*"

Then one of the "Sitting" men asked me, "See Rama, This is something we have been asking all the candidates and we would like to clarify this with you as well. If you are selected to work with us, then, you will be posted at remote places unlike your other batch mates who while working with Investment Banks and would be getting to work at metros and some flashy offices. So, how comfortable are you working at remote places."

"Remote places? Does Donne have factories there?" I asked, and thought for a while if it was worthwhile to say yes, because I had to mean what I said. "Yes, Donne does have factories there."

Only I knew the significance of this job, it meant passport to success and happiness, it meant Smitha, it meant end to the days of despair and ignominy. I said "Yes, I am highly committed."

"And what if you are posted in countries like Bangladesh and Sri Lanka?" asked the "Casual Look" man.

A touch of humor is always appreciated in an interview depending on the question, "Who does not want to go abroad?" I said and smiled, and they laughed, and they became serious.

And then one of the "Sitting" men spoke; I was spotting a trend now, "Casual Look" man and "Sitting" men spoke turn by turn trying to whack my concentration. He asked, "Who do you think could be a prospective competitor of Donne in future?"

A dose of illogicality seeped into me, and I knew the blunder had entered my mind, and since nothing was going my way, blunder made its way out, I said, "Parle".

The process of striking positivity got a severe beating with "Parle" as an answer and I realized it and closed my eyes.

"Parle? Are you serious?" said the "Casual Look" man squandering my point of view.

Illogicality was all over the place, I had to find logic to defend it,"I strongly believe that an unknown competitor is a serious threat than a known competitor for you already have a strategy in place for the known one. When a serious lot like you were shocked to see that Parle could be your competitor, then I feel Parle holds a significant advantage to make strategies which will shock you further. And I could have said Cadbury, but you asked for a competitor in future. Their brands could be serious competition to Donne's products in snacks category, especially in rural India."

Three of them did not respond to my reply, The "Casual look" man extended his hand for a shake indicating that the chance to put an end to the days of agony was over. I left the room without leaving sweat marks on the chair, reason, I was conscious not to lean against the chair.

***

I was not left with any courage to go and see another evidence of me being a loser, I decided to lock myself in the room and sleep away to glory, even Smitha's repeated calls could not break it now, and the battery faded away in sometime. In my dreams, some one knocked my head, only for me to realize that the door of my room was being hit madly by a bunch of rogues. I managed to push myself out of the quilt, opened the door while still half asleep. Om, Sri and Piyush were the rogues, and they threw a series of questions, "Where the fuck is your phone?" "What the fuck you are doing in the room?" "Smitha has been calling you like fuck." "You are fucking crazy dude!"

So many "fucks" were good enough to revive my senses, I said, "Fuck off" and said, "What happened?" Sri and Om hugged me violently whereas Piyush compelled himself to pat my back, it was becoming tough for me to understand what was going on when they broke the mystery of their weird behavior, "Dude congrats, you are through with Donne" Om held my face and said this while looking into my eyes.

A huge wave passed through my body, the pressure released from different nozzles from my head to feet, my responsive nerves went numb, the world was dead to me and a small drop of tear ran down my cheeks. Still recovering from the dream, I switched on my phone and called Smitha who was on the top of the world and asked me to come down quickly.

My world was changed, days of agony had ended, I saw respect for me in those eyes which cracked jokes on me, and above all, the first hurdle to get Smitha was defeated. The moment I met Smitha, she unlocked the emotions, she kissed my forehead, hugged me with pride, held my arms so tight that I felt pain, but I loved it and allowed her to do whatever she wanted. She took me straight to adda and we made love, and when I lay down with my head on her laps, Smitha said, "Baby, you will not leave me right? I still don't have a job." the childlike innocence blew me into pieces and I said, "No baby, not at all, in fact I was waiting for this to happen so that I could speak to your Mama."

And then what she said left me bewildered "But I have not told Mama that we have been seeing each other, you have to tell her that you proposed to me today and I asked you to speak to her."

"Its ok, trust me, you will be fine." I said realizing that I was taking a huge risk. "What if she says no?" I asked Smitha out of fear.

Anyhow, I was used to agony and fear by now, the last week of placement made me capable of handling uncertainties, life is so tricky; I had a different fear to handle till yesterday and today I have a different fear to handle. Fear was still the same, fear of losing Smitha. While I fought this fear, Smitha called up her mom and threw the phone at me, "Hello! Good evening aunty!"

"Good evening *beta*. Congratulations!" said Smitha's mom proving that Smitha had already informed her about my achievements.

Smitha held my hand and kept on kissing my shoulder, it gave me strength and courage to fight the fear, and I said hesitantly, "Aunty, I always waited for this day to come so that I could propose to Smitha, I did that today and she straight away asked me to speak to you. Please let me know aunty what you have to say."

"It is ok *beta*, but before I say anything, I would like to meet you. Is it ok for you to come to Delhi with Smitha?" With some light visible at the end of the tunnel, I said, "Sure aunty, we will be there during Diwali." and I gave the phone to Smitha who continued to discuss something else, but only thing I noticed was the smile on Smitha's face which did not fade for a single second, indicating that all was well.

Smitha disconnected the call, came to me and sat on my lap, put her arms around my neck and kissed my cheeks and said, "Baby, I am sure Mama will say yes, else, she would not have shown any interest in meeting you." My eyes got lit up and we kissed again.

11

The Maiden Meeting

"Will you get converted?"..... Booom.... That was it; I did not know what to say as all I could feel was Smitha slipping out of my life. "Yes, I love her. Anything for her!! Take my word, I stand by her thick and thin", said a troubled me. Illogicality had struck me and I did not know what I had agreed for would change my life forever.

Mama (Smitha's mother) was happy and so was Smitha because she was going to spend her life with someone whom she had loved for almost a year now. "Eat *beta* eat", Mama said decisively as I just enjoyed the tunes I was dancing to. She served me some more mutton. I had told Smitha zillion times that I am not a born non-vegetarian, I can't eat rubber like meat, I was fine with chicken and I was sure her mother would have known this fact, but still, she made a deliberate attempt to cook mutton. Her serving and royal treatment continued.

I thought, "Is it a test I am undergoing to prove that I am a real Christian and I am absolutely comfortable in eating what all was available in my class nine biology book." I felt I was being treated like Sunny Deol by Amrish Puri in *Gadar* when he is being asked to shout Hindustan Murdabad. The only difference was that I could not react the way Sunny did. He could do that because he was already married to whom he loved and the stage was set. I was neither Sunny Deol, nor Smitha's home had a hand pump stationed which I could uproot to vent out my frustration.

All was fine with me because I loved Smitha like Smitha loved her Mama. She could do anything for her parents and I could do anything to keep Smitha happy. I suddenly became Mama's darling; hence, she did everything she could to make my stay as pleasant as possible. She asked Ranjan, Smitha's younger brother, to leave his king size bed for me to sleep.

"It is really cold in Delhi during winters, here is your quilt", pampered Mama. "Has she forgotten the fact that I stayed in Delhi for twenty two years" I thought. "Thank you Mama, good night." "Good night *beta*", she kissed my forehead. I looked for Smitha, because I wanted to give a return kiss to her. She was invisible as she was busy preparing Mama's bed. Mama left and I switched off the lights to sleep.

It was actually colder than what I found Delhi was during my twenty two years there. I was satisfied over the fact that I was able to win Mama's confidence which would make Smitha mine and no force would ever be able to wound the relationship. I felt proud of myself that I could take such a drastic step of getting converted (My name is Rama Chandran Iyer, I come from a Tamil Brahmin Family) for someone I loved. I could not have given a better token of love to Smitha. I smiled at my future and my accepted wisdom said, "Sleep now".

My phone rang and I thought it was Smitha, who had sneaked out of her Mama's clutches and was standing at the door to give me a good night kiss. I looked at the phone to see "Amma calling" flashing on its screen. Amma is my mother and she is a jumbled "Mama."

"Hello, yeah tell me", I spoke half asleep even when I had not slept. Those were my Diwali vacations and I was supposedly going home but I chose to come to Delhi to meet Smitha's mother. I lied at home that we had just a day off at college and every day counted because of my short attendance due to all the time I had spent on interviews during placements.

"How are you doing? Why did you not call up the entire day? Why was your phone switched off? Why are you sleeping so early, its only 11, you sleep by 1 right? Aren't you feeling well?" Amma had asked me five questions in one go and I was wondering which one to answer. "I am not feeling ok. Have a slight fever." I answered the first and the last. "I have taken Crocin, and was sleeping, is it ok if I call you up in the morning?" Amma was worried and said "Yeah sleep properly and take care. Poor you could not even enjoy Diwali." She hung up.

I felt irritated that I was on a lying spree. I had eaten mutton, not Crocin, I was not sleeping and I had no plans to call up Amma in the morning. "Why am I lying to Amma? I am not doing anything wrong. I love Smitha and if I have guts to come and face her Mama, then why not my parents?" I quizzed myself. "Fuck you", I said to myself and switched on the lights, all to rewind what all has happened which was making me anti-parents.

Since my self-belief had taken a serious beating by accepting baptism, it took a logical equation to understand that my parents were accommodating enough and would accept whatever crap I decided if it did not harm anybody. However, the timing to reveal my love for Smitha and especially, the conversion factor to my parents was critical, I thought Smitha would help as I helped her save her ass by saying that I was the one who proposed and made her Mama believe that she had the most obedient daughter on the planet. With such strong faith in my love, I could sleep peacefully.

Only a bottle full of corex or two shots of vodka could have helped me sleep in a new place, and since nothing was available, I was left to enjoy my uneasiness the entire night. I did not even pee because I was ashamed of using others toilets thinking that they might not like the smell of my urine and what would they think of the noise which my urine would generate when it hits the pot, most importantly, a guest should not disturb anybody. I waited for sunlight, and slipped into a short nap before someone broke it.

Ranjan, who searched for something under the mattress, apologized for waking me up. Delighted to see that someone was awake, I came out of the quilt quickly and said, "Sorry dude, you had to leave your bed for me!" and before I could spot my spectacles and put them on, Ranjan finished his search job and pushed something into his pocket and said, "Its ok bro, I am going for a walk, are you joining?" I clearly understood where he was going, yes, he was going for a smoke, otherwise, who goes for a walk on a chilly winter morning of Delhi. He knew that I understood what he said; this meant Smitha had told Ranjan that I smoked. I joined him and I found him to be a replica of Om. It was unsafe to smoke with Ranjan, because there were clear chances that he might disclose this to Mama, but there were reasons that I found him as replica of Om; I struck chord with him instantly and trusted him.

***

"You have agreed for conversion, but what if your parents don't agree?" asked Mama while serving me *paranthas*.

Paranthas, mutton and a secular surname must have raised a lot of doubts. Smitha's dad (Mr Swaminathan) was a Tamil Brahmin; he got married to her mother (Suzzane Vincent), who was a Rajasthani Christian. And, Smitha's grandmother supposedly kept similar conditions in front of her dad, and he succumbed and became Swaminathan Vincent. So, the secular surname is a result of her dad's acceptance of the religion, paranthas are a result of her mom's North Indian roots!

"They understand me and they will agree, however, I will never say that let them not come to my wedding" I told her mother convincingly and wasn't she bothered to ask anything else. She gave me another Parantha when Smitha came and said, "Eat eat, its free." Honestly, I did not like the way Smitha said it, and there came Smitha's Mama to defend by blasting Smitha for her weird statement. The significance coming my way was overwhelming.

More was to come my way when Smitha's Mama asked me to get ready; they were selling off their Kirti Nagar's home for a flat in Dwarka. And we were heading for a house warming ceremony.

A series of events left me stunned, and will leave you confused to want more of Mama!

CAR: Without being aware of my driving skills, more importantly, without knowing if I knew to drive, Smitha's mother who had shown no signs of her character for me to be judgmental till then, asked Ranjan to move out of the driver's seat and ordered that the keys be handed over to me. Skeptical since I was not a good driver and my ass was busted when Smitha was asked to sit in the front with me. It would have taken a super computer to discover what was running in Mama's mind, because I did not have a clear yes till then, but what she was doing was nothing short of a yes. Was she trying to check if we lied to her that I proposed to her daughter just a month ago? No answer!

NEW HOUSE: Smitha and I waited in the car for Ranjan who would tell us when to come upstairs. This got both of us to discuss about Mama's opinion about me, which according to Smitha was positive till then. And just when I showed my concern for a final yes, emerged Ranjan to take us upstairs! And there was a yes upstairs, but that yes caused my head swirling; there was a Hindu priest (Pandit ji)! My eye balls almost dropped and took a close look at the priest to see if it was a catholic priest who got himself dressed wrongly as a Hindu priest! I looked for a cross around the neck but did not find one. I asked Smitha, "Is he relation?" Smitha looked a bit surprised and asked me the reason. "Looks like half Hindu, half Christian." I said. "Shut up" she said. Murdered by what was going on, I stood frozen at the door, when priest interrogated, "Is he the one?" and Mama nodded in agreement. I thought, "What me the one? If you want me to get out of your daughter's life, tell this straight to me, why are you treating me to this black magic?" And then came the first sign of yes, "Me the one" meant the one to marry Smitha because Mama asked us to hold each other's' hands and topple the bowl full of rice before we entered. I felt that I was in the middle of D-grade Saas Bahu serial where I was the new "Bahu" entering the house full of conspiracies and unwanted chaos! But, that gesture from Mama confirmed that I was the one who was getting married to Smitha! Smitten by her kindness, I hugged her and said, "Thanks aunty!" But my never ending curious nature made me ask this, "But aunty, why priest and all, do you follow Hinduism?" Mama said, "No *beta*, I just believe in this pandit ji, I look up to him for guidance." I bought the point but was not convinced, however, I thought that I should keep on bribing this priest till the time I married Smitha so that he kept on saying good things about us to Mama.

SAROJNI NAGAR: The date 8th November 2007 will never be erased in the history books published by me, because it was the day when Smitha was officially stamped as "reserved" by head of the government, Mama. Post house warming ceremony, Mama's juggernaut proceeded to Sarojni Nagar market; new house would need new curtains and all other things which are actually not needed in normal course of living. Of all the things Mama and Smitha discussed to buy in the car, I could not draw a picture of single thing in my mind other than curtains. Disinterested to the core in shopping, nothing I could do but conducted an eyes warming ceremony after house warming ceremony; Sarojni Nagar market boasts of the girls of all ages, species, sizes and colors. This was the place we chose from graduation days to rate girls. But sadly, I could not do that, because even the slightest of ill behavior would leave me ill fated. I was looking for music CDs when Mama called me and then arrived the command of the millennium, which left me, Smitha and Ranjan flabbergasted, "What are you doing there? Come here and choose the colour with Guddu which suits your bedroom." (Guddu is Smitha) and Mama left us and went to the other section. "Our Bedroom? Forget the bedroom, I did not even see the drawing room fully and whats going on? It is embarrassing, please ask her to stop this and where does this our bedroom come from?" I said with lot of concern. Smitha did not know anything either, though she liked the idea of our bedroom, and said, "Our bedroom baby" and blew a kiss at me and winked.

SURESH MAMA: This is the first character from Smitha's extended family, the family which went beyond boundaries of blood. I assumed that he was Mama's younger brother and expected a cross on the door of his house! But, as we reached his home for dinner, the name plate on the door read, "Suresh Garg CA LLB" I was about to faint then, I did not know what was happening, "How come he is Mama's younger brother? Is this family known for getting men converted? Smitha's dad took up Christianity, I was about to do the same, did Suresh Mama take up Hinduism?" The series of questions left me berserk and I gulped down three glasses of water to fizzle out the inquisitive fire within. Soon I was updated that Suresh Mama was their tenant earlier and also got informed about the stories of how he respected Mama which compelled her to consider him as her brother and forced Ranjan and Smitha to call him Suresh Mama. Suresh's wife, Babli as Mama addressed her was the most animated character of the family. I was sitting next to Ranjan, when Babli Mami took an initiative of dragging Smitha out of her chair, and forced her to sit next to me and asked Ranjan to take Smitha's chair and said, "They look good together. He looks tough and our Guddu looks so cute." I thought, "Where is Bunty? Why doesn't he take care of his Babli?" We were never hesitant to get close, but this entire idea of animation initiated by Mami was discomforting, and to multiply my fumes further, she took two five hundred rupees notes from her wallet and placed it on our palms, I said, "No aunty, I can't take this. Please. This is embarrassing." But Ms. Babli would not budge, I looked at Smitha's Mom, and she encouraged Babli Mami's animation by saying, "Take it Rama, you should never say no to what elders give you. Take it." I followed her orders and thought, "What if Suresh wants to give a red hot iron rod into my ass? Do I take that as well?" Spilling embarrassment everywhere, they started discussion on my snoring abilities, which obviously Ranjan disclosed because he was the one who had seen me sleeping in the morning. The discussion on snoring abilities was a welcome respite as this had diverted the attention from "How I and Smitha, in fact Guddu looked together" but Mama had different plans, she had sworn in the morning that before the day ended, she would either make me run away from Delhi or she would convince me that committing suicide was a better idea than to spend another day with them. She said, "Our Guddu will have a tough time" and after a pause, she continued, "Rama will not let her sleep, not because he is naughty, he will snore and Guddu will not be able to sleep." Her self-proclaimed terrible sense of humor threw everybody into laughter at our plight, I kept my head down and shut my eyes in disgust. The most difficult dinner of my life ended after a few more jokes on our private lives were cracked.

The onerous day tougher than the placement week was winded up with a call to Smitha's dad who was in Saudi Arabia, who called up Mama every night. He was the most humble man I had known till then, I wondered if he ran away to Gulf because he could not tolerate Mama's disgusting atrocities.

I said, "Hello Sir!"

He said, "Hello Rama!"

And then was the very famous pause as we did not have anything to speak. It became clear that Smitha's Dad did not have any say in deciding about the future of his kids, they were left to Mama's mercy, but still, this deliberate attempt of making Dad's importance feel to me was necessary so that I didn't carry unnecessarily wrong impression about the power structure in Smitha's family.

Mama prompted from behind to ask some irrelevant questions.

Irrelevant question no. 1 "Had your dinner sir?" (10.00 pm in Saudi Arabia, what do you expect?)

Irrelevant answer no. 1 "Yes, and you?" (12.30 mid night in India, and he knew we had gone to Bunty and Babli's place for dinner.)

Irrelevant question no. 2 "How is the weather there?" (How does it affect my life it rains or not in Saudi?)

Irrelevant answer no. 2 "It is pleasant. And is it cold in Delhi?" (No, it is a bright sunny night and I am running on the streets with my shirt off.)

Irrelevant question no. 3 "How is your health?" (He was not suffering from any ailment, I knew that.)

Irrelevant answer no. 3 "Oh! I am good and how is yours?" (Does he know that I smoke and will need chemotherapy sooner or later?)

Irrelevant question no. 4 "What time is your train tomorrow?" (How does it matter to you sir?)

Irrelevant answer no. 4 "Karnataka Sampark Kranthi at 6.30 in the morning?" (Whats the point in telling him the name of the train?)

And then we disconnected, Smitha's dad did not ask me the relevant questions like what my background was, what my future plans were. I thought that good it was that both her parents respected their daughter's choice.

***

Extremely satisfied with the results, Smitha and I were headed back to Hyderabad then. At the station, Smitha's Mama kissed our foreheads and hugged both of us and said, "From now on, please take care of my daughter."

Temporary bouts of stupidity kicked me at wrong times; I said, "Sure aunty, I will take care of her in the train and we will call you the moment we reach Hyderabad." Smitha's Mama patted her head in dismay and I realized that what she said was actually different than the way I interpreted and stubbed everything by just smiling and shying.

In the train, I asked Smitha at the door of the compartment, "So, sweeties, mission accomplished?" She hugged me and said, "Yes, I am really happy, but what did you tell Mama that she defended you like crazy?"

"Nothing, she asked what I would do if my parents did not agree" I said.

"And what did you say?" asked Smitha curiously.

"Nothing, I kept my head high and told her upfront that I will never say that let my parents not come for the wedding, and she was flattened with the way I said it, she probably thought that yes, this guy sounds tough." I said with confidence and I smiled.

Smitha did not appreciate what I said and transferred herself into a murderous mood suddenly, "What do you think of yourself? Just because my Mama did not say anything and accepted you easily, you have assumed that you have crushed her. She is my mom and it is better that you start respecting her, flattened by toughness? Bull shit!" and she left to sleep and even avoided the dinner.

Troubled by what had happened and realizing that I had committed a mistake by saying a few words against Smitha's Mama, I decided to apologize. "Baby, I am sorry, get up and eat something." I hushed while waking up Smitha in the midnight without waking up the fellow passengers. "I have not slept yet." said Smitha, "Promise me that your parents will not stay with us once we get married and I'll have dinner." Smitha threw me into a tizzy and out of motley of things running in my mind, making her eat was the most important, and so I said, "Yes I promise sweetie, please have your dinner now." Smitha smiled and got up quickly to eat. She was happy because she knew that I was a man of my words, but only I and my god within knew that I did not mean what I said.

12

C Me Baby

Since you have understood the emotions around my placement, it is imperative that you be introduced to the consequences of Smitha's placement. Unlike all other B-schools in the country, ours was known to fuck around with the heartbeats of the students in one way or the other. And one of the ways to do it was to spread the entire placement process over three months instead of shutting it up in a week.

Sadly, Guddu (Yes, Guddu, I started calling her Guddu as that was more private and full of love) was yet to get placed, thanks to the confusion of the job profiles and the organizations she wanted to work for. But the fact which she would never admit, not even on her death bed was the mismatch between her abilities and profiles she applied for.

The analysis of the profiles would last for hundred light years before applying, and even when the application was submitted, the analysis of the application would not even last for a second and the result, reject!

We were loaded with so much management *gyaan*, one was always expected to use a bit of it after paying such a heavy fees, fees which would cut down the pay cheque for next five years if you chose EMI! But Smitha, probably due to no EMI education, decided not to use any part of what was forcefully fed to her. The food was SWOT analysis; it had become indispensable for her to see what her strengths were and work on her weaknesses. But Mama's Guddu had lost it to ego and miscalculations; she continued to apply for analytical profiles, and frowned at profiles which had anything else to offer!

Guddu studied science in higher secondary, BBA marketing for grads, and MBA in finance. With this kind of a confusing background, she wanted to work only as an equity analyst or an investment banker. All other profiles were as good as toilet cleaners, for micro moments, I felt that I would be head of housekeeping at Donne. And to toughen it further, she had a break of two years when she chose to serve her ailing mother! Yes ailing mother! The mother with a pacemaker, she was so loud with a pacemaker, she would have been as buzzing as crowd in Eden Gardens before she got the machine!

Absolutely low on confidence, timid by nature, and little slow with the thought process, Smitha found the going tough by being unable to crack GDs. After one such GD, Smitha walked straight to the lake (a small water body in the college premises) ignoring me like I was not there. I kept on following her and knew that the sweet girl was not in her senses; I could empathize with her as I knew how tough it was to move without a job! And tougher, when it happened to a lady drunk with ego.

Smitha was a tricky character, she knew that she was not up to the mark, but if someone advised her on the same, she would not appreciate that. And that someone was me; I could not see her dying gradually. The humiliation of not getting a job was defeating her, and before she was destroyed morally, I decided to give a fuck to her ego and ensured that she realized what she was up to. Most importantly, her fast declining attitude would demolish the relationship as well.

"Listen Baby, stop crying first!" I tried consoling Smitha while putting my arms around her shoulder, but she did not speak.

I hugged her and rubbed her shoulder, her tears got intensified and she pushed me back, I would have chosen death over seeing my love cry, and I said, "No baby, no. This will not help you to resolve whatever is going on, we need to understand where it is going wrong."

"Wrong?" Smitha asked surprisingly as if she had never heard this word before.

"What is wrong with you dude?" Smitha shot back at me with vengeance, "have you gone blind?" she continued and she paused.

"Can't you see that the entire system is wrong?" Smitha held the system responsible for her losses. "They have politicized the entire process; they are pushing in their guys only." Smitha justified her allegations on the system.

I wanted her to get a reality check done instead of making baseless remarks which would do nothing to reform her. "They" I asked, "Who are they?" I continued being quite aware of the answer.

"They, who else?" said Smitha.

"Who are they baby?" I asked.

"Neelav Bose, Supriyo Bannerjee, Haimonti Moitra, Prithviraj Raychoudhary" said Smitha. For those who might wonder if this was the bench strength of Kolkata Knight Riders, they were the placement officers of our college and as far as I knew, every student was so poor to bribe them to get themselves pushed, but I was not sure if there were other favors offered to them. And most importantly, like all Bengalis do, none of the placement officers promoted Bengalis. Then where did the question of politicizing the process rise from?

"No baby, it is not like that. I think these guys are pretty indifferent, and why would they favor anyone of us? They have been into this job for almost a decade now, we are just headcounts for them, and it does not really matter to them if it is Smitha who has got placed or anybody else, for them, what matters is number at the end of the day." I offered an explanation which Smitha found worth adhering to.

"Baby, there is not a single company coming over the weekend. Lets go to Granite, I want to get really close to you." It came from nowhere; I was zapped and wished that if Smitha screwed up all the interviews and GDs and I would be with her in Granite over the weekends.

"Oh baby! Sure, we will go tonight, get an application for your warden." I told Smitha while being trapped.

"Screw you! All you men are like that; my career is at stake and all you can think of is sex! Screw you! I was just checking what's running in your mind!" Googly was out fashioned, Smitha believed only in carom balls now! And there she left snatching her bag from me.

***

It was an offense to study once one got placed, and everyone was committed to this offence once they got placed. Authorities realized quickly that the professors were getting their pay cheque for nothing because most of the classes were abandoned by two sets of students; one who got placed and two, who were running around to get placed!

The outcome was a notice which read, "It is to inform all the students that a minimum of 75% attendance is required per subject to be eligible for any class tests, viva or any form of marking system. The notice is applicable only to the students who have got placed and will be applicable to those who get placed with course of time."

"This is an absolute shit of paper." I said while reading the contents loud. Smitha's ability to read between the lines caught something which I did not, "But let's say if I get placed late, will my attendance be calculated from there on or will they do everything retrospectively?" said Smitha with the same childlike innocence.

To get that clarified, we went to meet the Admin officer, who confirmed that it would be calculated from the day one got placed and clarified that I was inviting serious trouble, "When did you get placed?" he asked.

"It has been three to four weeks sir." I said pensively knowing what was coming.

"Are you attending classes?" he asked.

"No sir, not as regular as needed." I said and he asked me the reason..

I chose not to answer the question with Smitha around and left. "Why didn't you answer him?" asked Smitha. "You have all the time in the world to attend classes, I can't understand why are you messing around." she continued.

The series of questions to churn out the reason out of me continued only to end with getting onto my nerves and I yelled at her, "Can't you just stay quiet for some time? I don't have 75% in any of the subjects right now; I am just thinking how many zeroes I have added up in the class tests. I have already screw up my GPA in the third semester which you are quite aware of and the fourth semester looks like a complete dud as well."

"But who is stopping you from attending lectures? What are you up to?" asked Smitha.

"Nothing, you are not placed yet, how can I leave you alone to do all the running around? Plus, I have to write assignments for you as well, make your presentations, make my presentations and amidst all this confusion, somehow find time to attend classes." I told Smitha with lot of concern.

"So?" asked Smitha looking for some more from me.

"So what? Everything has gone into the drains, none of my presentations and assignments stand eligible to be graded, but you are at least safe in this regard even if you are not placed. I have submitted all your assignments and made your presentations and even if you are low on attendance, you get grades because you are not placed yet." I spoke nervously and said lot of "YOU ARE NOT PLACED YET" unknowingly and thus called for trouble.

"Great, thanks a lot, no need to write any of my assignments anymore, I did not know that you were keeping a count of whatever you did for me and I realize that your grades are more important for you than my placement." Smitha was swift to leave.

How much so ever ego one might have, but if the gain can be sensed, the ego is sensitized, especially when the one who is going to make gains loves you madly. Even when I am writing this, I am not sure if Smitha was under the grip of the same philosophy. But Smitha's anger on my statements was not as acute as it was during my stamped misstatements of the yore! But how about the temptation of effortless and timely submission of assignments?

Probably the temptation had forced Smitha to sponsor the breathing space for me and an opportunity to apologize. "No baby, I did not mean to hurt you, just that I have been scoring shit for the last three semesters, I have been a good scorer throughout, don't like Cs and Ds in my grade sheet. So, slightly disappointed that none of my internals till date would count because I don't have even 50% in any of the subject, and I need to pray that these brainless profs don't hold any more tests till the time I reach 75%, and for that I need to be really regular in attending classes, but I don't want to leave you alone to do all the running around, I just hope that you get placed quickly."

"It's ok, you attend your classes. I'll see how I can manage. Let me check with Sri if he could help." said Smitha. I was sure that she had got nothing to do with Sri, it was a gimmick to garner my attention. Letting Smitha bank on anybody else would have sent me to the pinnacle of embarrassment. I picked Smitha over my grades and as she said, "I was already placed and like before, the externals would save me and a bit of C and D in internals will help me get through."

"No baby, nuts or what? I am there. Relax." I said and Smitha was content.

***

"Elimination, rejection, goof ups, messing up" such words were part of Smitha's vocabulary then till she came across a firm called TASK Wealth Advisors. This company promised fund management and some good money, good enough to lure Smitha to put her best. Coated with my support, and with regained confidence, Smitha decided to pull this one into her kitty.

I always made an effort, even if Smitha felt terrible; to know the questions she was not able to answer in the interviews. I also inquired about the situation she was put in, and what was the most comforting thing in the interview. The gamut of information was good enough to establish a Data Warehouse; I was only required to prepare a questionnaire which helped Smitha to scientifically crack the interview!

On the eve of TASK, we took up a task to see if questionnaire really worked with Smitha; the document had the questions, both technical and general which Smitha found tough to answer, the clearly laid flow charts which showed the situations which drew Smitha into defensive groove. It made Smitha conscious of her flaws and approach in the interview. All she had to do was to carry this consciousness till the interview! And she did that.

"Baby", said Smitha and stood frozen after the interview. "How?" she asked "How?" she asked again (stretching how this time). Trying to comprehend with a simian face, I asked, "What?" and the reply was an adjective. "You are a magician baby, they just asked me the questions you helped me prepare yesterday." said an over ambitious Smitha.

And the result was not a surprise, yes, my love was placed; thereby marking an end to bad moods and arguments. It was a victory for both of us, for the fact that we were the couple with the highest package put together. Such feelings were deserved to be relished, and we relished it in Granite, and there we crossed all inhibitions!

8th Oct, I got placed. 25th Nov, Smitha got placed. In these fourty five days, professors had carried out a massacre, killing all those who got placed. Despite the warning by the general, I invited suicide by not attending classes. And the result on 26th Nov was as follows:

ME		*Grades out of 10*		
Subject	*Attendance*	*Assignment 1*	*Assignment 2*	*Assignment 3*
International Trade	40%	0	0	0
Brand Management	25%	0	0	0
Mergers and Acquisitions	38%	0	0	0
Commodities	60%	0	0	0
Financial Statements and Analysis	56%	0	0	0

SMITHA		*Grades*		
Subject	*Attendance*	*Assignment 1*	*Assignment 2*	*Assignment 3*
International Trade	40%	9	8	8
Brand Management	25%	8	7	8
Mergers and Acquisitions	38%	10	10	8
Commodities	60%	7	6	6
Financial Statements and Analysis	56%	9	8	9

For you, above is the sign of an idiot, for me, this is a report card of my love; the love for which I could go to any extent selflessly. My sacrifice would have made no sense had Smitha not recognized it, but my love would never let me down.

"I love you baby, I promise that I will never leave you, not even in my dreams, I can't do what you have done, screwed up all your grades just to stand next to me throughout. But, please ensure that you don't mess up your externals now. You have to score really well to even think of a B," said Smitha quite sensibly.

Whole technicality around the grading system was no rocket science; but it made a lot of difference! Even though externals were for 100 marks, whatever one scored was halved and then the internal scores out of 50 were added to arrive at the total out of 100. Therefore, if any one scored 40 out of 50 in internals would require only 60 from externals to take his total to 70 (internals 40 plus 60/2=30 externals).

I was out on a limb and needed a miracle to even think of C, forget B. I had a total of 46 from internals, most importantly, 46 was a summation of all the subjects put together! I was deteriorated and headed for a complete disaster; if not the lowest, this total was obviously amongst the lowest.

I had no option other than to go full Monty, the only thing which kept on bothering me was that even if I scored a 100 in all of them, it would be reduced to 50, and my total would be no more than 50 change in any of the subjects including internals. And by the time, externals arrived, I was out of steam, and got my senses together like all those losers and thought, "Let me get off the hook, let me enjoy these last days in the college, let me not die with the books, it is going to be bad bad bad world outside. I am not sure when I'll be able to spend such good times with Smitha, Om and Sri. Sri and Smitha are going to be in Hyderabad, Om in Bangalore, and me in Gurgaon. Screw these books, grades and profs. I am content with C, but this time is far better than Cs and Ds. Live it up."

13
Manhandling Love

My union with Smitha, Om and Sri ended in February 2008 with everyone heading towards their respective career choices. Om flew to Kolkata to be at home till he joined, Sri to Mysore, Smitha remained in Hyderabad, and it is purely illogical of you to think that I headed home as well if Smitha stayed back in Hyderabad.

Smitha had to find an accommodation for herself; as per Smitha's fantasies, "The accommodation should be located close to her office (Of course a posh area), it should be furnished, it should have power back up, preferably a studio apartment, not on sharing basis and most importantly it should be in her budget." And guess what the budget was? Not more than 5k!

The mindset always wanted more; more value for less money, however, Smitha was introduced to reality in two weeks' time that what she wanted was not only more, it was unjustified on account of poor landlords! In those two weeks, Smitha made me travel by autos, buses and on the bike I borrowed from Sri (he left his bike in Hyderabad itself as he was about to return to the city to join his work). I wondered at times if she was really a rich dad's daughter! And there came Smitha's sluggish financial acumen, she spent almost 3k to 4k in two weeks in search of flats, instead of settling with something good and on a sharing basis!

Finally, Smitha found out that there was some girl who was about to join the same organization (TASK) from some other college looking for an accommodation, and what else do you want if the girl was a Christian as well? So, the flat was chosen which was to be shared with Cecilia! Smitha did compromise, but she still remained under the budget. Mission accomplished and next job was to buy the household stuff for Smitha which would include utensils, boxes for pulses and spices and curtains etc.

Smitha bought utensils of lowest quality. Reason: She was not going to stay in Hyderabad forever.

Smitha bought the cheapest cooker. Reason: Just for dinner, why should she buy an expensive one?

Smitha did not buy a bed. Reason: She took my mattress and she already had one.

Smitha bought simplest curtains. Reason: She was not staying in a bungalow.

Smitha bought a stove with cylinder attached under it. Reason: It was enough for two of them (Smitha and Cecilia).

Smitha's miser acts tormented me and I could not stop asking her this, "Why the hell you are planning this way? Why don't you eat your breakfast and lunch outside and arrange tiffin for dinner?"

And she said, "I need to save and send Mama Papa on a world tour on their 25th anniversary."

"Wow! What a wonderful daughter!" I thought and recalled when was my parents' silver jubilee and what did I do for them?

Once Smitha's settlement got ensured, I decided to go to Bangalore to be at home till I joined. But the ecstasy of being at home was way less than the pain of being away from Smitha. When things did not go my way, I thought, and thought hard to get them my way. And tried harder!

"Amma, I might have to go back to the campus", I told my mother forcing her to raise her eyebrows!

"Why do you have to go? And then why did you come back?" Amma asked. Amma always asked multiple questions giving me a choice to answer one or all of them.

It was not worth answering the second question, "I have to go back because my guide wants me there, he has asked me to do my management project under him."

"Has he asked all those under him to come back to Hyderabad? What about those who have already started working?" Amma asked me multiple questions again.

"Obviously Amma, only those who have not joined have been called. Please Amma, I have to go, since I have scored slightly less, I want to score really well in Research Project" I tried to convince Amma.

"And when will you be back? Where will you stay there? And when are you joining? How long will you stay with us before you join Donne? Don't we miss you?" Amma displayed concern by multiplying inquisitiveness.

"I'll be staying at Sri's place and would be back in a month and I have to join from 1st April, relax I'll be back by then and will stay here at least for a week." I answered Amma's queries.

"Ok then, as you wish, ask Raghav to book your tickets." She said and placed her palm on my head.

Raghav is my elder brother and would book tickets any time for me. I loved him for this and owed it to him for handling my adhoc requests.

After exploiting Amma's innocence to my advantage, I was back in Hyderabad within ten days to be with Smitha and become a male partner in a live in relationship!

Even though Smitha and I used to be together from dawn to dusk in the campus, yet this feeling of staying under the same roof, cooking together, sharing the same bed, wearing clothes of each other's choices, good morning kisses, good night kisses was closing any gap we might have had.

I can't remember a single night when we did not make love; the physical inclination had become so lethal that we made love even when Smitha had periods. After every beautiful night, Smitha would get up quite early before me and would wake me up with a Good Morning Tea and a kiss on my eyes. After finishing my tea, I would go to sleep again while Smitha would take bath and wake me up again, and then she would rope me in to be a part of the most exquisite thing of the day! More than what we did every night!

After bath, she would call my name repeatedly to wake me up and extend her hand out from the bathroom while keeping her body behind the door for towel. I had seen it in many Bollywood movies and always wanted to know why women could not carry the towel to bathrooms like men do and why do they try to hide their body behind the door when they make love with the same guy every night who hands over the towel to them? Stupid logics peculiar to women, she would come out wrapped in a towel and would ask me to get her shoes and would say, "Make sure you lock the door" reminding me that Cecilia was the third member in the flat! Before I could get the shoes, Smitha would have taken off the towel and would be struggling to put her bra hooks. "Please honey! Can you just do this for me?" she asked every day. I thought, "Sure, what a stupid question? Why would I say no?" She will put her shoes on, and swear on anything, with her lingerie and shoes, for me she could beat any FTV model! Smitha realized quickly that I was not comprehending this entire idea of putting shoes first, therefore, she cared to update me, "Baby, I put shoes first so that I know what exactly should be the length of my sari." Yes, Smitha wore sari to office to be professionally elegant! She would ask me to hold her sari steadily at the bottom so that she could perfectly do the folds and push the same in to the waist and then she would say, "Done baby" and I would get up to acknowledge that with a long kiss!

For breakfast, we had corn flakes every day in the same bowl, which I forcefully fed Smitha while she would flip through the pages of

Economic Times. I would accompany Smitha till the auto stand and would see her off and would light up a cigarette on my way back to the flat.

Smitha did not hire a maid because of her money saving tendency, so, I would voluntarily do the housekeeping and would ensure that everything is in order other than Cecilia's room. Since Smitha was a money saver, it would not have been really surprising that Smitha skipped lunch every day to save thirty bucks to send her parents on a world tour. Therefore, I ensured that I prepared lunch every day (One of my hidden qualities, a good cook), packed it in a plastic lunch box which had Mickey Mouse stickers, took an auto to get down at some place fifty metres before Smitha's office, called her there and would hand over the lunch box to her.

Smitha would always disapprove of this "*Dabbawala* Concept"; not because, it was embarrassing but what would Cecilia think! Fare enough, that changed me from *Dabbawala* to a "*Maharaj*"(Indian cook) which ensured that Smitha need not go through the hardship of cooking after work. I had enough time in the evening after I worked on my project to cook for all three of us; it was logical as well for me who was at home the entire day! Even though Smitha was disinterested in me as a *Dabbawala*, but she liked me as a "*Maharaj*" which was proved by the number of kisses she posted on my cheeks, more important than the numbers, she was not hesitant to kiss me in front of Cecilia.

Smitha appreciated my cooking skills and even said in one of the love making process, "You are a good CEO who cooks well." For me, appreciation was encouragement and encouragement always turned into enthusiasm to do better. I decided to surprise Smitha with her favorite dish, delicious chicken curry and jeera rice. My talent as a cook was limited to vegetarian stuffs only, but I wanted to do that for my love because she had been telling me this for some time, "Its been quite some time that I had chicken, I miss Mama's chicken curry and rice. At least hostel mess served us chicken once a week" Limited talent required me to download the recipe from internet, buy fresh chicken and those ingredients of recipe which were not part of Smitha's kitchen. I did not carry enough money because I had come to Hyderabad at the mercy of Smitha only; hence I had no option but to take money from Smitha's wardrobe.

For the first time I washed chicken, I almost puked a couple of times, but gathered courage to complete the task. Amidst garlic, ginger and chicken aroma, for a few moments, I asked myself, "Am I being unfaithful to my parents by cooking non veg?" and then clarified the doubt by answering myself, "Dude, you had been unfaithful to your parents umpteen times. You were unfaithful when you smoked, you were unfaithful when you boozed, you were unfaithful when you made love with Smitha, you were unfaithful when you ate non veg, you were unfaithful when you did not go home on Diwali and you were unfaithful when you lied to Amma to come and live in with Smitha. So, why such a huge fuss about cooking the two legged bird which can't fly?" Muddling is expected when you are thrown out of your comfort zone; I did mess up the kitchen in the process of delivering the best chicken curry in the world.

"What have you cooked? I can smell something really yummy" asked Smitha the moment she entered the flat, and then the smell of chicken dragged her into the kitchen and to her horror, she found everything in the kitchen imperfect other than the chicken curry. Smitha was delightfully disgusted; delightful to see the chunks of white meat floating in the gravy, disgusted to see the terrifying kitchen, however, the delight had outdone the disgust.

Smitha had to find out how I made the chicken and she did the same in the night lying next to me, "Baby, the chicken was yummy. How did you make it? Where did you get the recipe from? Chicken was fresh as well? Did you have money to buy all that?" The multiple questions reminded me of Amma. "Downloaded the recipe from the net and yes, forgot to tell you, I took five hundred from your wardrobe." I said.

I had adopted the most hygienic way of cooking known to me, but something went wrong with Smitha and she freed herself from my arms, got up and asked me, "Do you have any idea of what you have done? You have no right to do this!" Unsure of what Smitha talked about, I got up as well to confirm, "What happened baby? What right are you talking about? This is something which we do every night." I said while trying to take off her top. "No, not this. You are sick, you always think of sex." Smitha confirmed that I had the right of sex with her but also indicated that she was talking about something else which drew my curiosity. I had acquired the art of deciphering subtle hints during my relationship with Smitha; I was getting what she was saying, but confirmation was mandatory, "Can you please be clear?" I asked. "You are not earning as of now, I have not got my salary yet, whatever money I have is not mine, it belongs to Mama Papa and you have no right to spend my parents' hard money according to your wish." Smitha spoke brazenly.

Absolutely confused, I looked at Smitha waiting for some more to come. She said, "It is ok this time but please take care from next time." and she adjusted her top and went on to sleep again without bothering what was going through my mind. The series of questions bombarded my brain and rattled me, "Should I have asked Smitha before taking the money from the wardrobe? When we spent on each other in college, whose money was it? Did she ever think who funded nights at Granite, we were not earning then either? Would she have reacted the same way had I spent the money from my pocket? When she forced me to come and stay with her till I joined, Raghav booked my tickets, was it worth coming and staying here? Will she fall short of 500 bucks from sending her parents on a world tour? Was it so important for her to give me her piece of mind for mere five hundred rupees? Is it my unemployment status right now which has forced Smitha to speak this way? Was she right or was I wrong?" Certain questions are good for everybody if they are left unanswered.

My outlook towards Smitha was shattered after what she said; I had come to Hyderabad with only thousand bucks in my pocket and was not sharing the rent of the apartment, I was not paying for the food either but Smitha had an understanding with Cecilia that she would bear two third of the expense till the time I stayed there. The ignominy of the situation had engulfed me, I felt small and worthless; self-control was difficult for me when my self-respect was raped and Smitha just did that. Insulted, a tear ran down my cheek and I could not believe that I cried.

I cleaned my face with my T- shirt and packed my bags quietly, put on my shoes and wrote a note for Smitha, "I am going home baby. I am not sure why you said that, but in my opinion, what I did was not a crime! I am hurt. I thought we enjoyed enough rights on each other, and need not be asking each other for such petty things. But still if you feel that what I had done was wrong, I am sorry. However, you will see 500 bucks stapled with this note, please keep that as a part of my share of the expenses incurred during my stay here. I know 500 won't suffice, I have calculated the expenses till date; my share amounts to Rs 4700 including rent… I will transfer the remaining money from my first salary. And trust me, I would not have repaid this if it was your money, but unfortunately it is your parents' money and even my self-respect says that I should not be spending your parents' money according to my wish. Thanks. Love. Take care."

I left the note under Smitha's palm and stepped out of the flat at 12.30 in the night looking for an auto to the bus stand. With just four hundred and fifty bucks in my wallet, I looked for an ATM and withdrew whatever I had in my bank account. I reached the bus stand at 3 am in the night just to find that the first bus to Bangalore was at 3.30 pm. Since it was stupid to wait for twelve hours, I recalled that the train which I and Smitha chose to come back to Hyderabad after meeting her mother apparently proceeded to Bangalore.

The train was to arrive at 8.30 am, and I was at the station at 4 am and had to wait for two more hours because as per the rules framed by railways, the counters opened at 6. In those two hours, I kept on wondering If Smitha would have realized that I was not in the flat and thought that if she did, why didn't she call me. Concluding that I was no more of any worth to Smitha, I somehow managed to spend two hours by smoking away a pack of cigarettes.

"One ticket Bangalore, Karnataka Sampark Kranthi for today." I said at the counter. The hopeless government official at the counter, who probably forgot to brush his teeth, still recovering from the sleep confirmed, "Chaloo ticket? Unreserved?" Even a speech from Dr Kalam would have sounded absurd to me then with my deteriorating emotions; "No first class AC… What a stupid question was that? Do you have anything other than unreserved? Why do you irritate people so early in the morning?" I yelled at the official "Why are you losing temper? It is my job to confirm, if I don't do that, then you will only come and point fingers at me!" he reacted and handed over the ticket making me realize that I was unnecessarily getting emotional. I collected the ticket and went to the platform and waited for the train to arrive.

The humiliation went beyond my normal self, more to push me to swear not to see Smitha again; just when I took my phone out to call Smitha to inform her about my decision, I received a call from Smitha which I answered.

"What the hell was that?" she asked, obviously indicating towards the note I left.

"Where are you?" she asked without allowing me to say anything.

"Stay wherever you are. I am coming to pick you up." she continued.

"No, I am going. Please don't stop me." I said with acute disappointment while beginning to enjoy the attention I got.

Smitha realised that I was badly hurt and toned down to say, "Baby where are you going? I am sorry. Where are you?"

"I am going home, I am at the station and the train is about to arrive. So don't even think of doing something stupid to stop me." I gave orders.

"Shut up. I am coming. Just wait there." Smitha dismissed what I said and disconnected. I thought of retaliating by leaving Hyderabad and decided to board the train.

I am sure that the hopeless government official at the ticket counter was related to Smitha and he looked half asleep because probably he conspired with Smitha all night long to hand me over a ticket with a wrong date; it was 18th March and he gave me a ticket of 19th March. I had no option but to stay back and gave Smitha all the chance to believe that I did not leave because she asked me not to.

It would have been wise to ask Smitha not to come to the station and go back to her place, however, the ego defeats all wise men in the world and I was far away from being wise, hence I decided to stay at the station till Smitha came there. Smitha appeared at the same platform where I had seen her off after the first semester. Decked up in sari, it seemed that she was rushing for office and had to mend ways to reach station.

"What is this? Why did you have to react so much? It was only me who said that and I think I had enough rights on you to say that! Here are the keys of the flat, come and drop me on the way" Smitha spoke herself, answered herself and decided herself that I was coming with her. I liked the spark in her eyes but was not convinced yet, still I obeyed her!

After dropping Smitha at her office, the next destination was the flat, the flat which was currently managed with the funds provided by Smitha's parents. The flat did not look same to me anymore; the comfort level had vanished and I faced the same uneasiness that I did on the first night at Smitha's home when I went to meet her Mama.

I thought twice before I switched on the fan, I took off my mattress separately and yet could not sleep. The kitchen was mine, but cooking anymore for me was not fine. I stood at the balcony looking at dogs play on the streets, spent close to one tenth of score there, witnessed one gentleman in the neighbourhood smoke and then managed to undo the choke. A bottle of vodka, a pack of cigarettes would help me evade the torture!

Lonely booze sessions to kill misery are really dangerous; the issues are nipped temporarily but they are not killed, they continue to breed and are likely to backfire so strongly that even the strongest of monuments be shaken.

Blood flooded with alcohol did not leave me the same, the ill transformed me was still at the balcony and was witnessing a reason for me to lose control forever and damage. A black Santro drove into the apartments in the evening, it stopped at the visitors' parking and then the head lights were switched off. My hobby of observing things after boozing got on to me and my eyes remained fixed at the Santro. They were fixed for some more time until the door of the car was opened. The opening of the door shook the fixed eyes. Smitha got down from the car.

"Hey baby! Whats up?" Smitha hugged me as I opened the door for her. On a fine day, I would put my arms around her waist and kiss her but not that day. "Hmm fine!" I said and went to the balcony again to drink. Sensing trouble, Smitha followed me to see the balcony muddled up with ash and cigarette buds and the swinging mood galloped her.

"What the fuck are you up to?" Smitha shouted at me. I looked on with red eyes and said, "May I ask you the same thing?" Bamboozled with my reply, Smitha said, "What have I done? If you are still sulking about what happened yesterday, then I think it was sorted out in the morning? Why do you have to do all this?" Nervous breakdown was something to happen next with me and I got hold of Smitha and pulled her to the wardrobe, opened it and said, "Look, your parents' money is intact, I bought booze and fags with the money I had. I am not a thief, do you get that?" my pitch was highest when I finished speaking.

"Shut up. Quiet, Cecilia might hear everything." Smitha dismissed my point.

I slammed the wardrobe's door and left while Smitha reminded from behind, "Careful, I can't pay for the damages you do!"

Reeling under supreme agony, I bought another quarter of vodka and smashed it in neat, returned absolutely sloshed and banged the door like a mad elephant. Cecilia struggled to open the door as her right hand had the plate; I stumbled and saw Smitha eating as well. Without giving a damn, I walked straight into the room. Smitha came in with the plate of food and kept it on the floor and slid it towards me like they do to prisoners in jail. Smitha's just enough transgression turned the anguish in me into measurable actions; I kicked the plate and said, "What do you think? Do I look like a dog? And I don't want anything from your parents' money."

Then surfaced the best weapon which a woman could unleash; silently cleaning the mess while shedding a couple of tears. I melted a little and when I was about to lend a helping hand, Smitha said, "Get away, you moron, what do you think of yourself? You will keep on throwing tantrums and I will take all the shit?"

"No, you won't." I said, "Because, I don't mean anything to you anymore, you have been secretly meeting somebody else and keeping me in dark" I continued while indicating towards the Santro!

"What? What the fuck?" Smith was astonished.

"Now, don't act innocent! Om was right, after all you are a Delhi girl, you keep associations as long as it promises gains to you!" I made baseless remarks on Smitha's character.

"What the hell are you talking about? What gains?" Smitha interrogated.

"Someone dropped you in a Santro today?" I started clarifying.

"Yeah so?" Smitha intervened, "What's wrong about that?"

"Yeah, nothing wrong about it, but it took you almost 10 minutes to get down from the car." I completed what I had.

"So? What do you mean to say?" Smitha asked a few more questions.

"Nothing. Who was it? And why did you take so long?" I asked.

"That was Thomas. Office colleague and a senior and he was just giving me a few tips, we were discussing something, that's about it!" Smitha started clarifying.

I was undoubtedly uncomfortable with Smitha's association with Christian guys, because I always thought that Christian guys always had better chances of impressing Smitha's Mama with their born Christian tag and god gifted abilities of eating mutton relentlessly.

"Is he single?" I asked Smitha showing my discomfort.

"Do you think I was making out or something with him in the car?" Smitha cross questioned by asking questions with obvious answers.

"Yes, I thought so!" I confirmed Smitha's doubt.

"Bull Shit. How can you even think like that? We have been together for almost fifteen months now and this is what you could accuse me of?" Smitha cited disappointment and I was quiet.

She continued, "This is just a result of what happened last night, you wanted some other reason to vent out your anger and frustration, all to show me down." Smitha was raising her voice.

"And if you think I made out with him, then yes I did." Smitha continued her oration.

"This just shows how broad minded you are! You are like those men who want women to be confined to kitchen only!" Smitha spoke like a woman activist.

And then she said something which brought the wildest animal hiding inside me, "Your mother was also working. Your father must have reacted the same way if your mother was dropped by her male colleagues, kids learn from their parents or probably your mother must have made out in front of your home........" and her speech was cut short.

A big palm as big as Smitha's face fiercely came down from a height of seven feet and stamped itself on Smitha's soft face and she was grounded! Yes, I slapped Smitha. She got up to push me and said, "Get out right now."

"Yes, I would but after showing you what you are! You slimy bitch! How dare you speak like that about my mother?" I said and strangled Smitha. Smitha started panting and I left her and she slapped me. The slap unleashed the beast from me and I tore Smitha's clothes, slapped her again and again, clutched her arms tight, shook her wildly, threw her on the mattress, left bruises on her arms and marks on her neck.

Smitha was lying on the bed with torn clothes; her cheeks had turned blue! And I stood at the balcony regretting what I had done!

After a couple of hours, I went close to Smitha who had shrunk herself into the quilt. She had not slept; I took her hand in my hand and said, "I am sorry! I am wrong; I should not have done it. I understand that I instigated you by making remarks about your character. I am an idiot to have accused you of two timing. Please sweetheart, I know the damage I have done to this relationship is irreparable, but, please forgive me, I commit this life to serve you forever. Even if you think I don't deserve you, allow me to be with you because I am apologetic of what I have done, and this can be corrected only if you give me an opportunity to be with you and serve you! Please baby, I am really sorry." I started crying and touched Smitha's feet, picked up my bag and left for the station.

14
Men Bonding

Back home and struggling to abandon the wrong doing, I called Smitha every day after every hour; she would answer my call but would proscribe the idea of being with me. What I had done was nothing short of a crime, and would not attract mercy even at the house of lord and Smitha was still a human!

It was words when I accused Smitha of being characterless, it was words when Smitha clarified, it was words when I dismissed her explanation, it was words when Smitha shot back by dragging my parents into the argument, but it was action when I hit back! Howsoever wrong one might be in his words, but the one who uses force first is wrong undoubtedly and no argument can help to undo the wrong. You can't murder someone because he was profane. And never ever, even in your dreams hit a lady, no shelter even in hell for such a scoundrel!

Dead confused equation with Smitha, a troubled mind, self-conflicting actions and embarrassment had arrested me strongly and I proceeded to Gurgaon under the same arrest! Gurgaon was the first destination of my professional choice.

Trouble had decided to be my shadow ever since I hit Smitha and I had gone from mad to stupid which was known only to me. Soon, the world where I had to be best was aware of it. Every new guy in an organization is treated to a worthless process called "Orientation" where the new guy is made to understand the business operations on the first day itself and Donne was no different! However, the treatment from Donne was amazing at which Dipti said, "Feels great. Isn't it? But I am tensed, we have to meet the director of finance." (Dipti Ahuja was my batch mate who got selected with me) She read the schedule for us. Both of us waited in one of the meeting rooms when a man, who resembled a tiger with piercing eyes walked in and said, "Good morning! So, how are you doing?" Dipti with a plastic smile said, "Very fine sir! Thank you." to which he nodded. I hated unnecessary prefixes and suffixes when one spoke, either you are fine or not fine, what was "Very fine"? That is Punjabi style!

"I am the CFO. So, what is the schedule for the day?" asked Tiger looking man. I wanted to ask him, "Dude, don't you have a name? CFO must be having a name."

I looked at Dipti who still sported that plastic smile and was looking like a complete idiot. Why do you have to smile unnecessarily all the time? We were not selected as flight attendants.

"We have to meet the director of finance sir. He is going to brief us." I spoke smartly, but little did I know that I was giving all the reason to the CFO to slay those casual and serious men who interviewed me.

CFO looked at me with a straight face and a bit of disgust in his eyes.

Within five seconds I regained that a CFO was nothing but the director of finance! Trying to envelope my idiocy, I made another statement which made the CFO believe that I was not only stupid, but comprehensively lunatic, I said, "Oh! You are the director. I forgot that director of finance and CFO are the same." and I smiled like Dipti did, plastic and idiot!

Later that day, when we were taken for a round through the amazing office, I saw two kinds of eyes amongst the employees; the hungry ones which were fixed at Dipti and said, "Please come to my department, we have no girls here." and the second were the pleading ones and said, "Please come to my department to share some load, we are short of manpower." Then we stopped at another meeting room where I could see one of the serious looking men who interviewed me sitting with a few other men who looked more serious.

A pretty lady who looked dumb, obviously from HR, said, "These gentlemen make the elite finance team of Donne, they will brief you about your journey with Donne." and she left us amongst the most serious men in the world who only meant business or pretended to be those meaning business, I was to find out soon. Relieved to see that their focus did not shift to Dipti, we wished them, "Good afternoon sir." Probably they waited for pretty lady from HR to leave to shift their focus to the pretty lady in finance; even though both of us wished them together, most of the "Pretending to be serious" men responded only to Dipti and said, "Good Afternoon" while exposing their well brushed teeth. I wondered what would have been their responses if their Super Dad, the CFO was there.

The serious looking man who interviewed me took me out of the mayhem in the meeting room and said, "Hi, I am Sumit Rathi, I will be your navigator throughout your management trainee stint. How are you?" I guess the others continued to fight on who would be navigating Dipti.

"That is good to know sir! And I am doing fine." I said.

"Sumit. Call me Sumit!" he corrected me. "Let's go for lunch." he said. I wanted somebody to say this, I was dying of hunger and thirst and idiot Dipti had asked me not to reveal my hunger and thirst as that won't have sent good signals about me. No logic, but accepted.

Both of us walked to the cafeteria (canteen in college becomes cafeteria in office), I saw the queue where who's who of Donne stood revealing their hunger and thirst proving that Dipti was wrong. Dipti could have been wrong, but as aforesaid, I was stupid. Smitha's memories did not attack me till the time I was busy, but the moment I was left on my own, she came to grip my mind, and I started dreaming of Smitha while looking at the flashy office and how great it would have been to get her there one day and impress her, she would have been really happy, but all I could give her was preposterous symptoms of mine. Sick! And suddenly I found myself to be part of the queue while Sumit sir walked straight to the table reserved for us to have lunch with "Pretending to be serious" men. He called my name repeatedly to join him making the public around me aware that I was stupid and I was Rama. A lady standing behind me said, "You are Rama I guess, he is calling you." and pointed towards Sumit sir.

Subsequently, after all the embarrassment, I joined him, and then joined all the "Pretending to be serious men" along with Dipti who was all smiles. Not surprising, Dipti had the licence to be amused with the amount of attention she got on the first day. I wanted to ask her who won the battle to become her navigator but dismissed the idea.

Everyone started relishing the food and slipped into a lighter mood, I enjoyed the food along with the conversation with one of the best professionals in the industry. The table was getting chirpy, I was buzzing with food in mouth when all the "Pretending to be serious" men became serious all of a sudden and stopped eating, I wondered what went wrong and looked for a cockroach in the daal, but what I saw was the Tiger once again. Their Super Dad, correction, our Super Dad, CFO had joined us! Everyone wished him, I wished him too with food in my mouth and he looked disgusted once again and me? Stupid of course!

The pretty dumb lady from HR emerged once again and said, "Excuse me gentlemen." All the serious men stopped eating and said, "Sure, please carry on." and the pretty dumb HR lady turned to us and said, "Let's go."

"What go? I did not have ice cream." I thought but said, "Bye and thank you sir." while they said, "All the best" which meant "Picnic over, start working."

The HR lady took us back to the same meeting room where CFO had greeted us; there were 2 folders kept on the table which we were asked to take possession of. I asked, "What is this?" and the HR lady said, "Open it, this has terms of employment, HR policies, salary structure and other forms like salary account opening, employee information and PF etc. I request you to fill these forms and give them to me." "See you in half an hour." She continued and left us in the meeting room. After half an hour, she returned with one of the senior HR persons who checked our forms and gave it to the HR lady and said, "So Rama and Dipti, as you are aware that as a part of your management trainee stint, you will have to work in different locations throughout your training period. Right?" and we nodded in agreement.

"Rama, you are supposed to join Delhi branch tomorrow and report to Mr. Sunil Tayal, the Branch Controller." he said. "And Dipti, you will be here at corporate office and report to Mr. Vijay Chandgotia" he continued and left the room. It looked veritable that Dipti would have stayed in head office for the attention she got by all the "Pretending to be serious" men. I looked at the dumb lady from HR and asked, "What next? What are we supposed to do now?" and she replied, "You can either go back to the hotel or go around the office. Try meeting the people and get to know whom you are going to work with." and she also disappeared.

Even if it was left for us to decide what was next, Dipti' s eagerness to impress one and all forced her to say, "Lets go and meet people." and I disagreed. "What meet people? Do you even know anyone of them? It would be so embarrassing to just go and stand blank in front of people and keep on introducing yourself even if they are not bothered about who you are!" I said "Try doing it, you would look so stupid." I disagreed strongly.

"No, but if we go home now, they would think that we are least bothered about knowing how things work." Dipti retaliated.

"How things work? Things do work but not the way you are trying to make them work." I said hinting at Dipti's apple polishing skill, "Also, what would I do by knowing people here, I am going to Delhi branch, important for you to know them and I can't do something which does not have any relevance. So, bye, see you then at the hotel." I said while packing my stuff.

At the hotel, I discovered that employees are entitled for a beer a day as per HR policies; I ordered for a beer and was trying to figure out if it would be a great idea to call up Smitha or not when someone knocked at the door. It was Dipti who pounced on the sandwich kept on the table as I opened the door and said, "Please order some Maggi as well. I am really hungry." while she still munched on the bread and I ordered Maggi.

I was busy switching the channels and looked at Dipti who behaved like a kid from Somalia. "So, how is Smitha? How is her profile and everything?" she asked casually with Maggi patronizing her lips. Tantalized at the very thought of Smitha, I said, "Yeah, she is fine." and lit up a cigarette trying to stub everything under the smoke!

Dipti hunched perfectly and said, "Is everything fine?"

Lying to a lady with kid like innocence was proscribed, I said, "No, not exactly, she does not speak to me regularly, things went a bit awry in the last week. I hit her."

"I am feeling so small and guilty about it. I don't know what to do!" emotions began to flow.

"How could you do that? Anyhow, try calling her from my phone." Dipti offered assistance.

"Hello. Who is this?" asked Smitha since it was an unknown number.

"Hi. Rama here. How are you?" fear hindered my speech.

"Yeah, tell me? Whose number is this?" Smitha's excitement declined

"This is Dipti's number. Will you pick if I call from my number?" I looked for confirmation.

"Yeah but what is it?" Smitha was still disdained.

"Sorry!" I said this zillionth time after I hit Smitha.

"Anything else?" Smitha expected something else other than apologies.

"I will be in Delhi for next four months at least. I'll be working in Delhi branch." I tried to keep Smitha informed about my future plans.

"Ok. That is good. Anything else?" said Smitha. This made me wonder that what "Anything else" was.

"No, That is it' I said rubbishing the thought of "anything else".

"Fine. Bye." and she disconnected.

"Can I order your share of your beer?" I asked Dipti.

"Gone nuts?" she argued.

"Yeah. Can I?" I confirmed.

"Ok." she said and exited.

Sprawled by stupor, I laid on the bed with thin line of tears going down sideways when I received a call from a strange number, strange because it was more than ten digits. It was highly exaggerated to believe that I got a call for an overseas job just with a day's job in Donne. "Hello!" I said expecting some surprise.

"Hi *beta*!" service providers introduced a pulsating voice.

"Hello!" I stumbled before realizing it was Smitha's Mama who was in Saudi Arabia then with Smitha's Papa, "Yeah hello aunty! How are you?" I said.

"I am fine *beta*. How are you? How was the first day at work?" she asked.

Speculating if Tiger CFO was acquainted with Smitha's Mama, I said, "Yeah. It was ok."

"So you will be in Delhi? That is what Guddu told me." she said and I was satisfied that I was still a topic of discussion between Smitha and her mom.

"Yeah, they have put me in Delhi branch for next four to five months." I informed the pre-informed lady.

"I know *beta*. So, where are you going to stay then?" Smitha's Mama was worried.

"Currently in the guest house, will move to chummery soon." I said.

"Chummery?" she expected a definition of chummery, but concluded "What is that? Sounds like some jail" and laughed at her own sense of humor.

"No, that is company's accommodation." I corrected her.

"Is that in Delhi?" she inquired.

"No, in Gurgaon." I answered.

"Then? How do you plan to travel to Delhi every day?" she raised a thoughtful query this time.

"Yeah, have not thought about it. Should be by bus", I said.

"Bus?" Smitha's Mama was astonished and I rewound slightly to recall if I said bus or jet!

"Why bus? Do one thing, pack your bags right away and go home!" Smitha's Mama exercised her discretionary powers.

And it took a while for me to realize that she was talking about the flat in Dwarka because for me, Bangalore was home!

"Ranjan is alone there. I'll be coming by mid of May. And you can travel by metro; your office is in CP right?" Smitha's Mama displayed rare instances of logic and a big opportunity to intertwine with Smitha's family; win her family if not her!

Disobedience was barred, yet I thought of confirming with Smitha who said over the phone, "Do as you wish. I don't know what has happened to Mama. But would be good for you if you stay with Ranjan, you can save on both money and time."

Time was fine but what amount of money I was going to save was known only to Smitha's financial acumen plus my parents' silver jubilee was long back and I did not have any plans to send them on a world tour.

"Fine I'll go." I gave way to Mama's orders and disconnected.

The instant chord stuck with Ranjan was still alive; the idea of hiring a cab was cut short as Ranjan offered to come and pick me up when I informed him about my arrival. "You stay there bro. I'll be there in half an hour." he said.

The half an hour wait was stretched to an hour's wait, and consequently I called Ranjan who was out of the coverage area as updated by the Airtel lady! "Must be driving" I contemplated.

From an hour, the wait multiplied many folds and it was midnight, and Ranjan remained out of the coverage area all this while. Someone told me that if you removed your sim card without switching off the phone, the phone proves to be out of coverage.

Fearing his loss of freedom, Ranjan would have discarded the proposal of staying with me, and therefore duped me. Rejecting to inform Smitha and her Mama, I stayed in the guest house itself focusing my thoughts on how the first day in the branch would be.

"Here are the keys, I'll come late." I said while leaving the keys at the reception.

"That is fine sir, dinner would be here itself right?" the well-dressed man at the reception confirmed and I replied in affirmative.

"Your cab is there sir." he said to my astonishment forcing me to call up the Donne office when they clarified that the cab service was there only for the first day as I was not aware of the route and should throw myself to the brilliant bus service from the next day. Brilliance lies in hanging and not travelling in the buses. I missed Ranjan for a while but was content.

Lofty man with a telling personality, against my imagination chaired the Branch Controller's cabin, dumbstruck with his appearance, I pulled my wrist watch up the arm as a sign of nervousness and said, "May I come in sir?" to which he smiled, I sneaked in and the much awaited day began.

"I am Sunil Tayal, joined in 2005 with Kolkata branch." he introduced himself; He let me escape the "Don't call me sir, Call me

Sunil" clause and I chose an agreement with "Sir."

The dialogue was chopped when I got a call from Ranjan which I disconnected since I was in the middle of first and most important interaction of my professional life. Ranjan would not budge, he called again and I disconnected again, but this time, for his careless act the previous night.

Mr. Sunil's knack of observing things was sharper than mine and he said, "Come on, don't be so uncomfortable and formal, we are going to work together. You can answer your call first." leaving it to me to judge if it was sarcasm or not. I decided it was not.

Ranjan called again, "Yeah Ranjan, I am in the office right now." I said sternly citing his careless attitude the previous night!

"Its ok, I'll call later, don't take me wrong dude, I met with an accident while coming to pick you and the phone got damaged as well. So, could not call." he said throwing me in a state of shock.

"What? Are you serious?" I asked.

"No, I am fine, air bags saved me." he replied.

"Fucker, are you serious about the accident thing?" I reiterated my question.

"Seriously, I want your help." he said pleadingly.

"Where are you right now?" I was worried, "I'll come." I offered assistance to the young boy.

"Wazirabad. Rana Motors. The car is smashed big time." he was jacked.

"Ok, see you in a couple of hours." And I disconnected.

Recouping from the shock, I went inside the cabin again when the carefully polished side of Mr. Sunil asked, "Is everything fine young man?" he observed the expressions changing on my face while I spoke with Ranjan.

"Well, not exactly sir. My flat mate has met with a terrible accident and I am afraid that I need to go, he just called up." I broke the news of my bunking the first day at work.

He said, "I hope he is fine because he himself called up." which was nothing but, "Don't even think about taking an off, this is your first day."

And then the intelligent side of Mr. Sunil inquired, "How come you have a flat mate? I thought you were staying in the chummery or guest house! Right?"

"Yes sir, but I am moving out of the guest house this evening and going to stay with this friend who stays in Dwarka, I am not opting for chummery because of the excessive travelling." I clarified the dishonest image which Mr. Sunil was probably trying to design.

I was confident that Mr. Sunil was shaken, whether for the decline of right of exercise on his subordinate or due to my carelessness towards the job on day one . Without waiting for his consent anymore, I chose to head towards Rana Motors wondering if Mr. Sunil would ring the tiger CFO to update him about my heroics.

Flirting with uncertainty, I took a metro train designing mentally the shit generated by Ranjan. Ranjan waited for me at the metro station, and hugged me in desperation the moment he saw me. The pressure from the twenty one year old was releasing, his body lightened a bit which inclined on me for support; he would have started crying had I not held him tightly to treat him like a grown up man, "So, what happened? Have you informed Guddu or Mama Papa about it? Where the hell did you meet with an accident? And police?" I asked him questions like mothers do so that he did not miss his Mama in the toughest of times.

"Fuck" Ranjan reacted resplendently.

And then he continued while we walked towards the Rana Motors, "Dude hope you have not informed Guddu about it, she is Mama's pet, she will spill the beans. I don't want Mama Papa to be informed about this. We have to clean the mess on our own. I think I can bank upon you?" This is called banking by default.

Looking at Ranjan's fucked up face resembled a request for a forceful adoption. Mama's pacemaker would stop functioning if she was informed about this and Smitha who was Mama's pet as per Ranjan would surely not think before deactivating the pacemaker!

"What to do?" This track played in my inner music system repeatedly before it got jammed to tell me, "Help him, and don't tell Mama or Smitha about it. The equation you share with him is not dependent on you relation with Smitha. Remember, the chord striking instantly."

"Fine then, but how did it happen?" I assured Ranjan and said, "Were you drunk?"

"Yes, I was drunk and the car fell from the flyover." Ranjan shocked me.

"What the fuck? How could you take off from the flyover? Which flyover was it? And such an asshole you are! Drunken driving? Shit man, what about the police? How did you reach here? You are screwed up big time." I was becoming insane!

"Listen, there is a slight trouble." Ranjan was exposing now.

"Some more trouble! Wasn't this enough?" I rebuked him.

"I was not only drunk, but had smoked up as well. That is the reason I lost control, it was flyover right after the toll gate." Ranjan gave me more reasons to not inform Mama about that.

I closed my eyes in horror and pushed him a little and turned to the other side pulling my hair, wondering what all mess needs to be cleaned up and how to manage the narcotics department! More than the car, I was worried about Ranjan's future and asked him a relevant question, "Bugger! Were you in possession of some stuff?"

"What stuff?" he asked innocently.

"Grass?" I whispered, "Let me know if you have any more surprises, charas cocaine?" I continued sarcastically.

"Yes, I still have it." he said and put his hands inside the pocket to show it to me which forced me to force his hand to remain inside the pocket and I dragged him to the washroom while saying, "Keep it inside you fucker."

At the washroom, I ordered, "Come on take it out now."

"Careful." I suffixed.

He took out a pouch full of grass, to which my senses deteriorated because the content of grass was more than I, Om and Sri smoked in two years and I asked him, "Are you into opium trade?" and he smiled.

"Fuck you! Is this some kind of a joke? How can you smile? Asshole!" I was going crazy and snatched the pouch from him and flushed it off before he could respond.

"What have you done?" Ranjan had the reasons to be terrified if he was seriously into opium trade.

"Can't you see? Have you gone blind as well?" I shot back and said, "Come, don't worry and this was important. If you were caught with this, you would have been done away with for ten to fifteen years!"

"But I got it from Manali, Kaala Gaanja." he was concerned and I looked at him sternly for he clarified, "I swear, I am not into trading, I got it for me but it was worth fifty thousand!"

A wave zipped through my body and I froze, said "fifty grands? Where did you get the money from?" waggled in hopelessness and said, "What next? Where is the car?"

Ranjan understood that I had lost it and said, "Smoke?" and I said, "Yes" and we walked out of the service station, and there lied shock of the day. While we walked out of the service station towards the lawn for smoke, I spotted a black Wagon R which looked like a rickshaw with a cross hanging inside, I stopped to ask, "Is this car yours?" and crossed my finger for Ranjan to be negative, but this was the best surprise from the Pandora Box he carried that day. "Sorry Bro, yes this is our car." and looked down in embarrassment.

I kept one hand on my forehead, the other on my hip and looked on in dismay, and said, "Anything else? Please I am not ready for any more surprises. Hope you have not crushed anybody. How the fuck you are safe when this is the fate of the car?"

"No, but there are two things, one is that police needs to be taken care of and the car bill! I have already paid the towing vehicle." Ranjan signed off the illustrious outcome of his gallant driving skills!

"Car bill? You have insurance right?" I asked.

"Yes, insurance is there, but" Ranjan said.

"But what?" I inquired.

"But we cannot claim it, because of two reasons, one is that insurance will be available only after the police is informed and they will book me for drunken driving, and insurance doesn't cover drunken cases." Ranjan clarified.

"And what is the second one?" I asked.

"Even if we are able to win the police by bribing them, and they don't book me for drunken driving, insurance cannot be claimed because the vehicle is in Mama's name, and the owner needs to sign on the claim papers." Ranjan confirmed that he was fucked and I was being dragged in the quest of instantly striking the chord!

"So, we have to tame down the police first so that no case is booked against you and the vehicle, and then arrange for the finance to fund the repair of the car." I confirmed the jobs on hand.

"Yes." he said easily.

"Auto" I called on the main road.

A green box with yellow top slammed brakes damn in front of us, an oily face on sweaty torso popped out to ask, "*Kidhar*?"

"Wazirabad police station" I said looking at Ranjan.

The oily bastard could decipher that we were screwed up and demanded ransom instead of fare, "hundred rupees"

I vomited all my anger for Ranjan on the oily bastard, "*Behanchod, Pakistan nahi Jana, 30 rupay le lena.*"

The oily bastard looked at me in vengeance and said, "*Bhikari, kahan kahan se aa jate hain*" to which I did not react thinking that his anger was justified after I abused him, but Ranjan thought differently who held the oily bastard by his collar and dragged him out to hit him. I intervened and said, "Leave him, we don't want another police case" to which Ranjan said, "How dare he speak to you like that?" and he turned again towards the oily bastard to get him and I stopped him again, "Chuck it, the disappointment what you gave is way too painful than what he said." I said and called for another auto and boarded it without arguing for the fare for I did not want Ranjan to pick up a fight.

Ranjan sat next to me and said ultimately, "Please help me get out of this!" and held my hand, "I will never repeat this, none of my so called buddies is helping me. Please." I looked at him with mercy and said, "Its ok. Once we crack this, we will party." and smiled.

We reached the police station, where Ranjan walked in with ease as if that was his school leaving me behind shivering a bit at the thought of face off with a species as tall as me with a paunch and rugged accent called Inspector. I stood at the entrance looking at Ranjan who walked straight to the "Species" and got him out of the chair after shaking his hands with him. Both "Species" and Ranjan then walked towards me, I stood at the door wondering if Ranjan told him if I was the one who forced him to smoke up.

The "Species" came up to me and extended his hand to me for a shake, I was petrified to think if it was one of the tricks from movies where the hand is twisted at the behest of shaking it, yet I shook hands with him, firmed up my face and body to say, "Hello Inspector! So how are you doing?" leaving behind the fear.

Baffled with my response, "Species" said, "Hello Mr. Rama. Hope you know why you are here?" I looked at Ranjan who seemed to have leaked out my name.

I loosened my tie a bit, folded up my sleeves and said, "Yes, I know. So, what is that you plan to do?"

"See, we have already told him what is required, we have found traces of alcohol in his blood samples, so, we have told him that he could be booked for negligent and drunken driving." Species said.

And Ranjan intervened, "Yeah, but sir.." and I took command to say, "Shut up, you have done what you had to, now, stay out of it when we are speaking." and turned towards the "Species" with a wrinkled face and said, "Yes, please continue. I understand you have told him certain things, but that was different, I want you to tell me what is the way out without bothering him or his parents, Let's talk business sir."

For the first time in my life, I felt my integrity was at stake, but nothing else sounded lucrative enough to save Ranjan, I continued, "He is a kid. Let's sort it out maturely."

"Kid?" Species retaliated and said, "Your kid was loaded with so much of alcohol that he turned the car into a plane to take off from the flyover."

"Yes, I understand sir, but I request you to consider the fact that his parents don't stay in India, and let them not do the running around for his ridiculousness, let me know what we could do to stub this." I pleaded then.

"Thirty thousand" he said looking at the other side, a normal style of asking for bribe.

"What?" I looked for repetition.

"Thirty thousand, no bargain." Species said again, this time decisively.

I wondered if I had to come to buy the bridal gown for Smitha and said, "Sir" with apologies in my eyes.

"Thirty thousand by tomorrow, I can't hold it for long." he said sumptuously and left mocking all my smartness.

"Where will we get 30k from?" I looked at Ranjan expecting him to generate some idea.

"We will sell my chain." he said while pulling his gold chain out with his thumb, "I will tell Mama that it fell somewhere."

"No, Mama will not spare you even if you give her stories, she will find out." I said dismissing his idea.

"Do you have some cash?" I asked Ranjan.

"Yes, I do" he confirmed.

"How much?" I asked.

"Close to 15k" he said.

"Fine, let's go to Chandni Chowk." I said.

"Why?" he asked.

"Shut up and follow me." I ordered.

Another metro ride of the day transferred the ill-fated us to Chandni Chowk, the busiest market place in Asia where even a Chai Walla is a millionaire; more importantly, there was no other place I knew on earth where everything found a buyer! But what was that I planned to sell was still unknown to Ranjan and me.

Walking in the by lanes of Jama Masjid in crammed streets made me feel like a gangster who had come to take the delivery of guns! The air was filled with the smell of mouthwatering delicacies, we could smell from kababs to jalebis, samosa to dosa, yet Ranjan, in the delicate of the situations could differentiate kababs in the air and said, "We will have some kababs once we finish the work." and I stopped to glower at him, realizing his carefree nature was not impressing me, he said, "Oops sorry!"

Terminated at brain, I needed a smoke and stopped at a paan shop to buy a fag when Ranjan spotted the kababs and said, "Till we smoke, let's have kababs as well." and I lost temper to say, "Get lost and get a plate for me as well." Ranjan returned with two plates of steaming kababs which he quickly got rid of to place one plate on my left palm, I reacted quickly to the heat by juggling the plate to my right palm. I was shaking my left palm brazenly to cool it down when I saw my wrist and stopped abruptly to see a Rolex clinging on, the needles pleading to me not to be sold to any tobacco chewing shopkeeper who has never worn a Citizen in his life! And I threw the plate when Ranjan said, "Dude, you could have given them to me if you did not like them." while he blew the steam from kababs, "Shut the fuck up and come." I said and pulled him.

"twenty five thousand." said an owner of a shop which bought and sold second hand stuff who looked like a pimp in the part time.

"What?" said Ranjan in excitement, "No, you are not doing this! Dude, this is Rolex, people die to buy it. Your brother has given it to you. Please don't sell it. We will sell my chain." he tried banning the sale.

"No, your mom will sense that something is wrong, I can see that your credibility at home is not great. I will do something and tell my brother one day what happened to the watch he gave, relax." I said convincingly.

"But" Ranjan looked regretful, "I promise that I will buy you a similar Rolex, no, one costlier than this when I start working."

Culminating the emotional show, I turned to the shopkeeper and said, "Do you know how much is this for?"

"Yeah, should be one to one and a half lakhs." he said and bent to take out a box, placed it on the slab, opened it and said casually, "I have so many of them, there so many like you who come here to sell it off." (the box had so many branded watches)

"But I need at least sixty thousand." I said firmly and, "Please we are in need of it." I said meekly.

"Fine." he said, took the watch swiftly, put it in the same box with its siblings, bent down again to keep the box back, and bent further revealing his low quality underwear.

"Here you go!" he got up and placed two bundles, a five hundred rupee one and a hundred rupee one, "Total 60k."

"Original notes right?" I asked for confirmation and he shot back brilliantly, "Original watch right?"

My heart bled tears and I imagined that how the needles bled tears in the box away from the wrist. "Sorry bro! I can understand your pain!" Ranjan extended sympathy, "Its ok, let's go to the police station straight and get a clean chit, its 3.30 now! We can even go to the service station and see what will be the estimate for repair" I said and looked at Ranjan who stood frozen while I walked a bit ahead.

I stopped and asked, "Come. What is bothering you? Its ok, don't lose heart, you promised me that you will buy me a new watch. Come" I sort of started liking Ranjan.

He hugged me and I rubbed his back to console him, "Come on, its ok. And I like those who trust me and you are one of those! Smoke?" I said.

"Bro! I was scared to tell you the money required for car repair, they have an initial estimate of eighty two thousand ." Ranjan dropped a log on my head.

"What the fuck!" I said and dropped shoulders.

"That is the reason I was stopping you from flushing the grass" Ranjan clarified that his intentions of carrying a pound of grass was not malaise, "We could have sold it to somebody." he displayed his ambition of becoming a drug trader.

With my face shrinking, brains cells stemming, body shivering, dishonesty got onto me and I was getting brilliant. Dishonest brilliance suggested me to sweep the money in my account to get the car repaired.

"What happened? Don't worry, I will arrange for the money." Ranjan tried relaxing me a bit.

"You speak again and I'll put a dagger down your chest." I was enticed, "No need to do anything, you will surely get into something illegal. Fucker"

"Then what do we do?" he asked.

We went straight to the police station and handed over the money to "Species", in exchange got all the case papers including the original FIR copy, and took a bus straight to Gurgaon.

After rubbishing the police, we were left with 30k in my pocket, 15k with Ranjan and another 55K in my account! Wondering how did I become rich? That 55K was the security deposit amount refunded by the college authorities!

With a stone, as heavy as the car which was reeling at the workshop, on my heart, I took out my cheque book, prepared it for 45k and gave it to Ranjan asking him to withdraw the money as and when needed, "Listen, keep this with you, once the car is done, you can use this to withdraw money. By the way, how long will it take for the car to get repaired?"

"Should take two weeks." Ranjan had apologies written in all languages on his face.

"So, hang on, I'll just pack my stuff and we go home." I said providing him a default banking.

And then Ranjan asked a germane question, "Tell me something, Is everything fine between you and Guddu?" and I was stunned, he continued without allowing me to answer, "No, please don't mind just that I did not see you speaking to her at all today."

"No, no man, nothing of that sort, did you leave any scope for me to speak with her?" I joked.

"Ok, here you go!" he said and dialed Smitha's number and gave the phone to me. Clueless of how to react to this wonderful gesture from Ranjan, I speculated if Ranjan be informed of the physical abuse I unleashed on his sister.

"Hello Ranju. How are you?" said Smitha.

Wondering if Smitha would faint, I said, "Hey, Rama here."

"What?" she reacted as if I stole her brother's phone.

"Didn't you go to office today? Don't you have work?" Smitha bombarded questions.

"No, actually…" I searched for an explanation.

"And what are you doing with Ranjan's phone? I hope that you have not told him what happened between us." Smitha was still in the enquiring mode.

"One sec, speak to Ranjan." I gave up.

I obviously did not hear Smitha's side of speech, but I could make out the essence of conversation by listening to Ranjan's side of speech.

"Di, I met with an accident."

"Yeah, I am serious."

"Car is smashed big time."

"It is in the service station."

"No, I did not tell Mama Papa, please you don't tell either."

But didn't he ask me to hide this from Smitha as well as she was Mama's pet? Whatever, he was self-contradictory, I witnessed a monologue.

"No, nothing happened to me!"

Smitha was unbelievable, she first enquired about the car and then about Ranjan. Pragmatic she was!

"No, I am not taking insurance. Rama helped to tame the police; he sold his Rolex to fund the bribe."

"Yes, I am serious Di, he is the one who is paying for the car."

"Yeah, we are going home only, but I have a request."

"Please marry him, he is very nice." Ranjan testified, the first member of her family was won without deliberation.

15

Walking on the Water

The discharge date of the car and Mama's arrival looked like clashing; those days were marked with Ranjan's repeated visits to Rana Motors to push the things and the visit to my office while on his way back home. On one such afternoon where the car was the topic of discussion usually, Ranjan, for the first time, raised alarm about the pace at which the car got treated at the hospital.

"They are taking good amount of time, I am not sure when they are going to deliver the car." Ranjan talked as if he was buying a new car for which the waiting time was supposedly long.

"Obviously, the car looked raped and fucked, they might be conducting all sorts of tests on it, plus it needs a surgery due to multiple fractures" I said sarcastically to illustrate the damage done to the car.

"Shut up, but Mama will be here in a week's time, the car should be there before she comes." he said.

"And it should be functioning well!" I completed.

Ranjan decided to ramp up the frequency of his visits; the hard work would undoubtedly bring in results, but the modus operandi of declaration of the result bamboozled me. Forcefully stretching myself at work had become a regular practice, and on one such practice, Ranjan rang up, "Hi bro.. yoohoo" Ranjan sounded out of control, I was contemplating another accident with his flowing energy and asked, "Hey hang on. What happened?"

And there was a pause, the pause was meant for Ranjan to complete his drink in one shot; after bottoms up, he said, "dude, I don't want another accident. I am drunk and I am at IP extension. Please come and pick me."

"Accident, oh ..so, you got the car? But, why drunk?" I asked.

"You said that we will party, so, I am partying." he said.

"Fine, I'll be there, but don't you dare drink and drive." I said and boarded a metro to get hold of the young lad before he took off from another flyover.

Smitha's Mama was supposed to arrive the next morning and it was the last chance for us to party, more importantly the ecstasy of getting the car at the nick of the time was to be celebrated. A crate of beer found its way down through our esophagus and we hit the hay challenging ourselves to get up on time to reach the airport.

The exaggerated lady stepped out of the airport with two king size suitcases which could accommodate ten girls of the size of Smitha, and she did not delay in exhibiting those qualities which made me wary of her.

"Why are you standing there? Come and pick up the suitcase, idiot!" this one was for Ranjan.

"Why did you book a cab? The car is already there." this one was for both of us, I hated those who baselessly placed their wisdom far above than those of the others. I intervened and said, "We knew that you would be carrying such massive suitcases, and Wagon R can't accommodate these. So, we thought of hiring a cab as well so that you could go home comfortably."

Ranjan looked at me with popping eyes, it seemed that no one dared to cross question or spoke against Mama. But, I did. Should I anticipate some backfire? The time would decide so.

We drove into the same flat where Smitha and I were made to kick a bowl full of rice; the extravagant lady possessing a nose of a dog could smell cigarette! Ranjan had explained about this quality of smelling things down which Mama mastered at, hence, we stopped smoking inside the flat some ten days ago, yet the never ending suspicious nature of Mama asked, "Ranju, you smoked right?" she charged at Ranjan and I was dumbfounded how she was so confident about Ranjan's smoking habits and how beautifully Ranjan defended. "No Mama, swear on you, I did not smoke." he lied blatantly and I still looked on like an idiot.

She turned towards me to scare me, and, she asked, "He did not smoke right?"

It was like asking one thief if his partner thief was actually a thief, and did I look stupid to say yes? I said, "No no aunty! Not at all." with confidence oozing from all holes god gave me.

You would not be surprised at all and must have happened to each one of you who would have ever even thought of loving a girl. The clause is evolved by default and you have no choice but to give in, because either you give in or you cave in! The clause is put by girl's Mama, and in my case Smitha's Mama "Shut up! What is this aunty aunty? Call me Mama!"

I twisted my tongue, adjusted my vocal chords, a somersault in my stomach, and I threw, "Mama. Yes Mama!"

If Mama were to be an output of a regression equation, it was absolutely difficult to decipher the variables which defined her behavior; she would be poignant once and then she would be a heartbreaker, she would be logical and then she would be utter nonsense, she would love me once and would not care for a second to rebuke me! Since her character cut across mine, I was heading for a complete disaster by staying with Smitha's Mama under the same roof; also, the quick outburst to clarify the cab at airport might have lingered somewhere in her mind.

Me: Undisciplined, Unhygienic, Shameless and a Liar

I was grateful to the rent free stay, the free food, free laundry but I did wrong by slipping into the shoes of a family member because Mama thought the other way probably. If the stay was for a day or two like it was when I came to meet her during diwali, I could have managed to put up a disciplined act by not being my natural self, but it was not possible and not required when I was staying for almost over two months.

I would drop in my shirt into the washing machine every day after I returned from office, however, I noticed over a week that everything in the washing machine was getting washed other than my shirt; I did not bother to ask why and thought that I should not have taken everything for granted. On a Sunday morning, I took the collection of shirts over a week and washed them before taking bath. When I went to the balcony to put them for drying, Mama went to the washroom and screamed as if she spotted a ghost. I rushed to the bathroom in a hurry to check what was wrong, all to witness Mama standing high and steady. I asked her, "What happened Mama? Why did you scream?" and she said, "Don't resort to these cheap tactics."

I replied in astonishment "What tactics? What did I do?"

"What is this soap water doing on the floors?" she behaved like a mother in law straight from the family movies on dowry, only difference was the victim was male this time.

"Nothing Mama, I was about to clean this after I put the clothes for drying." I clarified.

"Shut up. I know you are upset that your shirts are not being washed." she exposed that what happened to my shirts was deliberately done.

"No, but since you have brought it up now, can you tell me why my shirts were not being washed?" I said citing disappointment at discrimination.

"Because you are so unsystematic. Why can't you unbutton your shirt and then take it off? said Mama clarifying that she was pissed off with my habit of taking off a formal shirt like a T-shirt, "You just unbutton the first button and throw it in the washing machine and I have to sit and unbutton the entire shirt before washing it, my nails get damaged, do you now that?" she explained the enormous pain she undertook to wash my shirt.

"Yeah, I am sorry about that. But did I utter a word? Albeit, you could have told me this straight on my face, I would have surely done the required." I offered an apology.

"Shut up. I am not your mother to teach you this. Your mother should have taken some pain to make you disciplined." Mama took a direct dig at my parents and she reminded me of Smitha who did the same when she took a shot at my mother's character.

I wanted to hit back like a mad wolf, but thought otherwise and left the house in a rage wondering what was forcing Mama to behave the way she did.

I went straight to Connaught Place library to do away with whatever happened. And then Smitha called.

Yes, Smitha and I were back to normal terms conditional on the support I rendered to Ranjan to get through the mess. However, Smitha referred to the dark incident whenever she wanted to shut me up during an argument!

"Hi" I said in the lowest of voice.

"Hi, where are you and what do you think of yourself?" Smitha opened fire leaving me to hunch perfectly what she hinted at.

"I am in the CP library." I informed Smitha and thought of not telling her what I thought of myself, as she was a better judge of it.

"What are you doing there? And how did you behave with Mama?" she asked a bit worriedly.

"I am reading and will go to office in second half. Have a meeting" I said, "And there is no point in telling you how I behaved with Mama because she must have already told you" I offered no explanation.

"Yeah but what was the point in leaving home? Would you have done the same thing if it was your Mama?" Smitha acted like a catalyst between me and her Mama.

"First of all, my mom would have told me what was wrong instead of resorting to these methods of behaving hysterically, plus, I did not have any complaints, I just washed my shirts, I forgot that I was not a family member and one thing..." I said and Smitha cut me short.

"What one thing? Why did you slam the door and leave?" she asked me and I was grounded.

"Who slammed the door? Who gave you such stories?" I asked Smitha and wondered if Mama was the same lady whom I met during Diwali.

"You mean to say that my mom is lying?" Smitha confirmed that it was Mama who was cooking stories.

"No, I am not saying anything. But one thing is that she spoke about my mother unnecessarily and I don't approve of it. Just because I have decided to get converted, but it does not mean that I will take any shit against my parents." I took a firm stand and Smitha signed it, "And who knows better than me?"

"What?" I asked for repetition.

"Nothing, but why office? Today is Sunday!" Smitha changed the topic.

"We have an audit beginning tomorrow, so boss has called for a meeting where he wants to brief us. The entire team is in office, since I am just a trainee, I am not required. But, I thought would be good if I join." I informed honestly.

"Ok sweetie, don't get hyper please, at least for me. We have to get married na?" Smitha tactfully tamed me down finally.

I felt terribly bad for Smitha, she was, for no reason, becoming a negotiator between two emotionally charged people. Therefore, I decided to surrender and went home after the meeting got over.

Me: Fraud/Intentionally Lethargic

Ranjan opened the door for me and I said, "Hi, so how is everything? All fine right?"

He smiled and held my shoulder tightly and I called for Mama forgetting everything that happened in the afternoon, but, Mama was the cousin of some WWF fighter, who would fight till the last breath, not to win the fight, but to settle the ego!

I went to the room where "Her Majesty" rested and people like Amitabh and Rekha performed for "Her highness" on TV through a movie called "Silsila".

"Oh this is a nice movie. There are Jaya Bachchan and Sanjeev Kumar as well in this movie." I said while lightening the air.

"I know that, and don't you have manners not to make noise when someone is busy watching something?" she insulted me again. "Your mother has not taught you this either." she degraded my mother again, probably, trying to check how I reacted. But I ignored thinking that

"Out of mind" lady would torment Smitha. However, I wondered why Mama was trying to provoke me repeatedly, and that too by talking shit about my upbringing!

I stayed calm for some time trying to push down the poison Mama hurled at me and then said, "What's for dinner Mama? I am hungry." and Mama sent another snorter, "Am I your servant? Just go and see what's there in the kitchen. Eat and make sure you clean the plate."

I, as shameless as I could be, all for Smitha, went to the kitchen, opened the cooker, and saw red chunk of meat floating in the gravy. It certainly did not look like chicken, and I thought of confirming with Ranjan, who said, "Sorry brother, I told Mama that you don't eat mutton, she asked me to shut up. Anyhow, I have something for you. Will you come down for a walk?"

Mama raped my self-respect and tested my patience at her will, throwing me into obscurity, squatting magnificently that who was asinine! But Ranjan sprung surprises, he went straight to the car at the parking, opened it and handed over a full medium sized pizza with a bottle of Coke and said, "Eat, Guddu told me that you don't eat Mutton, she asked me to get something for you." and he smiled.

My emotional meter was on the extreme and I could not avoid shedding tears and I broke down, Ranjan rubbed my back and said, "Come on. I am sorry for what Mama did."

"No, I am not feeling bad for what Mama did but I am grateful that I know you and Guddu." I reconstructed myself and messaged Smitha, "Thanks sweetie. Thanks for the pizza. You still think about me." and Smitha replied, "My dear *Shona*, its ok. Love you."

After luring my taste buds with the efforts from Pizza Hut, it was the turn of Mama to bud my growing attachment for the family. "Why did you not eat the food? Do I look stupid enough to have cooked this for you?" Mama was still crazy to keep the high tension alive.

"No Mama, nothing like that. I don't eat mutton. So...." I began to elucidate when I looked at Ranjan who waggled his head slightly, popped his eyes out discouraging me to speak the truth. "So, I ate before I came home." I said completely missing the fact that I was the one who begged for food, but Mama caught me there, "Then why were you so excited about what was cooked? You just wanted to show that I am sitting here as your servant cooking according to your taste buds." she spoke hysterically.

I wanted to tell her that I had eaten Pizza which Ranjan bought, but the truth would have led to Ranjan's sudden assassination by the hands of Mama, hence, I decided to gulp down the poison hurled at me and looking at Mama's agitated face, I was sure that she was not through, "I am sure you did not have any work either, you knew that we were washing curtains today, and it would have required efforts from you as well to take the curtains out and put them for wash. So, you just escaped the hard work. Ranjan did everything all alone. You are not only undisciplined, you are lazy as well" Mama's list of demerits about me increased.

For the first time, I thought seriously about leaving Smitha, "Why am I doing this with myself? Why am I allowing Mama to destroy me? Is Smitha more important than my honor? Does Smitha even appreciate this? Does Smitha deserve this? Is it worth tolerating when future looks dim? Do I settle scores by replying to Mama's shameful remarks about me?" And then I thought which negated the above thoughts, "Is the fate testing me by punishing me for what I did with Smitha? I am probably paying for hitting Smitha."

Such was the after effect of the dark night that it haunted me to make me feel miserable, and any idea to leave Smitha looked many miles away as I promised to commit my life to serve her forever! I wished to be apologetic!

All such belief to be committed to Smitha was squandered when Mama, who mastered the craft of taking the wind out of people, revealed the reasons for her wicked behavior, but she would not spill the beans in one go, a phased methodology was adopted without giving me anytime to react as I was fast getting ready for office. "The director at Papa's office is very young. He studied in Harvard, he is just twenty eight " Mama gave away information which I wrongly assumed to be worthless.

"Ok." I said while concentrating on my tie knot.

"He looked at Guddu's picture and said that he wanted to marry her" she dropped the log on my head, and the first result was a poor tie knot by me who perfected it!

"Mama but you are not serious about this right?" I asked for an unusual confirmation, at the time when comparing myself with the director was not only sin, but crime.

"No but..." Mama jigged with my emotions, and I denied her speech.

"But Mama, I will do my best, I am just twenty four, by the time I am twenty eight, I might not be a director, but some one efficient enough to keep Smitha happy." and offered myself trouble.

THE INDIAN SHAADI CHAIN

If all the women from A grade colleges of India married men from Harvard, Stanford and Kellogg, all the women from B grade colleges married men from A grade colleges, and all the women from C grade colleges married men from B grade colleges, then all the men from C grade colleges would be either left unmarried or settle with women who are not at all educated!

"OK. Now stop crying, wipe your tears and leave for work. Come on." Mama seemed to melt, and I saw tears in my eyes when I went to the mirror to tie the knot again.

GOSSIPMONGER

I called Smitha the moment I stepped out of the flat to investigate if she was aware of the proceedings.

"Hi Baby, good morning." Smitha sounded at ease and please.

"Hi, good morning." my words trembled.

"What happened shona, why are you tensed?" Smitha stretched her words.

"Nothing, you just got up?" I asked.

"No Office?" I asked again.

"Yes, I do, will go a bit late. Thomas is coming late. So, if the boss is late, we can also go late" she revealed the reason of her "Ease and Please".

"But what happened to you?" she asked firmly and I began to cry while walking garnering the attention of all the office goers.

"Oh stop crying. What happened?" she asked again while getting herself out of the slumber.

"Nothing, do you know that Papa's company's director wants to marry you?" I asked Smitha.

"Oh is it?" and she laughed, "Why didn't he tell that before I met you?" Smitha said presuming that she was the funniest lady in the universe.

"Please tell me, what is going on? He wants to marry you and he saw your picture it seems." I asked for some more information on this chapter.

"So what? I don't want to marry him, I will marry my baby right?" Smitha helped me regain my senses by addressing me as her baby.

"Thanks dear, but were you aware of this?" I began to ask unnecessary questions.

"Yes" she said casually.

"Then why did you not tell me?" I started probing and Smitha hated it.

"There was nothing to tell you, there could be thousands of them willing to marry me. But there is only one I am willing to marry and that is my baby. So, I thought it was not important" Smitha displayed sensibility.

"But why this is in Mama's mind till now? Please never leave me" I questioned and pleaded.

"Ok, baby, I'll take care of it. You go to office now, I am in the toilet and Cecilia is knocking, she wants to use it." she said, "Love you."

My inquisitive side wanted to ask that Cecilia had an attached bathroom, then why was she knocking on Smitha's bathroom, but decided the other way and acknowledged, "Love you too baby. Bye."

Professional pressure outdid the personal pressure and I was relatively fine when Mama called up to dismantle the relief and said, "What do you think of yourself? And what did you tell Guddu?" It was Mama's turn to ask me the same questions which Smitha did the day before.

"Nothing Mama, I did not tell her anything" I answered the first one and thought of not telling her what I thought of myself, as she along with her daughter, was a better judge of it.

"Stop gossiping about our family! Did you get that?" Mama talked imperatively.

"Who is gossiping Mama?" I pleaded innocence, "What are you talking about?" I said.

"Stop acting smart!" Mama ordered and I wondered how both mother and daughter spoke the same stuff.

"You told Smitha that I am looking to get her married to Noel Kelly?" Mama updated me that director's name was Noel Kelly.

"No Mama but I just asked her if she knew about it", I explained.

"Shut up, Guddu called me up and asked me not to torment you with these things" she reprimanded.

"How dare you conspire by making my daughter speak against me? She has never dared to speak or question me, and today, all because of you, she has the courage to question me and give away orders for people like you. You are trying to create differences in our family by resorting to such things. I thought you were a strong man and would have kept that to yourself." Mama was charging.

"But Mama, I had no such intentions." I said inoffensively.

"Whatever, listen to me now, I have asked Guddu not to speak to you without asking me and you will also not speak to her without my permission. She promised me. Do you get that? And I will see if you are the right guy to get married to Guddu or not." Mama was blowing it out proportionately and exponentially and in whatever way of multiplication known to mankind.

"But Mama, I love her, I can't think of not getting married to her." I beseeched.

And she disconnected without wanting to know if I had ideas to obey her or not. Probably, it did not matter.

And next I called Smitha to confirm if she actually promised or Mama mustered her art of cooking up.

"Hi, Mama said that you promised that you will not speak to me? What crap! Is that true?" I asked.

"Yes" she said.

"But do you mean it?" I confirmed.

"Have you gone nuts? Mama keeps on saying hundred things, I can't obey her every time." Smitha established that promises are meant to be broken, and I wondered how "A world tour for parents" kind of a girl was losing respect for the promise made with her mother! Did I taste victory in love?

But Mama was the queen of all detectives, a thousand drops of Sherlock Holmes's semen would have been needed to fuse her existence with reality! Within five minutes after I called Smitha, Smitha called back and was fuming.

"What the fuck did you tell Mama?" Smitha asked me aggressively (Fuck was the only word which found place in Smitha's vocabulary when she witnessed hopelessness)

"Nothing. Why are you going mad?" I wanted Smitha to cool down.

"You told Mama that you can't think of anybody else because you have slept with me?" Smitha was going head over heels!

"What the fuck? Have I gone mad? First of all, I said that I can't think of not getting married to you. Second, I am not an idiot to tell a girl's mother that I have been sleeping with her daughter, and third, even if I did, do you think things would have sounded so normal till now? She would have killed both of us. Why is she on a lying spree and behaving weird? I am sure that I can't get this clarified with her because, she, very smartly, has taken a promise from you not to speak to me and if I go and ask her, you will be in deep deep trouble. She will come to know that you spoke to me! Good luck baby, we are screwed." I lost temper and thought that was enough for a face off with Mama.

"Sorry" Smitha said and disconnected.

On my way back in the Metro in the evening, I understood that locking horns with Mama was futile; I decided to apologize for something I did not do, for some who are drunk with ego can be tamed with an over dose of ego!

"Mama, I am sorry." I held her hand and she turned her face the other side, exhibiting melodrama.

"Mama, please, Mama, please." I had completely changed from some one who gave a fuck to people throwing tantrums, and for that short lived moment, I thought, "When did I say sorry or please to my mother?" Yes, I had changed, but was Smitha recognizing this effort?

"Mama, please" and I stretched "please" this time while tears began to fade my vision.

"OK, first wipe your tears." Mama sensed emotional victory, but I was not crying for the fear of losing Smitha, but I was giving her a free licence to overrun my ego.

Certain tactics are artistically built and consciously applied which leave you brooding if they are god gifted or learnt willfully, and one such tactic Mama engineered at was to charge somebody's weakly balanced emotions and then skillfully scratch them till they become a visible wound leaving one tired and eventually cave in. She asked me a perfectly timed question which then looked like something out of nowhere.

"Do your parents have any property?"

A lower middle class family was my identity and my parents did not have anything under their belt, they owned a house which was sold off to clear the debt which surmounted during the period after my father was laid off by his employer as a part of right sizing the company. My mother in an endeavor to brighten our future, suffered twice with Tuberculosis. Bare minimum necessity was a hardship during my upbringing and education looked luxury, I earned my education by working from class ninth, sometimes as a newspaper boy, sometimes as a private tutor, sometimes selling burgers, sometimes selling credit cards and savings accounts! I was a self made man, and I believed in myself, but this collaboration with Smitha's family was unearthing the ghostly past which I had buried deep under my efforts. With such a past, anyone reading this will call me a maniac to have accepted conversion and "your parents will not stay with us" clause, at a time when I was the only property my parents had!

Such questions not only tortured me, but made me feel small and worthless, after all the efforts I had put in to reach the level where I was, how necessary it was to know what my parents owned or not? Was Mama comparing me with what Noel Kelly possessed or was Mama trying to evaluate my worth to marry Smitha? I, certainly, did not have anything on my comparison with Noel but I had things to tell about my worth for Smitha.

"No, Mama. They don't own anything." I said and helped to sharpen her memory, "I told these things clearly when I had come to meet you during Diwali, where does this come from now?"

"And what savings do you have?" Mama asked something worthless

"Nothing, I just got my first salary. How can I have savings?" I replied intelligently.

"How much do you get every month?" She got personal, and I wanted to throw my salary slip on her face the way she was hurling poison.

"Sixty five thousand" I said plainly.

"And you spent all the money? She interrogated the ends.

"Yes, since this was my first salary, I sent some money to my mother to buy a ring for herself. I said while concealing the online gifts I purchased for Smitha and a few overheads on the car repair, which if exposed would not have left the Sis-Bro pair breathing. In an effort to save them, I put all the mud on my head.

"What? You eat here, sleep here, you have no expenses other than the metro pass, which means you bought a ring worth fifty to sixty thousand for your mother?" Mama was showing her derogatory view point and losing whatever residual regards I had for her.

If her daughter could dream of sending her parents on a world tour, how illegal it was to buy a ring for my mother, moreover, it was my call where I spend my money; my mother was not even aware of how much I earned, forget about the spends. And if my mother aimed to be aware of my savings, with what ease I could reveal the gifts I bought for Smitha and the expenditure on the repair of the car. Few truths remained embedded in my inner core; had I exposed them, my life would have been a bit easier! I told myself, "I love Smitha, it is ok."

"And your mother did not even stop you from buying such expensive gifts? What kind of mother is she?" One mother proclaimed the licence to degrade another mother despite the truth that the gift for her daughter was costlier than the gift for her daughter's would be mother-in-law. I remained silent.

"I plan to get Guddu married in two years' time. And you have all the time to match up to her, currently you have no status to get married to her." Mama dictated terms of the wedding.

"Status? Let me tell you that I have been a topper throughout my life and your daughter has been changing streams, I got placed much before her and I am earning more than her, I studied from a top college in Delhi University and your daughter was BBAing somewhere, I am a good writer, orator, and your daughter is highly timid and meek, I funded my own education and she was born with a silver spoon, keep the parental achievements aside, and then compare." I wished to say all this but all I said,

"OK. What am I supposed to do?" I anticipated no mercy.

"Your Salary is sixty five thousand, you have to save a minimum of fifty thousand every month from here on and save at least twelve lakhs for marriage, because we have plans to spend twenty five lakhs on the wedding." she signed off!

ANY TAKERS FOR SUCH ATTROCITIES?

16

I Dream of Genie

"Fifty thousand a month"

The herculean task kept singing in my ears along with the phenomenal objective it would culminate into worth twelve lakhs. But, phenomenal objective was destined to be raped by obstacles which either happened or were made to happen! I could never be au fait with.

Hyderabad Monthly

During my last reeling days of stay with Mama in Delhi, Smitha's birthday fell on one of the days and she made me promise to her that I had to be the first one to wish her, and not on the phone but while being on her. Did Smitha love me so madly that she could break the promise? The promise not to speak to me looked like dick when I had an open invitation to make love with her. With Mama hovering over my life, how to make it possible was left on my brilliant dishonesty.

"Mama, I have to go to Jaipur on Tuesday, there is a new product launch." I said.

"Jaipur? Why are they taking you?" she was astonished; she probably thought that only directors (read Noel Kelly) deserved to be invited for product launches, and I worked with housekeeping!

"You didn't tell me before? Why?" she was exercising her supremacy and what was I supposed to tell her? That her daughter could not stop getting fucked! I did not say anything, all for Smitha.

"Just got decided and I will go from office itself! I will take my bag along in the morning!" I lied further.

I lied to my boss for taking an off next day, he asked questions which won't have changed my decision, and finally I took an auto straight to the airport after work. My mental peace was badly disturbed that it showed when the cabin crew gave out precautionary instructions before the flight.

"Next time they ask me to use the cushion to float in the water during an emergency landing, I am gonna screw them up. What do they think? Everyone here possesses one fifth of Superman's DNA. Assholes!" I said to my fellow passenger loud enough to be heard by two to three rows at front and behind. I realized it quickly and hid my face in embarrassment.

Wine, roses and a cake is generally an easy job to attend, but it is tough when you have to chase for it late in the night! With everything in place, I was at Smitha's doorstep just five minutes before 12, and I knocked at the door. Smitha opened the door to make me weak in my knees, she was dressed in a super sexy black silky gown, her frame visible so nicely, her wet hair added to the beauty and the lip gloss gave the ultimate touch needed!

I kissed her, we drank wine and then we made love till I was drained out; it was almost after four months, the longest after college that I saw Smitha. I could not stop my hands getting off her, I could not stop eating her breasts, and I could not stop telling her how down I felt during my stay with her Mama.

"It is ok baby. Mama loves us, she is like that only." Smitha cajoled me, and planted a kiss on my cheek.

"But what about 50k baby? How will I manage? I have education loan and my phone bills are so high." I displayed issues I had.

"Hmmm. That is something which you will have to do now shona! Mama is generally very serious about those things." Smitha stamped her Mama's decision on my head.

"But baby you should tell Mama and try to save me from this. How will I manage?" I pleaded.

"Lets see. Send her your expense statement every month and she will understand. She is not cruel." Smitha gave false suggestions! And yes, cruel was an understatement for Mama's abilities to fuck happiness!

I got up next day to see Smitha getting ready, struggling to put her bra hook, I went ahead and kissed her and then helped her put the hook and asked, "Baby why are you going to office? I have taken an off for you only."

"Baby, I will come by second half, they are celebrating my birthday. Please shona" Smitha kissed my forehead and I dozed off again.

At around 1 in the afternoon, Smitha called up to inform me about her colleagues decision of taking her out for lunch and that she would be back by evening. I was not fuming, because I was used to worthless treatment by then! So, I waited all alone.

It was 8 in the evening and I started feeling the torture. Smitha made me feel worthless and my repeated calls got disconnected and then she messaged, "Stop irritating.. I'll be home and I am safe"

I waited at the same ill-fated balcony, and saw the same black Santro driven into the apartments and Smitha again took ten minutes to get down from the car, but this time I chose to keep quiet and drank the agony! But I chose to keep a tab on what Smitha was up to.

"Hey Baby!" Smitha entered home and I smelled alcohol.

"Wait. You are drunk?" I interrogated.

"Yes. Any problem?" Smitha was blunt.

"No, but you said that you boozed only with me. So, why are you picking up this habit? It is not good." I advised to someone drunk with ego and alcohol.

"Shut up. I am not a kid. I know what I am doing!" Smitha ridiculed me and I felt like jumping from the third floor balcony and get hold of bastard Thomas and do a Mano Mano with him and give him a dose of my strong fist, "He was changing Smitha" I thought.

I decided to keep a track of Smitha, because the way things were moving, I knew they were not moving my way. So, the probability of Smitha leaving me for bastard Thomas could not be ruled out.

"I will come to Hyderabad every month from now on." I said.

"Really? Oh! So sweet of you baby. This is the best gift you could give on my birthday. You promise me."

Smitha was excited and before I could give my hand for promise, Smitha dozed off leaving me to think that was it correct in taking an off by taking the whole amount of risk. Mama was right, "Only directors deserve to be invited for product launches."

One reason I thought Smitha was lucky for me; life brightened whenever she gave me words of confidence, and here she asked me to cope with the problems and provide Mama with an expense statement, but fate had its own ways. My boss kept my transfer orders ready and my next destination was Mysore. I felt like what Nelson Mandela would have felt like after twenty seven years of prison, happy and on top of the world, but Mama could not have liked it and she shook the ladder to bring me down from the top to the bottom and I thought, "How Mama and Smitha thought alike?"

"Mama, I am getting transferred. I have to go to Mysore." I said with excitement running in my body, but I chose not to express it.

"Yeah, I know, you would have requested for it, your home is closer from there. You can go home every week and spend the way you want to." Mama's bitter tendencies were not over yet.

"I will have to go home, what will I tell my parents? Bangalore is hardly 3 hours from Mysore or else I'll call them to Mysore." I spoke to someone who was not listening.

"Yeah, so your parents can loot you even if you don't want to get looted." Mama accused my parents again, but I thought, "Let her bark, I am flying out of this jail in a couple of days. Who wants to see her again?" But wasn't I wrong in thinking like that!

"Listen, I want to see every month how you are going about your savings? If I see that you are not going in the right direction, then I'll get Guddu married to somebody else!" Mama took a leaf from corporate strategies and decided to break the long term target into small must win battles.

"So?" I expected more to be generated from the lady.

"Send me your bank and savings statements every month from now on." Mama instructed strictly, and continued, "Remember, 50 k means 50 k."

I knew that 50 K is 50 K and it was not 49K or 51K, I was a finance guy and not she! But, I was relieved that the expenses to meet Smitha would be slightly lower as Hyderabad could be reached by bus from Mysore and I would not be required to listen to the crap shared by the cabin crew!

My Dad Turning Sixty: A conspiracy!

Just a week after I landed in Mysore, my parents, Raghav and Geeta (my sis in law) visited me and we enjoyed a nice city tour and on the Sunday afternoon, when we lay on the bed after smearing sambhar and curd rice, a wonderful idea came to Geeta and such ideas found place in woman's head only! Like a world tour for parents!

"Appa is turning sixty." Geeta said ecstatically.

"Yes!" I said citing astonishment, oldies have their birthdays as well, and in the hardship of celebrating their kids' birthdays, their joys and birthdays are lost somewhere and females like Geeta are needed to find and celebrate them. Geeta was another kind of woman I knew. She was the daughter in law and loved my parents more than we did and I am ashamed till date.

"We need to celebrate it." Geeta decided, certain qualities peculiar to all woman, they speak and they decide. But some decide for the good and some for the worst!

Geeta was a "Good" decider though and we all appreciated her thought and the concept of "Remarriage at sixty ".

"We do it in December depending upon the *Muhurtham*." Geeta went on deciding.

"Yeah sure." we all agreed.

"Let's chart out a budget." Geeta, an active lady did not waste a second in opening my laptop bag and got the laptop and a note pad.

When Geeta and Amma started putting down what all was required, I wondered if Mama was right in demanding twelve lakhs! But I had a valid question, "Tell me how much will be required?" and Geeta said, "A lakh." and all I could gather was "Ok!"

Mama was controlling my life through satellite connections even when I was remotely located, and during one such control procedure, I informed her, "Mama, my dad is turning sixty and we are conducting a small function on this occasion."

"And I am sure you must be spending, how much?" Mama did not waste a pulse before exposing her cheap attitude; she wanted to know the expenditure before even thinking of wishing me or my parents. Taking anymore crap against my dignity was forbidden, and I gave an edgy reply, "I'll spend whatever it takes. I don't think you should be having any problems, I expected you to wish me first and then get into these rounds of discussions." And I disconnected without getting moved by what Mother-Daughter pair would think about the so called "Act of misbehavior" which in human terminology is known as "Protecting your self-respect".

Cell phones started playing a major role in gripping my life and in no time, Smitha called and no prizes for guessing that Mama would have bitched about me more than I expected.

"What the hell?" Smitha preferred "What the hell?" over a "Hello".

"Nothing, hell was in Dwarka. I am fine here." I said bluntly!

"Shut up! How could you not have any gratitude? The home which gave you food is hell now? Just that you are closer to home now, you have got some attitude. But let me tell you that this ceremony is a mere excuse from you not to save 50 k and escape." Smitha spoke illogically and I did not know what was wrong if I was getting the lost confidence back.

"Listen, I will not tolerate any nonsense against my parents and you will have to respect them equally" Smitha rolled out the verdict.

"You would not have had the guts to speak like this if I was not respecting your mom" I tried to correct Smitha but instigated more trouble for myself.

"Whatever, no one is forcing you. Anyhow, I just wanted to convey that you will have to save 50k in any case and Mama is not up for any nonsense. The monthly income and expense statement has to reach Mama whether you celebrate your father's any birthday!" Smitha demanded respect for her parents while she joined her mother to disrespect my parents!

And she disconnected without completing the cycle of communication. The gimmick was enough to send shivers down my spine and I started designing the ways to optimize my contribution towards the ceremony but the courage to put this across to Raghav and Geeta was drilling me.

Amma vs Mama

While I made Raghav aware of my forcefully built false intentions about the ceremony, Amma was falling prey to stones in her kidney. The way Raghav explained the situation at the hospital, reminded me of the scenes from the movies where a doctor, who would have acted as an advocate in some other movie would explain the complications around the surgery.

"Doctor said nothing to worry; she has to get admitted for a week's time, and then would be the surgery after getting her sugar levels under control." Raghav updated me about the happenings in the hospital.

"Ok, do you want me to come there? Or can you manage?" the most shameless question I could ask; my mother was in the hospital and I wanted a confirmation if I was required! Where were the slippers?

"Yeah, could be great if you can come here for two or three days as it would become very difficult for me and Geeta to be at the hospital after work, We cannot leave Appa alone there, he is old." Raghav was sensible enough with his cause of worry and I agreed abandoning the negative energy against my parents which evolved in the minds of Smitha and her mother.

Willingly or unwillingly, I was bound to call Mama twice in a day, one to keep her happy and second to take the instructions on how should I breathe, pee and duck! And in one such conversation, I fed the ears of Mama with something which the ears did not want, "Mama, I am going to Bangalore, taking a three days off, my mother is in the hospital."

"Oh! *Beta* I thought if I could request you to come here for a day or two to take me to the hospital. I might have to get admitted as well." Mama was competing with Amma and it was trivial to know if the request was genuine or just fake to keep me away from my family.

"Mama, how about Smitha? Is she not coming? And Ranjan?" I asked about other possible care takers.

"It is ok *beta*, if you cannot come, then don't be bothered about anybody else. I thought I could bank upon you. I will see what needs to be done." A lady who shouted slogans of "Hail Hitler" with a stick in her hand was showing shades of Gandhi.

"No Mama, I just meant….." I started speaking and Mama disconnected and I wondered what cards she would play.

Mama took advantage of Smitha's promise of not to speak with me to her advantage, and gave away stories which bred in her head, and Smitha transformed those stories into negative energy and screwed our equation.

"Mama just wanted you in Delhi to take her to the hospital. You cannot even do that." Smitha was complaining.

"Yeah, I could have gone but I have to go to Bangalore to be with my mom, she is getting operated as well." I tried introducing logic to Smitha.

"And why don't you go?" I asked her.

"See, I have back to back meetings with clients and I have not met targets, and Ranjan is going to Gujarat for some interview during that time." Smitha meant that I had to do all that which she and her brother could not do for their mother.

"Ok, but I have to be with Amma as well." I cited confusion.

"Your brother and Geeta are there. Why can't they do that?" Smitha said and I thought, "You and Ranjan are also there, why can't you do that?" but I said, "Fine, let me see." which was as good as commitment.

"And, are you paying for your mother's surgery?" Smitha asked an irrelevant question and I knew what was running in her mind.

"Yes, of course!" I said.

"But do remember that you need to save!" Smitha said.

"But if I go to Delhi, I will be spending on flight tickets. Then what?" I checked with Smitha for double standards.

"I don't know, it is up to you to go to Delhi or not and see how to save even if you pay for your mother's surgery." Smitha signed off.

SHAMELESS were those days when I did everything which left me fighting with my principles, I could not bounce on what I said, "I'll commit this life to serve you."

I chose Mama over Amma and flew to Delhi while paying half of the surgery amount to Raghav. But does a monetary help suffice for the responsibility I had towards my mother? No answer, I looked for slippers again!

Astonishment waited to greet me when I reached Delhi; carrying a picture of an ailing mother with dark circles in my mind, I saw an over pumped mother munching on cashews and walnuts! The pacemaker mother looked hale and hearty and the entire gimmick to get me to

Delhi looked like a trick to keep me away from family. I cursed myself.

"Mama, how are you? I thought you were bed ridden." I asked upfront.

"What did you expect? I would be coughing here and keeping medicines next to my bed?" Mama started laughing and I was fuming.

"Ok, do one thing, get some samosas from the market, some Pepsi, my sister is coming from Gurgaon and yes, do behave yourself in front of them."

Ordering samosas when I had spent 12k on flights itself was murderous, and asking me to behave myself was absolutely uncalled for. "Screw her." I thought.

When I returned from the market with samosas and Pepsi, I saw a gang of six to seven over grown men and women laughing hysterically over some joke which I am sure would have been cracked by Mama, and I entered like it was a house of aliens, and bowed slightly to wish everyone and looked at Mama to help get through that chaos.

"Come *beta* come, this is Rama, we have chosen for Guddu." Mama introduced me to the gang and made simian faces while her eyes said, "Come on, and touch everybody's feet." and I tested my back by bending it 6 times.

I felt like one of those cereals getting grinded in a mixer, and wondered am I really the one chosen for Smitha and if yes, do I get discounted for 50k every month task, but fate had its own ways to torment me. Before I could finish my feet touching exercise, Mama sent down another googly, "He is from IIM Ahmedabad" and I looked for some body else who would surface. And then realised that I was the one from IIM Ahmedabad. I was scandalized to see that Mama lied.

After the gang left, Mama dived back into her bitter attitude and started off, "So, how much have you saved?"

"Mama, its been only a month you gave targets, I will do it, but 50k is really tough, I have an education loan of 10k every month, then food and phone bills. 50 k is really tough." I spoke my heart clearly.

"So what? I know your other bills. All you want to do is to send money home. What will my daughter do if you keep on giving money to your family?" Mama thought that she was sane.

"Ok, I'll see! But where did the IIM-A come from?" I wanted the source of lie.

"Nothing, Guddu's reputation is at stake, people might not think well about her if they come to know that she has chosen someone from her college. These affairs are not good for a girl's reputation." Mama had reasons for everything.

Ok, Is that the reason you are giving me? If a girl chooses someone from her college, her reputation is at stake. Pity on such thoughts! What is so remorseful about choosing some one from your peer, your school, your college? Why is our society yet so wary of accepting such facts when it is happening everywhere! And is IIM the only college in the world where one should pass out from? And eventually, won't this be leaked when the relationship gets solemnized? Or did she expect everyone to join her in misrepresenting the facts? You are mentally deranged lady, who will buy that you have chosen a Hindu Brahmin and he is ready to get converted? Do such things happen in arranged weddings? Mama though being disapproved by me, was becoming a laughing stock.

"And, listen, when you tell your parents about Guddu, tell them that they should also say that you are from IIM." Mama expected my family to be slavish as well.

We went to the hospital, and it took only 2 hours for the entire diagnosis, and we were on our way back when she said, "Rama, come what may, you will have to save and start reading Bible as we will go for conversion somewhere in Jan."

I had another must win battle which would ensure my status to get married to Smitha.

17

Shut up and Bounce

The demands seemed to have no end; all they knew was to accelerate! Accelerate so fast that they would crush anybody who came their way! And when you keep on accelerating while minding to put your feet on the brakes, the car is certain to go off track.

Here I was the car; Smitha and Mama were drivers (they drove in turn) and soon I was planning to throw myself off balance. This car never back fired at the drivers, it harmed itself!

The latest after status, savings and manners, which Mama discovered as something not with me was a car and a home. My targets changed every day without allowing me to concentrate on any one thing at a time. 50 k a month, then mugging up of what Jesus and Moses did, then a car and a home; it took me no wait to understand that I was expected only to save, how and where the resources be mobilized was left to Mama's good judgment which was erratic!

A week after attending Smitha's jubilantly ailing mother, I reported my income and expense statement to Mama; where I used all my accounting and financial skills to fudge up the report and reconciled it with my bank statements and other saving avenues. Fudging was important to accommodate my smoke, booze and phone bills. Had I revealed smoke and booze, no mother would allow the daughter to get married to me. And had I revealed my phone bills, Smitha would have fallen in the radar and would have got accused of breaking the promise, another possibility was that I could have got accused of two timing.

Hence, these smoke, booze and phone bills were changed as "Money Sent to home"; the safest for me to negotiate. But, as expected, Mama was devastated to read this line item, "Your family continues to loot you, they are not bothered about getting you married, instead of encouraging you to save, they just take money from you."

I had developed amazing immunity against the poison, even a snake bite would have need the snake to be hospitalized. Instead of taking the shit head on, I chose to live with it and find ways to adjust the demands.

The real shock came when I had to go to Hyderabad to meet Smitha to keep up the promise of meeting her every month. To spend more time with Smitha, I zeroed in on air route and thus, the task was to misrepresent this expense, credit card was one option but how long one could depend on a 37% interest rate source of funding?

The money to buy a car, the funds to pump in a home, to arrange for air tickets, contribution at home, my ailing mother, Smitha's pace making mother, smoke, booze, education loan and the shark objective of 12 lakhs to solemnize the wedding! Boy, wasn't I getting jacked? I realized soon that my pay cheque was not so heavy to take the burden of what was needed.

Multiplying my source of income was one way of meeting the needs, but what was it that I could do was not striking my head which was in the middle of turmoil, the best I could think of was during one of the booze sessions in one of the pubs in Mysore.

I looked at the bouncers, and I had looked at the bouncers in Delhi, difference was startling, here bouncers looked a bit polished and did not look like those resorting to force without waiting for a second, but Delhi bouncers were different, they would at times end up beating the wrong guy as well! And I being a polluted Tamilian was a blend of polish and bash up!

That night, I spoke to one of the bouncers, Shiva (name perfect for someone to bounce people up and down), after the pub got closed, "Hi! What a wonderful profession! You look so normal in normal clothes." and Shiva smiled and extended his hand and I took my hand of my pocket and shook it with him. I gave him enough reason to believe that I was tough as well; being taller than him, I had an angle of depression while I spoke to him.

"Hi, Rama" I said.

"Hi, Shiva" he said.

"So, how long you have worked here?" I asked.

"Almost six months now." he said while we walked out and stopped at the pan shop for a smoke. (How can a smoker identify another smoker!)

"Cool, is this what you want to do?" I asked.

"No, I am studying and have a financial crunch at home, so, trying to fund my expenses." he said and I struck chord; I could relate to him.

"And what do you do?" he asked.

"I am working here, done my MBA." I told him.

"Great, MBA! Even I want to do it." he said, the young guy looked ambitious and his eyes sparked off dreams and out of nowhere, I compared him with the boy having a silver spoon, Ranjan. Contrast again!

"Can you help me in getting a job here? As a bouncer! I am really well built." I asked which left Shiva in tatters.

"Dude, what the fuck! You must be earning good!" He said and then without saying a word, he understood that there was something which forced me to resort to something I did not study for!

Being a bouncer sounds exciting, but visualizing from the bouncer's perspective is a pain.

You stay amidst the best of the alcohol and don't booze!

You stay amongst the women smelling off delicious perfumes and can't relish them!

You stay amongst the skimpily dressed females and don't touch them!

You are the best dressed male in the pub and females don't look at you!

You are the savior of many and they think you are the goon!

You can beat up anyone and the manager half of your size gives you orders!

You are educated and don't need this!

I could give up on all of the above but the last one! Fighting my self, but for my love, I decided to become a bouncer, but reaching the pub at 7 needed some juggling at office, and I told my boss, "Sir, I will come to office at 7 every day, and will have to leave by 6 every day, have to study in the evening. Would be great if you can allow me for the same."

Natrajan, my boss, was a humble human being and had zero attitude about what he was. A typical of a Tamilian, education was the best excuse to get anything done and he said, "Yeah, no issues, study well."

And only I knew that I was supposed to study the wrong doers and show them the door in the pub.

My life was screwed from top to bottom, there was a visible pattern in my schedule, busy always till the weekend, and would make up for all the sleep I lost during the week! I would leave for office at 6 in the morning, for which I would get up at 5.30 every day (I felt that I was back to college), reach office by 7 and would remain on my toes to complete everything in time (but of course, whatever I did was never up to the mark as I stopped concentrating on any one thing at a time); a sudden call during the office hours by Smitha to reiterate 50k and other surrounding objectives would leave me panting for the rest of the day.

And then I would rush by taking the fastest possible route to the pub, the normal formal clothes would get replaced by all black suiting and shirting! And I would don contact lenses; I got them specifically for the job (how ferocious a bouncer would look with plain powerful glasses!), spend the entire time walking around the tables, mugging up the names of the drinks which I had never heard of, and then, Shiva, who became a good friend held the responsibility of dropping me at a place where I would get something to eat and then walk down to my home.

Though sixteen thousand was a good addition to what I earned every month, yet there was an absence of peace of mind, and at times, I felt like a fighter surrounded by snipers and my job was to evade the shots taken at me for the job I resorted to could not be revealed to my literal and metaphorical well-wishers. And I was soon becoming the villain, one who ran away from relationships while being in an effort to build relationships.

With an earning spree from 6 in the morning to 1 in the night rendering me hardly five hours of sleep, I required special energy and time to mend out ways to be able to speak to my family and Smitha's family including Mama!

Smitha would inconsequently complain of her being kept at bay, "Why don't you speak to me regularly these days? Are you seeing somebody else?" Smitha pleaded and then shifted gears to say, "If this is the way you plan to treat me, secondary to your family, then I think we can't continue any further."

But I could not tell her what kept me busy for the fear of something which was nothing.

Mama would go a step further and would never let an opportunity go to launch missile attacks on my family, "You don't tell me what is happening with your savings. How much bible have you read? I am sure you are continuously talking to your family and they are brain washing you to get over with this relationship." and I had to tell her, "No, my parents don't even know about it." and I would think, "Brainwashing? Who is brainwashing? My parents? You must be kidding!"

Amma called up to know my whereabouts, I was fast getting detached from the family; screws were falling and she was sensing it, "You have stopped coming home on weekends, you don't call up the entire day, even if I call, you disconnect. Is the pressure too much at work? Hope you are eating well! Take care and come home."

There was a sparkling difference in the approach of two mothers! One chose blame game, the other chose concern!

Raghav believed in practicality of the proceedings and assumed the same for me, "Its ok! You have work, better you concentrate on work, no point in travelling just to spend a day in Bangalore. However, whenever you have time, come home."

My brilliant dishonesty masqueraded the queries by popping up one reason or the other for the complaints my well-wishers began to construct.

Out of the 4 complainants above, Smitha was the only complainant who talked about consequences if complaints were not addressed. The fact that I could not talk to Smitha during the evenings, threw Smitha into obscure behaviors, most of them fuelled by her mother as she thought that her daughter was not speaking to me.

Smitha would doubt me for infidelity; she would get emotional if I was getting close to some other woman, which once clarified would result into accusing me of intentions to dump Smitha, that would suddenly transform into her anger for my parents, who by then, according to Smitha as well, were trying their best to brainwash. Once Smitha got tired of complaining, she would redesign herself as a strict interrogatory officer who knew just one question to grill someone in remand, "How much have you saved? See, I can't argue with Mama if you don't end up saving at least 50k."

With repeated arguments and clarifications, I wondered what was holding me back from telling Smitha that I was the first bouncer in the world who held a Post Graduation in Management!

But the post graduate in management forgot that he was answerable to many other than Smitha and Mama. Professional life was as important as personal life, and professional life was the only factor which could drive money, which in turn could drive the possibility of marrying Smitha.

In a hustle to put things in order and control, it did not occur that I was still a management trainee and my confirmation did depend on how well I performed in the interim review. Barely a week before the review, I fell back on my professional stint to realize that I had done nothing concrete till now, which could be piled up into a meaningful presentation. I was assigned with day to day tasks, where I did not attain perfection either.

Someone who knew nothing below 9, someone who disowned a below par performance, someone who did things sincerely was withering off and was all set to cover up his newly developed inefficiencies through a presentation made by one of the disturbed minds of its times. To make the presentation, I even gave up on another two hours of sleep every day and was now sleeping at 3 in the morning. To ensure a superior performance, I stopped talking to Smitha who hardly understood the dynamics I lived with. And the outcome was a product which had no sense, no logic and was meant to act as filler in a series of presentations on the review day. For anyone with a wee bit of commonsense, it would have been a cake walk to open up the loop holes in my presentation. I knew that, yet I believed that was the best I could do.

From the time I boarded the flight till I reached the presentation room, my heartbeat continued to rise, then things seemed to normalize a bit as the presentation was taking place in the same room where I and Dipti started. My confidence was getting restored at the sight of Mr. Sumit Rathi, my navigator! But the confidence graph which was on an upward trend had a nose dive when I saw the Tiger CFO.

Tiger CFO looked absolutely disinterested in what I presented; he must have attended thousand such presentations by thousand such losers, so, he discovered with the first slide that it was crap which was coming. Even I did not know what I was presenting, the lack of confidence the absence of proper sleep, a weak foundation in the company and a confused job (bouncer or finance) was clearly visible in the slides which had neither a correct beginning nor a correct end, and the content was way too loose!

I could not answer a question which the esteemed committee asked, I kept on observing each one of them who waggled their head in dismay, the looks which they passed sideways declared that I was screwing it up and they were bothered how their Super Dad would burst up to the comedy going on! The most fucked face was Sumit Rathi's, who for sure was getting slayed in the evening for I was his find for the organization.

By evening, entire finance fraternity and the management trainee gang knew that I was the black sheep and did not deserve to be a part of them. I had no one to blame, and so I could not smile. It was me who should have been cautious about what I was doing with my life. From the front liners, I was soon falling in the category of complete duds and accepted that I was the laughing stock. My self confidence was devastated; I hated myself, thanks to those who declared I was the descendent of good for nothing race!

Smitha called several times after the debacle (which she was not aware of), but I did not reply, more sensitive was the issue that I did not go and meet Mama even when I was in Gurgaon for the presentation, which amounted to grave misbehavior and it was my destiny (which was getting penned down by Mama) that I be reprimanded to have not to put an attendance to her majesty.

And finally when the mercury cooled down, and I acquainted with senses, I answered Smitha's call who by then was fuming, "What the fuck? Why are you not answering my call?"

"Nothing, I messed up the presentation" And I broke down.

Smitha realized that I was not in the correct frame of mind, and it was vain to argue on topics like "My Mama is the best", albeit she said, "Its ok sweetheart, this is not the last company in the world. Mama has been asking you to send your resume to Papa, he will fix a job for you in his organization and we will go there." An attempt to console me was an instigating statement as well in disguise; falling to Papa's favors would have been the last thing I would have agreed with, and I outrageously replied, "Screw your Papa's job, I'll stay here and prove that I have it in me. You stay assured; I'll fulfill all the demands which your Mom has, all those who thought that I am hopeless will wait and watch."

"Shut up. Just because I love you and have agreed against my parents' wishes to marry you, you can't just speak anything which comes to your mind. Stop cribbing about what has happened. I have been seeing that you keep on avoiding me, accept that you were not good and needed to concentrate more on your work so that you could be perfect with your presentation. And, when you were not speaking to me, you should have invested good amount of time in preparing this. I am sure there is something which is going on behind the scenes." Smitha said, and I thought, "Was I the one whom Smitha called a CEO material? And I am the one who is no good today!"

If this was not enough, Smitha had a nuclear bomb in the store for me, which for sure was developed with Mama's neural structure, for the fact that I did not visit her, and I did not speak to Smitha properly for almost a month now, which for sure was enough to plant more ideas against me in Smitha's brain. I expected the brain to mellow down with time and accept my family, but that was turning out to be undesired!

"Listen, I really don't trust you anymore, I need an undertaking signed by you stating that you agree to the demands and conditions." Smitha demanded brazenly!

Yes. Undertaking, I heard it right and you read it right. "Undertaking? What? You must be kidding." I said while laughing nervously.

"No, I am not kidding and yes, I need it on a stamp paper that you will do what is required." Smitha sounded firm.

"Yeah, I'll do what is required, but does it actually require an undertaking on a stamp paper? Baby, we love each other and will an undertaking prove it?" I said.

"I knew that, if you actually loved me and if there was nothing else behind the scenes, then you would have not even thought a second before putting up an undertaking." Smitha disconnected leaving me to justify why an undertaking was important, and as I had mended ways to adjust to demands, I developed logic behind the undertaking, "I was wrong to have hit Smitha when she spoke wrongly about my mother, and that seems to be the reason for her being against my parents. And she is timid in nature, and might be scared to stand up against her mother and say that she loved me, so, I am the tough one and need to steer it clear to the shore and assure a bright future for both of us, and if she is insecure and an undertaking would help her overpower the insecurity, then I am game for it."

I was living with hypothetical reasons, which never existed but they eluded me to live for them, I realized that I developed peace in my mind even when it was not around, and I developed agony even when it was not around.

I called up Smitha to inform her about my agreement for "THE UNDERTAKING", "Hi, tell me" Smitha said.

"Nothing, I just wanted to tell you that I will send you the agreement or undertaking in this case." I said indifferently.

"Hmmm, thanks shona. Muah" replied Smitha hurriedly.

I lived to be loved by Smitha and "Muah" rejuvenated the lost me, "Baby, when do we meet next?" I asked.

"We will talk about it later, I am going out now." Smitha said, hurriedly again.

"With whom and where?" I interrogated, "I wanted to speak to you." and I revealed the reason behind interrogation.

"With Cecilia to EXCESS." Smitha said neatly.

"EXCESS? This is a sports bar right? When did you start boozing regularly?" I asked a bit surprisingly.

"No, I don't booze much, last I boozed on my birthday when you were here but Cecilia does." Smitha shifted the buck on Cecilia.

"But as far as I remember, Cecilia never boozed when I was there" I got my intelligence into the discussion unnecessarily.

"Yeah. So?" Smitha wanted me to complete.

"Nothing! So you can speak to me till you reach EXCESS. Cecilia knows about us." I said.

"No, I can't." Smitha replied strangely and stretched "No" and ended "I can't" abruptly.

"Why? How are you going?" I asked.

"Thomas is coming to pick us up, in fact, he is there waiting downstairs in his car." Smitha reminded me of the "Black Santro" which made me hot blooded.

"Ok!" and I disconnected.

UNDERTAKING

I, Rama Chandran Iyer, son of Mr. S. Narayanan, hereby declare that I am willing to marry Ms. Smitha Suzanne Swaminathan, daughter of Mr. Swaminathan Vincent. Addendum, I undertake the following:

(a) I agree to take up Christianity as my religion, and I am ready for getting converted. I will not follow Hinduism after marriage.

(b) The marriage rituals will be completely based on Christianity and will not have any touch of Hinduism.

(c) Post marriage, my parents will not be staying at the place where I and Smitha will stay. They will stay with us only when Smitha Suzanne Swaminathan agrees for it.

(d) Even if my parents come to see me, they will not stay for more than 2 weeks at our place, and during such period, Smitha will be free to go to see her parents, and she will be free to choose not to return as long as my parents stay.

(e) The home where I and Smitha will stay will not have any effect of Hinduism.

(f) I will share all my expenses' and savings' details with Smitha and her mother.

(g) I will save Rs 50000 every month and will revise it depending upon the increment, and will contribute half of the wedding expenses which can amount to Rs 25 lakhs.

(h) All my financials will be handled by Smitha post marriage and she will be deciding where and how they are to be spent. It also calls that I will not have any right on Smitha's financials and will never question her on the expenses and savings.

(i) I will continue to find a suitable job outside India and will settle abroad for ever.

(j) Smitha will be impregnated according to her consent and I will never ever force myself on her.

(k) Our children will follow Christianity and my parents will never be allowed to influence them.

(l) I will never ever man handle Smitha and if it happens Smitha has the authority to exercise her right against domestic violence and can sue me.

(m) I will respect Smitha's parents the way she does, but it does not obligate Smitha to respect my parents in return.

I declare that I am not under any undue influence, coercion while undertaking the above clauses.

Rama Chandran Iyer

Pan Card no. : ANDRP34561

Once the undertaking was built and plotted on a stamp paper, I thought of giving the same to Smitha in person, to show her the pain in my eyes, to show how much I loved her, to expect that she would budge.

This made me travel to Hyderabad without informing Smitha, and it was late in the evening when I reached Smitha's flat and anticipated Smitha at the door, but it was Cecilia, and she smiled asking me to come in.

"Hi! How are you?" I was polished.

"I am absolutely fine, and where are you? You don't come often to meet your sweetheart?' she asked revealing her awareness about "all was not well" between Smitha and me.

"No! Nothing of that sort! Just occupied a lot with work." I answered honestly.

"Ok, but where is Smitha?" I asked.

"I don't know, I left office at 7." Cecilia answered innocently.

"But you guys come together from work. Don't you?" I asked.

"Yeah, we used to. Now, she comes a bit late. Just call her up and tell her that you are here." Cecilia looked like concealing something from me and wanted to stay away from Smitha and me.

"Ok, I will call her up, but you don't tell her that I am here. Kind of surprise visit." I requested Cecilia and left the flat.

I started walking towards Smitha's office and called her up and she disconnected. I called her up again and she disconnected, and then before I called her again, she messaged, "In a meeting."

I was baffled because it was almost 10 in the night, and what sort of meeting happened at such a late hour was slightly objectionable, and the moment I thought it was objectionable, I saw the same "Black Santro" with a cross and alloy wheels parked in front of 99 Dosas which was on the way to Smitha's office.

And I somehow felt that Smitha was inside the restaurant with the same mother fucker Thomas. I barged into the restaurant in a flash and a waiter came up to me and asked, "How many of you sir?" which I did not answer, as my eyes scanned through the restaurant looking for both of them, but I failed, and asked the same waiter, "Do you have something upstairs as well?" and he politely said, "Yes sir!"

And the upstairs had Smitha and Thomas munching on dosas, when I walked up straight to them and stood like a tower, all to catch Smitha's undivided attention and a fucked up face. Thomas stood up and like a real gentleman offered me a seat and asked if I would like to have something.

"Yes. A glass of chilled water." I said while my piercing eyes were fixed at Smitha.

"Oh! O." said Thomas trying to mock the emotions I went through.

But, I was the one whose emotions flowed without any inhibitions, "So, is this the meeting?" I asked Smitha.

"No, dude listen...." Thomas started speaking.

"You stay out of it, bastard." I abused Thomas.

"Ok" he behaved absolutely unmoved with the proceedings.

"Don't create a scene here!" Thomas ordered.

"You son of a dick, got issues with this, get out then." I was losing temper.

Thomas took some money enough to cover the bill, left it on the table and walked out of the restaurant, and asked, "Smitha, you coming? No point sitting here with this guy." and both of them walked out of the restaurant.

I hated such guys, those who under the shield of chivalry and decency, hit on other's girlfriend; they try to be the best buddies of the females reeling with their relationships, give them incorrigible solutions on how should they tackle their boyfriends, and act as if they are the biggest protectors, at the time when their dick would bleed if someone did the same with their girlfriends!

Thomas dropped Smitha at her flat, and I followed them in an auto rickshaw, at the gate, I said, "Dude, stop being with her, else I'll screw your happiness" and he left without uttering a word.

"What the fuck? What the fuck do you think of yourself?" Smitha opened fire at the flat.

"What do I think of myself? I think that I am crazy, idiot, stupid and one of his kind! But what are you up to? Why did you lie to me that you were in a meeting?" I yelled.

"Stop raising your voice, don't jump into conclusions, we were in a meeting, and while on the way, we thought of having dinner, but it is true that when I messaged you, I was at the restaurant." Smitha cleaned up the air, partially though.

"So, why did you lie?" I was irritated.

"Coz I knew that you will not like the fact that I was with Thomas and that would lead to unnecessary arguments, questions and answers. I did not want it, I wanted peace. So, I lied." Smitha transferred the weight on me, and even when Smitha was at fault, primarily it was my mistake to have forced her to commit something objectionable! Logic?

"The fact is sweetheart, if you loved me, and you knew that I did not like you being with him, you would have ensured that you are not with him instead of lying to me" I gave Smitha the real feel of concern.

"And Cecilia told me that you come at this time every day, so, you are in a meeting like this every day? Tell me clearly, if you like that bugger, I will walk out. I don't want to be screwed." I was about to break down.

"And here is the undertaking signed by me. Keep it" I said and walked to the balcony.

Smitha was completely scandalized by my behavior, and was negative about me when she read through the undertaking; therefore, it was not surprising that she was able to find flaws!

"Did you read it?" I asked.

"Yes, I did, but I have highlighted the changes, you are very smart with words." Smitha replied and I wondered how quickly she could forget what happened and take my case again. If I had been deceitful towards her, the earth would have rotated from east to west, and even a police complaint would have looked like mercy.

"What changes?" I asked.

"See, first, you have written I am wiling to marry, that should be I will marry. Second, you say that you will not follow Hinduism after marriage, in fact, you should not follow Hinduism once you get converted. Third, your parents should not stay for more than two weeks, and any extension will be decided by me and we never decided that I will be free to choose not to return as long as I want. Fourth, you will continue to find a suitable job, the deal is not to keep on finding a suitable job, it should be that you will soon find a suitable job overseas, and if nothing clicks in six months, you will take up a job in my dad's organization. Please get these changes done and give this undertaking again" Smitha had no shame, no fear, and no dignity when she spoke and I was losing all the respect I had developed for her over the years.

And then she got a message on her phone, which was lying next to me and Smitha was changing then. It was crime, but I did it, the message read, "Has that moron left? What about TDS this weekend? Excess was fun! What say? It was fun to booze with two beautiful ladies. But Cecilia will not be around this weekend I guess. So, it would be two of us only! C ya. Gud nite and let me know what did that moron do?"

Smitha came out and saw my red hot face; burning eyes with her mobile phone, "What happened?" asked Smitha.

"Read this, and you said you don't booze." I probed.

"I did for the first time on my birthday, not after that" Smitha clarified, "And for god's sake, he is my good friend, stop doubting please!" she continued.

"I am the one whom you plan to marry, you never boozed with me! Chuck it, I am gonna screw him up. I am calling him up." I said and dialed Thomas's number.

"Hello! Who is this?" said Thomas.

"Your dad, you bastard!" I said.

"Oh! Rama?" he confirmed.

"Yes, stop going around with Smitha, will not be good for your health." I commanded.

"Stop being a blabber boy on the phone. Got balls, do a man to man and I will teach you a lesson for what you have been ranting about!" He hit back.

"Oh! Is it? I'll be there at your place, tell me your address." I got charged.

"Ask your lady, she knows it. I am waiting." he said and disconnected.

I looked at Smitha furiously and asked if she knew where he stayed, and she said, "Please don't do this. Please baby. He is my colleague!"

"But he doesn't behave like a colleague and you did not behave either. You have given him unwanted space, and I'll push him out from that space today!" I was on a rampage.

And I pulled Smitha by hand, called for an auto rickshaw and went straight to Thomas's place, who seemed to have slept and did not expect me to come, because I had a lady to pull me back.

The second half asleep Thomas opened the door; he was shocked to see me standing at the door, and then looked for Smitha who stood behind me. I picked up my bouncer stance, stood with my hands folded and raised my eyebrows. "So, I am here! Do you want to do man to man here or on the road?" I said.

And before he said anything, I caught him by his neck, dragged him violently out of the gate and threw him on the grill of the garden.

He got up quickly and ran towards me and banged his head into my stomach, the boy had power, and I fell down. There is an age old theory that you should never fall in a fight, because a series of kicks never let you get up, so, never get pinned down! And probably Thomas knew this theory as well, he kicked me on my face and then on my chest. He then punched me on my nose, by this time, the fearsome beast was awake and I got hold of his neck which I pressed with my thumbs and Index fingers and pushed him down and rolled on to him. I sat cross legged on his stomach, with my knees on his hands, denying him any movement, I punched him incessantly, if someone had a timer, he relished my knuckles for good two to three minutes!

I carried a knife in my socks for self-defense, something given to me as a bouncer; I took that out and pointed straight into his eyes and said, "Listen you bastard, I can finish you off this very moment! But this is not your fault! Your over smartness brought you this state! Fuck off! And stay away from Smitha!"

During this entire male tussle, Smitha shouted, "Stop it please" probably more than thousand times, I even found that in tandem when I punched Thomas. "A punch, then stop it please, then a punch, and stop it please, punch, stop it please, punch, stop it please, punch, stop it please!"

I held Smitha and went back to the flat where Smitha stood frozen, I said, "I will send the revised copy of the undertaking. And, yes, listen to me, when I am doing so much for you, I expect you to be attached only with me. Do you get that?"

"Get out! Get out right now! I don't want to see your face anymore!" Smitha shouted while pointing at the door. "How will I face him from tomorrow at work?" she continued.

"Whatever!" I picked up the bag and left to catch Karnataka Sampark Kranthi to Bangalore.

Back to work, daily mundane job, and then walking around the tables to look for any wrong doer in the evening signed off those days when Smitha hardly spoke to me, definitely angry over that incident.

As my stint as a bouncer, I constructed strange anger towards the guys who hit on girls in the pub. Whenever I saw a man approaching a woman, I visualized Smitha in one of the pubs with bastard Thomas and men trying to be close with her.

A bouncer was not required to intervene as long as women were fine with men approaching them and flirt. Over a period of time, I started believing that it was women who instigated men and they enjoyed the attention which these flirtatious men gave. I used to stand with Shiva and we waggled our head in hopelessness, "This bastard comes here every weekend and picks up a new chick!" said Shiva pointing at one of the flirtatious guys I talked about.

"Amazing talent! Isn't it?" I said and winked.

"What talent? Look at him, my dick looks more handsome! If you are loaded with money, even an angel will fall!" Shiva said.

"Oh! Is it?" I asked.

"Yes, I have seen the pattern here, the bill what a guy pays is directly proportional to the number of chicks he has picked up till date!" Shiva knew statistics as well.

"And you know what? Most of these beautiful ladies have boyfriends back home. Bloody sluts!" and he went towards the other corner of the pub.

And when I started slipping into what Shiva said, I was called by the manager, "Listen Rama, just stay around table no. 34, there are few guys on that table who are creating trouble for the ladies on table no. 36. Just hang in there."

"Do I use force?" I asked.

"No, only if needed. This is the last drink we are serving them; the waiter will come with the bill there. Make those guys pay and then somehow make them move. You are smart enough! Take care of this!" and he left for his cabin!

While I walked around the two tables, 34 and 36, one of the guys from table no. 34 called me and gave me a tissue paper and said, "Please give it to that girl."

It read, "You are the hottest chick with such big boobs, I want to suck them and you suck my dick. Can I have your number?"

"No sir, I can't pass this on. If you want to speak to the girl, please do that outside the pub." I told him amicably.

"And Mam, if they trouble you again, please call me out, I am Rama" I told the lady while pointing at my name badge!

"Hello listen, I asked you to pass on the paper, not to read and decide." said one of the guys from Table 34.

"Sir, you are arguing unnecessarily, and calling for unnecessary trouble. You can speak to the lady and I will not utter a word if she approves. But I think they are not pleased by your remarks which you have been passing for some time. So, please stop it here." I tried pacifying the drunken guy.

In the meanwhile, the waiter got the bill, and handed it over to me and left. I placed the bill on the table 34 and said, "Request you to pay before we serve you further."

One of the guys was the semen sample of one of the millionaires of Mysore, he took out his wallet laden with currency notes, and started throwing it on the bill, I counted it and gave back an extra 500 rupee note which he threw.

"Sir, this is extra what you have paid!" I said and gave the bill amount to the waiter.

"This is for you. Keep it, and don't interfere, give this paper to the lady over there." he ordered.

"I am a bouncer sir, and not a middleman! And we can serve you further only if you shift from this table to the table at the corner. Else, I am afraid that you will have to go!" I said while smiling.

"Oh shut up! You bastard!" he said and slapped me.

I looked at the manager who gave thumbs up, which meant "Use force" and then I looked for Shiva who came running for my aid and slapped the guy who slapped me.

I held two of them by collar and pushed them out of the pub, and Shiva threw another two out of the pub.

Those guys continued to shout, "You will pay for this you bastards! Wait and watch." Something happened to Shiva; he ran back and kicked one of the guys and then patted on my back.

"We will take a different route today." I said while we changed.

"Why? You are scared of those threats from drunken bastards, relax, they will not do anything." Shiva said. Being local, I trusted him and said, "Ok!"

And while we zipped on the empty streets in the night, a Scorpio speeded and ran parallel to us, and I was right in asking Shiva to take a different route. Yes, Scorpio had the same bunch of guys whom we mauled at the pub! It had rained slightly and when Shiva started speeding to avoid the drama, we slipped because one of the guys hit our bike with a rod from behind.

Since I was prepared for the assault from behind, I jumped off the bike few seconds before it slipped, and was safe. However, Shiva hurt himself badly and Scorpio braked powerfully in front of him to make us feel part of a movie scene. But, it was no movie, those four guys got their few more friends along, with Shiva retired hurt, I was no Arnold to beat all of them up and run away with Shiva on my shoulder!

The best way to come out of it was to surrender, and I said, "Listen guys! Let us not fight. What happened at the pub was our job. That is what we are paid for. Please!" and I tried extricating Shiva little by little but those guys were in a murderous mood and the one who threw currency notes kicked me on my shoulder and I dropped Shiva again who suffered in grave pain.

I was almost in tears, I knew those guys could at maximum, beat us up, but I could not see Shiva bleeding! "You guys tried to be hero in front of those chicks. Bastards!" one of them said, and began to kick Shiva whose head was still under the helmet! Therefore, any attack would have broken his bones, but his head would have been safe. We saw cops patrolling every night on that road, but why is it when needed, you don't get cops!

I held the feet of one of the guys, not to throw him, I did not believe in action then, albeit, "Please, please, he is bleeding, let us go. We were just doing our duties." I pleaded.

"You were ok, but this asshole slapped me and then he threw me out and then he kicked me." said one of them.

I said, "Enough" and took out the knife I had for self-defense and ran it on one of the many feet which kicked us ruthlessly! (Remember the theory? Never fall during a fight, you will never be able to get up!)

Those guys had no balls, the moment they saw the blood of one of them in their gang, and a knife in my hand, they got scared out of their wits. I shouted, "You bastards, I have been pleading to let us go. He is bleeding and if he dies, I'll get you to the court!" And then I deeply slit one of the many palms visible. The gang eloped from the scene!

When I could take out Shiva completely, I was relieved to see that he could stand, and had no fracture, but, had bruises all over the body. I picked up the bike again and drove to a hospital and got Shiva treated and a first aid for myself. I sat next to Shiva and said, "I asked you to take a different route and you were wrong in slapping them back, and it was crime to kick them once they were out of the pub! They were the customers. Why did you lose your temper? We should thank our stars that we are safe. They had no issues with me; they wanted to beat you up. You are one cool chap and I have never seen you lose temper, what happened today?"

"Nothing, I broke up and last weekend, when you were in Hyderabad, my girl came to the pub with the guy whom I slapped and kicked. That bugger knew that the girl whom he came with was my girlfriend!" and tears ran down his cheeks and I stared at him wondering how wrong Shiva was and instead of slitting those guys, should have slit Shiva's girl!

18

Confession by a Snake Oil

The respect for Smitha was getting depleted, and I was rediscovering myself. I could tolerate anything but infidelity, which I was not sure of on Smitha's part. Therefore, even if Smitha decided to speak less frequently, I developed the courage not to encourage Smitha by not calling her up.

It happens that you realize how prized a commodity is when you lose it. And Smitha speculated that she was getting endangered in my world, there lies the beauty of love, and I call it the pinnacle of any relationship when we take each other for granted. Smitha assumed that come what may, I was there forever, and only when it occurred that I was not immortal in her life, she felt terrible!

"Hi.... Can you call? It is urgent, I don't have balance." Smitha messaged, my good memory says that it was the first communication in any form from Smitha in ten days.

"Don't have balance? You have not spoken to me for ten days? Where did the balance go?" My intelligence was getting recovered when I was not speaking to Smitha.

"Now, can you tell me what is it? I am busy right now." And I did not lie; I was doing the bouncer job.

"Nothing! Call once you are free!" she replied.

"??what non sense? You said it was urgent! Now tell me what it is." I ordered.

"Oh! So, you need reasons to call up now." Smitha melted. A spark in my eyes and a shine on my face generated.

"Fine! I'll call later." I replied.

"Buzz off!" She replied; it was evident that Smitha was missing me; she was missing all the importance she enjoyed! There was no one now to dance to her tunes.

And I smiled at Smitha's childlike innocence which I fell for.

"Love you Baby. Will call." I messaged.

And she sent a smiley.

I fell for Smitha's decision to leave her ego and give me hints that she missed me and found ways to kick off the regular communication with me. Howsoever muddled our relationship was, howsoever one tried to screw it, howsoever one created hindrances; they could never diminish the underlying force, the force which bonded Smitha and me. We loved each other, our conscience knew it. No Mama, No Kelly, No Religion, No Thomas could have been strong enough to quake that! I found reasons again, hypothetical or not, only time would tell!

The over ecstatic I called up Smitha, "Hi baby!"

"Hi" she said indifferently.

"Oh! Baby you are still angry. Ok, I am sorry." I offered an apology even when I was not apologetic.

"Shut up. What took you so long to call me up? And yes I am still angry." Smitha wanted to be pampered more, as if I was the only one who was wrong for the increasing distance between the two.

"Please na baby. I told you I am sorry. But I don't like it when you meet Thomas. Please baby. Please. Hmmm, please!" I pampered as much as I could do.

"No, I am still angry." Smitha said with no anger.

"Ok baby, tell me what should I do to make my baby smile?" I tried to be nice.

"Marry me and you will never talk about Thomas and irritate me." Smitha took control.

"Yes, baby, I will marry you. But Mama has to agree right?" I was logical.

"Baby, One more thing. You will not get angry right?" Smitha was opening the missile box, the latest in her possession.

"What? I'll not get angry." I got a bit serious, expecting the unexpected.

"Sure? Promise?" Smitha was childish.

"Promise! What is it?" I asked.

"I told Mama that you came to meet me and the fight you had with Thomas." Smitha said that breathlessly and expected me to generate emotions.

"What? What the hell? You are….." My senses fell apart.

"Then what did she say?" I continued

"She first scolded me for staying out with Thomas for long and then she was upset that I lied to her about speaking to you." she said.

"So, what do I do now?" I asked her.

"Mama wants to meet you. Can you go and meet her over the weekend?" Smitha asked which I thought was a command more than the request.

"Do I have a choice?" I said sarcastically.

"Now, don't give me that nonsense. Please! Can you go or not?" Smitha confirmed.

"Your wish is my command" I signed off my acceptance.

Another hit of 15 to 16 k, and without being aware of what was in store, I headed to meet her majesty, and this time I was informed that the master of her majesty was present at the venue. And since that would have been my first face off with the unknown, whom I had presumed to be the most humble man, I was scared because all my presumptions have been proven wrong blatantly.

Till now, male characters in Smitha's family looked more like actresses in Hindi movies, cardboard figures. Suresh Mama looked like a sensible one against the animated Babli, the characters which forced me into feet touching exercise also looked with brains, and the exemplary one was Ranjan, whom I could claim to know in and out, but was paying for the surname given to him.

"Listen, if this is the way you plan to live, Swami, please remove your surname against his name, we will disown him." I heard Mama yelling this, the operating tool was Swami (Swaminathan Vincent, for a second, I was fainted if she actually addressed her husband as Swami when she taught her daughter to treat her husband as Daasi)

And moreover, who is so cinematic to disown a son and remove the surname! I wondered how it would sound if my mother said this to my dad in the most dramatic way, the only result could be my father bursting into laughter. Anyway, as I said, cardboard figures don't do much.

Shunning the drama going inside, I covered the smile and rang the bell. It was a tall fellow, who resembled a senior artist in Indian Cinema, perfect for father roles! His shining head showed the trauma he lived with, his grey moustache showed the pressure he reeled under, his simple attire showed the humbleness. It took me no time to understand it was Smitha's dad and I smiled, "Hello sir!" and he said, "Come in."

"Boss, what come in? I have stayed in this home more than you!" I thought but I managed to smile only.

I went to Mama, hugged her and winked at Ranjan, whose expressions said, "Thanks for coming and cutting this drama short!"

I was sure Mama would have elaborated each and every thing to Papa, who when spoke to me, seemed to carry something in his mind. I, who was becoming very critical about me, felt like getting scanned. I longed before they could tell me what was it they wanted to discuss for which they made me fly to Delhi in such a short notice, and "Boss, I am not on a vacation, have to go back to Mysore. So, please break the ice." I thought.

They had not discussed the topic I anticipated them to spend the maximum time on, but they sent a "Doosra" this time, which goes the other way, and you have no option but to play at it, "We want to meet your parents and discuss about you and Guddu."

And the only way I knew to react was to get up and scan the faces in shock, and I looked at Ranjan if he had any idea, but looked absolutely out of sync.

How do I react? Because this is what I wanted, this what I worked for, this is what I was getting converted for, this is what I betrayed my parents for, this is what I devastated myself for, this is what I worked double shifts for, this is what I travelled extensively for, this is what I slit feet and hands for, this is what I picked up fights for, this is what I distanced myself from Sri and Om for! But, yet why is this feeling not flowing down smoothly, why there is a sudden feeling of fear? What is wrong if they wanted to meet my parents? I was about to cry, because an undefined fear struck me!

"But Mama, what do I tell my parents now? And what about the conditions?" I was digging my own grave.

"No, Papa thinks that it is high time that we get some confirmation from your side as well, we can't just allow you to hang out with our girl." Mama was so just!

"Meeting your girl once a month and catching her red handed with somebody else is hanging out? Please define hanging out." I could not say this!

I thought her part of insecurity as a girl's mother was well justified, and more than for her, the sensible Papa could send his point down my head.

"See Guddu is a year elder to you, and if she continues to wait for you to set up things, and if you turn hostile later on, our Guddu might not be able to take that and also, she will be quite old to be accepted by others, and also, since most of our relatives know that you are the one, so, it is important that there is something from your end as well" Mama's such logical words were murdering me, "Please god please, please tell me what is the source of this incarnation?"

"Dear old lady, did you get that how important is it for you to save your own ass, if I were to walk out from your daughter's life? I need not be bothered about any society, any relative. But, you the stupid one have told you relations that I am the one whom you are planning to get your daughter married off to! Also, your diminutive acts of telling that I am a Hindu guy ready for conversion would have clarified it to them that it is not an arranged one! So, why is it that I have been oppressed all this while; do I give it back to you? Also, what proof are you talking about? Your daughter already has an undertaking signed by me, the original copy of which she must have sent to you by now which must be safe in your locker!"

I was absolutely sure that Papa would have intervened and enlightened the stupid lady to curb down the attacks on me, because there is a limit to which one could be stretched, and he must have realized that it was high time that I hit back. But, he belonged to the same league; therefore, to place the money on him outrightly was a quick decision. So, I decided to play myself in.

"Mama, but I have not saved much yet; I hardly have 3.5 lakhs with me, and if I go with the same pace, I will pile up good money." I played my first card.

"That is ok, but you should at least get your parents' word on this one." Mama said.

(Oh is it? When did my parents' word become important? First, my parents need to be important. Right?)

"And yes tell them that we want to schedule the wedding in December." Mama gave me a few more inputs.

"But Mama, December? How will I arrange the money?" I raised concern!

"Yeah, that can be taken care of." Mama raised some hopes.

"How Mama how?" I was beginning to smile seeking some respite!

"We will do one thing; you just call your parents for the wedding and don't call any other relatives. As it is, they will not be able to appreciate the Christian ceremonies. So, you will not have to contribute much basis your share." Mama's super intelligent side was overflowing and causing floods.

(Öh! Thanks a lot your highness for being considerate enough to allow me to invite my parents' for the wedding. Are you done or do you have something more to guide me about?)

"And one more thing, make sure that you tell them that you were the one who proposed to Guddu, and then she asked you to speak to me, and there were certain conditions which were important for the wedding to happen." Mama continued, and when she continued, nobody could stop her; she became the woman possessed with Mask!

Uneven talks found their way out at the wrong times, my striking was poor, "Mama, did you keep the same conditions when you married Papa? Did you ask him to leave his parents? Didn't his parents have any issue while he gave in for everything?" And then I looked at Papa and asked, "How did you manage to convince your parents on the conversion front? How did you agree for the clause of your parents not staying with you?" I opened fire without realizing retaliation, and was caught off guard!

Mama was charged enough and clarified, "Papa loved me so much that he could do anything for me and he did not make it count ever, in front of me?" (Ok, so you want a goat that should give milk and should not utter a word while getting slaughtered. Got it, but I thought I was doing enough to show my love for Smitha. And please understand that keeping a point is not making things count, and Mama, I liked your "In front of me" thing, and you did not care if he hurled abuses at your back!)

How could she read my mind? Therefore, she continued, "And his parents are so lovable that I could never think of asking him to leave them." and I looked at Papa's face for confirmation and I laughed crazily (of course, it was my inner side laughing), she carried on, "His parents were self-dependent and had self-respect not to depend on anybody, and it was their choice not to stay with us, in fact, they stay alone in Mumbai. But, I adore them. We love them so much." she stressed on adore! (Ok! No need to dramatize now, I accept that you love them. But I fail to understand that I have been displayed in front of half of the population from your side, but none of the Papa's relatives have given a go ahead till now! Go ahead is a dream, they have not even seen me. Your parents are no more, so, morally, I should be meeting Papa's parents before I met the entire circus crowd. And why Papa does not go to Mumbai when he comes to India? Forget Papa, you are the one who stays in India; I have never seen you calling them up or going to Mumbai to meet them, and I remember Smitha frowning once when Papa asked her to call up the oldies. I might be wrong here and I accept what you said! Adore.)

And then she came to defend Papa, "Papa was very hard working and was on his own before he married me, and he was confident from day one that he would get converted. Plus, how dare you speak like that to him? You must not forget that he is the head of the family." (Fine, he is hard working and I am hardly working! What do you expect now? That I should be pulling a rickshaw? Not your fault, you don't know what I am up to! And excuse me! Did you say head of the family? Which family? And where did I misbehave? If this is the respect you command for him, then am I wrong in thinking alike?)

Pandemonium did not stop; Mama resorted to her ultimate weapon as she knew that I would always get opened up to this one, "And if you can't respect Papa, then forget that Smitha will ever marry you." This was enough to push me in a defensive mode, "Mama, I did not mean to disrespect Papa. Please, I just wanted to know how do I gather enough courage to tell this to my parents and more importantly, how to tell my parents!" I softened.

"You had enough courage to go and beat up her colleague, are you a rogue? That shows the kind of family you come from! Street fights and arguments! Next time you do that, I am sorry we might have to rethink our decision!" Mama told straightly.

Kind of family? Why are you taking shots at my family for no reason? Ignorant highness, are you even aware that your son was carrying grass worth 50k? Do you know that he took off from the fly over? Do you know the rounds he made to the police station? Does that mean that you brought him up this way? Certain things happen, and you can't control them! I have a gentle upbringing and I hold my head high for I have been taught to stick to my words and never fall back on my commitment because relations don't evolve by conditions!

But I knew well beforehand that it was futile to attempt any kind of discussion with someone so authoritative with feet licking listening skills! In a situation where the objective is made lucrative and the means to achieve are relaxed, there was an invariable chaos of the correct decision with the fear of getting trapped.

"Ok Mama, then, I'll tell my parents about this. Is this what you called me from Mysore?" I told her and asked her a question instantly.

"How sarcastic you are and is this the way you talk? Is this what you called me here for?" Mama repeated the question in a different tone altogether. Actually, I wanted her to interpret it like that only!

"No Mama!" I said.

"Papa wanted to meet you. Do you need more reasons?" Mama made a valid point; point that I had gone from bad to worse without even meeting the head of the family. I was slightly worried to think about few more conditions which Papa could have rolled out for me.

I paused for a while to collect whatever happened after I came to Delhi. The conditions which my wedding was dependent on were still alive; however, the conditions on which conditions worked were slightly modified now. Did Papa tamper with them? I did not know then.

"Ok, yes Mama, I never realized that I had never met Papa. I have spoken to him many times, so I never felt that I have not seen him." and I smiled..

"Fine Mama, I have a flight early in the morning tomorrow, I'll go and meet a few friends." I told her while trying cool down everything and thinking to present the case to my parents.

"No, we don't trust you. You will not go anywhere and you will speak to your parents in front of us" Mama was micro managing.

Can you please write the entire script which I need to vomit to my parents?

I somehow wanted to delay everything which was being rushed earlier forcing myself to indulge in one thing or the other, the only idea was to defer the confrontation with my parents! As Mama had perfectly pointed out, I had all the courage in the world to sock up Thomas, I had all the courage to take the bold steps, but what was coiling my mind? Was it required to speak to my parents in front of the highness? Was it required to tell my parents about all the conditions which were enforced? Was Mama stubborn enough to force me to speak against my parents? Did Smitha deserve enough to enjoy this importance in my life? But I did commit this life to her!

The commitment was solid enough to slope me into the transmission form; to inform my parents about everything I decided, decisions which are going to rock the future! How will they react? I did not know, but sooner or later, I would have told them. So, why not at that particular moment? It asked for the concentration of all the senses and energies, I did that and rang the number.

"*Amma, Rama pessarein.*" I said in Tamil as if I was kidnapped and Mama started jumping to prompt me to speak in English. Her lips moved without any sound saying, "English English"

I thought, "You unhinged woman, even if I speak in Tamil, your husband is sitting here to translate it to you, therefore, stop animating." but I waggled my head.

"*Rama, Yenne Aachu*?" In a pulse, she picked that there was something not confirming with me.

"Nothing Amma, wanted to tell you something." I started the foundation work and switched to English.

"What do you want to tell me? Are you coming home this evening?" Amma asked because that was Saturday and it had been ages I went home.

"No, I am not coming home. I am in Delhi." I began to open up, while my eyes met Mama's eyes which were fixed at me.

"Delhi? You did not tell me that you were going to head office" Amma asked innocently.

"Amma, please! The head office is in Gurgaon and not in Delhi." I said while I rolled my thumb on the middle finger nail.

"Oh! Ok. I am sorry. Then what are you doing there?" she asked.

"I am at Smitha's home." And I ended abruptly and waited for Amma to react.

"Why? What happened? Is everything fine?" she was worried for this weird behavior.

"I proposed to Smitha and have been seeing her for more than 2 years. I love her." I said in one shot and looked at Mama, who looked furious for something which I ignored.

"Ok that is really great! So, you have gone to meet her parents? Right?" I could not believe my ears, was I getting trapped in another plot?

"Yeah, yeah Amma. I know her parents well before, I stayed with her family while I did my Delhi branch stint." I bought time to let the feeling seep in.

"But there are a few conditions." I gave her the feeler.

"Conditions? What conditions? She also loves you right?" Amma was right in saying that there are no conditions in love.

"Yeah she does, but the conditions come from her parents." I made efforts to keep Smitha clear.

"They want me to get converted to Christianity! And…." I continued but was cut short

"And what? And you agreed for it?" Amma asked or confirmed was unknown.

"Yes Amma. I am sorry Amma but I did not have any choice." I said and realized that there was no one on the other side…. She disconnected.

And I sat down, my head down rewinding the proceedings in the relationship and speculating if everything could be reversed and I become the same old Rama; Mama said, "Who asked you to tell her that you had been seeing her for two years? What will she think about Guddu now?"

I chose silence as an answer and thought harder, "Think about Guddu? She will think that Guddu's parents are extremely fortunate to have a daughter like her who obeys her parents and gives them the top priority. I am worried what would she think about me? And how can you be so stupid? If I don't tell her that I have been seeing her for such a long time, won't it sound stupid that I am ready to get converted in a relationship which had lasted only for a week. Use some sense. Oh! I am sorry, you don't have any!"

And when I raised my head to give it back to Mama, my phone rang and it was Amma.

"Amma. Why did you disconnect?" I was on the verge of breaking down .

"And I don't want to lose you! Please don't be angry." The love for the family was unwinding.

"It is ok. Never fall back on your words. If you have agreed, stick to it!" Amma was traumatizing me by not reacting.

"Thanks Amma, I knew that you will support. They want to keep the wedding in December." I started spilling the beans!

"Great, please let us know the dates as well if those are decided." Amma was correct to vent out the anguish through sarcasm.

"Why are you talking like that? But this is not the end of it, there are a few more!" I had few more to confess.

"What?" Amma was certainly getting jitters.

"They want to spend close to twenty five lakhs for the wedding as they are quite rich, and they want me to contribute half of it and if I am not able to do it, I should not be inviting all our relatives, only the limited guests should be invited. Also, the wedding should happen by Christian rituals only" I was the most shameful and Amma was, no doubt, in the middle of a heart attack, but she pointed a genuine idea.

"Ok, fine, we will have a wedding in our way as well, then there should not be any problem I guess." Amma beating me up with a cane would have been lot more easier than what she was doing then; I expected the mother of a swindler to be a bit more emotional, instead of suggesting me ways to tackle the nuisance I was engulfed with.

"Amma I am sorry but that will not be possible, they will not be agreeing to do with any Hindu rituals. In fact, they will not allow Smith to be treated to any Hinduism. Also, it is required that our kids will not follow Hinduism at all." I gave some more shocks to Amma, who was all ears to the bull shit I ejected.

"What are you saying? Are you sure about what you are talking about?" Amma desperately needed a confirmation and I was quick at giving it.

"Yes." I said without a hitch.

"Ok. I don't know what to say, come home next weekend. We will speak then." Amma tried to handle the delicate situation.

"We will speak for sure, however, Smitha and her family might come to Bangalore and would like to meet you then and decide on the dates and other formalities." I updated her further.

"But, we have not even seen Smitha yet?" Amma raised concern, "Oh! You have seen her, she has to be good, your choice." Amma answered herself.

"Bye!" I said.

"Bye!" she said.

The most complicated conversation after the placement interviews was concluded and I silently went out of the room while noticing a victorious smile on Mama's face. The smile was synonymous with bringing down one more man to their feet, to their terms, the victory of the feminists! Was it? I did not know then, all I knew was to commit my life to serve Smitha.

Amma's miffed face was the only visible thing at that point of time, how to fight the anguish and ignominy was fighting with the love I developed for Smitha. My no man stature made fun of my erstwhile authoritativeness! Amidst all the conflicts, Mama, whom I never expected to hurl words of encouragement, threw another one to shake me up, "*Beta*, make sure that you come again to Delhi after two weeks, you will have to go through the process of conversion! You have to be a Christian before you enter into any sort of customary rituals with Smitha."

I looked at her sinfully, and went on to pack my bag and said, "Good night Mama, I am going off to sleep. Will leave early in the morning."

19
Converted

I was summoned to the capital so that witness to my confessions were pure and my plight could not be missed, but, the fresh in the agony list was yet to arrive. And the arrival was scheduled two weeks after I landed to take the much anticipated stick from Amma. But Amma continued to throw chaos by being absolutely satisfied by my behaviour. I took it as a sign of acceptance and stepped to move ahead in life. Move ahead with opposite to my upbringing!

Barely two weeks after the return from the den in Delhi, Lady Don called for me again, this time; I was left to be treated by some Pappu uncle.

"*Beta*, is it possible for you to come to Delhi this weekend?" Mama asked me during one of our not so regular phone conversations.

"Managing fifty thousand out of sixty five thousand was also not possible, but wasn't I doing that? So, this request, or command I say, will be adhered to as well your highness."

"Yeah Mama, I will come. But what happened?" I accepted while thinking of the extra rupees I could have made over the weekend as a bouncer.

"*Beta*, Pappu Uncle has arranged a date for your conversion process and that is the only date available. And since you have not written your exams completely, he is trying to find out a way to make your conversion process a bit easier." Mama informed me about the wellness showered at me.

I surely missed Mama and Pappu uncle when I got my driving licence done, because you need such middlemen for such jobs. However, let me not degrade the prestigious title Pappu uncle held. He was a priest in one of the Churches in Vikas Puri! And so, he held the responsibility of looking over the conversion experiment. I felt like a rat which was subjected to the maximum experiments in the biological labs.

My resources meant for wedding, home and to maximize the presence of my relatives at the wedding were getting screwed for my impertinent visits to Delhi which were rescheduled at the will of some Pappu uncle who had no relation with me other than to row my boat of Christianity. During the times when huge noise was made for Smitha's job, I was forced to take leaves without prior notices and then ridiculously asked to reschedule everything.

I was asked to contact Pappu uncle, who would give me instructions of what all was needed, "Hello, am I speaking to Pappu uncle?" I asked shamefully while smiling a little while I said, "Pappu uncle" but self-restraint was important then.

"Yes, Pappu uncle speaksing." He said freely and I for a moment thought that "Speaking" was a tough word to pronounce as it needed the tongue to touch upper part of the inner mouth, but....

"Hello uncle, how are you?" I asked.

"I am fine, thanks you." he murdered the language again and I ignored that again considering it was not my problem.

"How ij you?" he pumped another one out. First, a wrong use of tense, and then wrongly pronouncing it! I started to beliebe that he waj someone likes me, who hailed from a non krishan background, but later on moved on to become one and finally graduating to become a preesht!

But I won't give up so easily; I continued to speak in English knowing that he will give an eye for an eye without feeling the glaucoma.

"Mama asked me to speak to you and said that you would be telling me what all is required for the conversion process." I confirmed the reason for calling him up.

"Yej Yej, get a kurta pajama. bhite colours." he started off. (Colours??)

"But, I doubt if I get a kurta pajama in Mysore, and even if I do, will be costly. Can't I get my white tracks and a white T-shirt?" I raised concerns.

"No no, you hab to get new dress. Becauje this ij phor goad. You sood not wear old dress phor goad funcson" he rubbished my application, and then he gave a suggestion, typical of a middleman, "I bill purchaje the dress four you in Delhi and you can do the payment aphter coming."

"No, its ok, thank you. I will manage." I chose not to fall into the trap of middleman! "And what else is needed?" I asked.

"Bring underbear and tobel also." Pappu father ordered leaving me to expect a swimming round in the conversion process. I thought, "Am I appearing for mega model hunt?"

"Fine, I will get everything. I will reach Delhi day after tomorrow in the morning. What time will I have to be there at the Church?" I asked.

"Bhery good. You come to church at 1. Ok?" Pappu uncle confirmed.

Flights booked on a short notice are costlier and airline operators had no special love for me, even when I was a frequent flyer. With just a Sunday available, I looked forward for maximum exertion; Mysore to

Bangalore by road, Bangalore to Delhi by flight, visit to den, then the passing of exam without writing the exam, then sign off at the den again, back to Bangalore, and then to Mysore.

I buckled up for the step confirming my knot with Smitha and reached Delhi. Since a pit stop was scheduled at the den, after the breakfast, I was supposed to move to Pappu uncle's place, who was designated to accompany me to the venue. I recalled my days of struggle for driving licence when my driving instructor accompanied me to the RTO for getting the licence.

"*Beta*, here is the address, please go to Pappu uncle's house and he will take you to the church. He will guide you and you will not have to do much of the running around." Mama took care of me.

I had done enough of running around, now, even if she asked me to swim across the English Channel, I was capable enough of doing that, however, it was very helpful of her to spare me the horror of running around at the Church. In fact, I think it was her responsibility to do so.

"Hello uncle, I am on my way to your place. Can you please guide me a bit?" I called up Pappu uncle asking for instructions.

"*Beta*, pleaje get down at Kirti Nagar metro stason and you come to Ford sowroom. I bill come there." Pappu uncle continued to slaughter the language!

I waited at the Ford sowroom, and then I saw a man hardly weighing half of the quintal on a Bajaj eterno coming towards me, barely managing to stop the vehicle as it looked heavier than him, helmet double the size of his head, "Rama?" he confirmed.

"Yes. Pappu uncle?" I confirmed.

"Yej. U hab helmet?" he asked.

"You did not ask me to bring it. I have towel, underwear and kurta pajama." I said and smiled.

"Ok, buy one." he said and pointed towards one of the helmet seller on the footpath; typical of our country where helmets are available for fifty rupees. I bought Stailbard! Mock of Steelbird.

And then the thin man powered all his skills to navigate the scooter with a heavy pillion, took a stop at one of the notary registrar office, who surprisingly was open on a Sunday! And the middleman Pappu uncle seemed to have links there! He barged straight into the office while signalling me to follow him. He said something to the guy typing documents and then turned towards me to interrogate.

"What ij your phather name?" He asked.

"What is this?" I was unaware.

"*Beta*, this ij aphidavid. You are habing no problem for krishanity." he said which I interpreted as my willingness to accept Christianity. That was hilarious; people go and get affidavits done for their acceptance to one religion without any undue influence. But, my acceptance was influenced by Mama. So, should I tell Pappu Uncle the reason for my conversion was something I contemplated! I also thought if he actually knew that I was the one who was selected for Smitha to get married to? If he did not, he was not to be blamed; he was just doing his duty or did Mama get certain commission to get people introduced to Christianity? And when it occurred that I was thinking illogically, I asked something more illogical.

"My father's name or Smitha's father name?"

"Bhaat?" he was amazed.

"Nothing, Mr. Narayanan." I answered.

"Your date ophh birthday." another one.

"28th Feb 1984" I said and asked, "Why is an affidavit needed uncle?"

He looked at me and smiled; probably, he admired my inquisitiveness or he expected the question. Gosh, I should have asked something else. "Compulsory for conberjan becauje Hindu group keep a check on thij thing. And they attack iph they come to know about Hinduj getting conberted."

"Why didn't you tell me before, I would have reported this to these Hindu activists. They would have taken Mama's case and my job would have become a bit easier" I thought but I said, "Correct. So, where do we go next?"

And then came the surprise of the day, a freaking one, if not for my low degree patience, I would have stoned Pappu uncle to death!

"*Beta*, be bill not go to Church today." he said casually and gave the affidavit for me to sign. And I only had fire within which I wanted to spit at him! However, the prudent was to ask him the reason for abandoning the process that day.

"Why uncle? What happened? It was happening today only?" I wanted to know the reason.

"*Beta*, today be bill complete the paper bork and I bill take you to dipherent church." he gave me stories, but the reason was missing.

"We had arrangement for mass conberjon today, however, the newj waj received by some hinduj, so, they hab surrounded the church to stop us." he talked about some riot like situation which got me excited as this was the only thing missing in my otherwise not so exciting love story!

And "Mass Conversion", you must be kidding me! He actually meant that there were few more idiots like me who had decided to resort to Christianity. Did that mean that most of the girls had mothers like Smitha's? But I failed to understand the concept of "Mass Conversion"! How can a certain set of people take pain to influence another set of people, get affidavits to justify what they are doing is correct, conceal everything from the other set of extremists who resort to vandalizing of the minority buildings as a sign of precaution! Religion as of today has become a way of life. I put a holy thread around my torso and need to have lived certain promises, but I don't. I am a frequent carnivore, smoker and a drinker! I am just a Hindu Brahmin by birth, but my actions don't approve. Similarly, what is the point in imposing a religion on somebody if he is accepting it half-heartedly? Look at me, I am an atheist, neither I knew god nor I knew any religion, but I was getting converted and keep on faking throughout my life that I love the religion which Smitha follows. The irony is that Mama was a post graduate in political science and was teaching Civics in a top rated school in Delhi before she retired or got thrown out.

And all the stories that Pappu uncle was taking extreme pain to do it specifically for me were bull shit. I began to swallow that there were many more middlemen like him under the name of a priest whose pay cheques depended solely on the number of conversions in a month. Like sales targets! Otherwise, who would be considerate enough to burn petrol? And this brought me to ponder that how could he expect me to roam around in underwear in front of the other applicants carrying affidavits along with underwear! It should have been labelled as mass ragging.

"But Uncle, I just have a day off. I have to report to office tomorrow. You will not understand that I have loads of work to do." I said. In fact, I meant that I had better jobs to do than him who just had to find goats for conversion! It did not make any difference to him if it was Sunday or Monday.

"But you bill hab to come tomorrow and be bill go to different church!" he crooned the same thing again.

What did he mean by a different church? Will it have a different paint or different interiors, the benches must be better there! The self-proclaimed protector and seller of the religion remained ignorant that if god was there, he was there everywhere. He did not ask people to mug up bible and vomit it on the questions papers maintained to judge ones understanding of the religion. Mama cleared exams of political science, did she practice it? How can a written exam ensure the interest and acceptance levels of the religion? Greats made religion and humans made rules!

"Be bill not go to Connaught Place Church, be bill go to Vikas Puri Church and I bill do your conberjon", he said. Ok, the middleman himself had licence to issue licences and was maintaining an office away from the knowledge of Hindu activists. I wanted to pass on the address to Hindu activists who would come and bash him up. But sadly, they would damage the institution which might have sheltered some innocents as well.

"I can't assure my availability to you tomorrow, you were supposed to help me out with this one today, we will see." I spoke to him just like I spoke to the middleman who got my licence. And I handed him over the helmet which he could use in future to tap more goats, boarded a bus and left for the den where I had kept my bag.

The middleman had few more traits; he had an impressive image with Mama's dumb head. He used it to spill negatives about me; he reported my misbehaviour and my disrespect for the religion.

Mama, with a regular frowning face opened the door for me and the balding Papa stuck to his chair looking at the proceedings. "Expected this from you!" and she left for the dialogue to build where I had to say, "Sorry Mama" and she would speak at length. But there was a change in the script, at least temporarily!

"Expected? What was expected?" I cited ignorance.

"You don't want to accept the religion and that was very much evident from your behaviour today. Pappu Uncle told us everything. He says that you disrespect the religion." Mama was best at complaining.

"When did I disrespect the religion or anybody Mama? Why don't you see that I travelled so far only for a day for this occasion?" I tried to make the empty head understand.

"See there is no compulsion for you to take up the religion"....."Oh! Is it?"

"You should accept Christianity only if you have pure faith in Jesus"..... "How can you expect that in a year's time?"

"It is only up to you to accept the religion, we are not forcing you"….. "So, does that mean you will get Smitha married to me if I don't get converted?"

"Yeah, but don't expect Smitha to get married to you if you don't get converted!"….. "Does not that amount to force and compulsion your highness?"

"Mama, when did I say that I won't get converted? The only problem is that I cannot extend my stay further, I am not supposed to take leaves during my training stint, I thought that things would get over today and I could join the office from tomorrow. But…" the script became real.

"So, you should not be complaining then, things do get here and there, you have to meet god, god will not meet u!"…... "I know that, I have been coming to meet you, you are not coming to meet me."

"And Pappu uncle was so much angry with you that he even said that he won't get someone converted who does not have faith and respect for god." Mama gave me horror stories.

"He is very strict and particular when it comes to religion. So, you should not be arguing with him."…….. "Everyone should be strict and particular about their job, of course, not me. My job is to chase your daughter. Fine, he was upset because his pay cheque was at stake because of one less goat in his basket this month."

"Ok, I will cancel the tickets and book a new one and inform my bosses (Pub and Factory), that I will report day after tomorrow." I said with a sunken heart.

The next day had more excitement in store for me, because I carried only one extra underwear which was required during the conversion. So, I had to repeat my underwear, repeat my clothes, and repeat the entire activity. The reason to carry underwear to the church was yet a mystery, probably I would be asked to swear on my underwear to do away with Hinduism, and it will be burnt.

Mystery was to unfold soon, when I turned up at the church. Church was a mystery itself, the address which was provided had a residential establishment, with a board "Beware of Dogs" I made rounds of the establishments, but was never convinced that it was the centre for conversion. So, I applied my neural science, thought that the address was wrong, therefore, went looking for the same building number. but in a different block but could not find any. Finally, got defeated and called up Pappu uncle who was eagerly waiting for his commission (That is me) at the stipulated address.

"Uncle, the address what you gave does not have a Church. It is some Kapoor's house. I saw the name plate at the gate." I informed Pappu uncle whom I called for directions.

"Yej Yej *beta*, that is the Church. The houje is of Kapoor. We hab taken it phor rent! So, come to the same plaje." He was giving me shocks, and a point to think. Place belonged to a Kapoor, and it had a Church.

So, the rented building was a lab, where conversion processes were being carried out under the banner Kapoor; which did not raise any eyebrows, hence was the safest bet!

And surprisingly there was no dog inside; however, it did shelter an old couple whom I thought to be Kapoors and said, "*Namaste* uncle", but I saw a cross hanging around the neck of the old lady and thought if the old couple was Kapoor of the yore and is now Cooper of the present!

I was thrown at the will of Pappu Uncle who had gained an upper hand by threatening Mama that he would abandon the conversion process. Hence, I was likely to fall to the antics which Pappu Uncle would resort to, he could settle his scores for my misbehaviour, it was his victory! He had a goat, his pay cheque was ensured, and he made me bow to him instead of the God!

He looked a bit rude, because he knew I was not running away, so, he could even strip me off if he wanted to! Did I say strip???

"*Beta*, take oph your clothej!" ordered Pappu uncle.

"Take off my clothes? Why? It is so cold!" I retaliated, when he reminded me that I had to wear *Kurta Pajama*.

"Take this oph and bear *Kurta Pajama*!"

"Ok. Where is the changing room?" I asked.

"There is no change room, go to the last of the church and there ij a pond there. You can do the changing and then coal us." Pappu uncle said.

I changed quickly, not because I was dying to get converted, because I wanted to get rid of this nonsense as soon as possible, and catch my flight. "Uncle I am done." I called for him, when the male part of Cooper said, "Why does he call you uncle? He should call you father."

I thought, "I had already instigated him sufficiently, why do you want to screw this up further? Why don't you do your own job oldie?" But I was scared if this old couple was somehow related to Mama, and my day would be nailed.

Pappu uncle seemed to ignore the uncalled for advice from the oldie Cooper and took out his weapons of conversion which included a wooden cross with beads, the holy bible and a small bottle with some liquid.

He asked me to climb the steps and stand near the small pond, and said, "Phold your handj phor the goad and listen to the phrayer! And bhen I say amen, you step into the bhater."

"What? How deep is it?" I knew how to swim but it was always good to be knowledgeable.

"Don't bhurry, it ij note bherry deep." and he took the bible in one hand, opened the chapter which he intended to read (he must have kept a bookmark, that is his daily job!) and held the cross and beads on the other hand and started reading something which I could understand barely.

"On this holy day of January!" he began when I for a second thought if it was holy day or a holiday!

I kept my hand folded kept on looking at the sun, recalling all the days I grew up as somebody else, my mother's holy chants shouting in my ears, the fight for the prasadams I had with Raghav, the compelled visit to the temples when slippers became more important than the god for me, the grown up me who would take Amma to the temple and would stand outside proving that I was an atheist, the belief in Bhagat Singh who said that the god created religion and religion divided people. All the thoughts were draining when I heard "Amen"…. "Amen", and louder "Amen" which brought me back to my senses and I submerged into the pool.

"That is the epphect of Jejuj! You bhur loast in him that you did not even relaije when I said Amen!" Pappu uncle day dreamt and I nodded my head sarcastically.

"Thij holy bhater….." He recited…(Holy Water? You actually called this algae ridden pond as holy? Nice, very nice)

"Thiy holy bhater bill clear all the sinj which he had done, Lord Jejuj pleaje phorgive him and take him in your armj today, shower the blessinj and the lub the way you hab been doing it on uj! Amen!" he completed and asked me to take a dip in the smelling pond. I thought underwater!

What sins did he talk about? He actually meant that all religions other than his were sinful! I did not think so and what did I do for which god was supposed to forgive me? Yes, god should have actually forgiven me for betraying my parents' trust! There is only ultimate power which has been showering blessings and love on every one, so, what is the need of conducting these dramas to prove that god was attending to Pappu Uncle's call only? There must be thousands of conversion going on in one part or the other, in one form or the other; Hindu to Muslim, Muslim to Hindu, Hindu to Christianity, Christianity to Muslim, so on and so forth! If God was one, was he listening to all the calls simultaneously and showering whatever he was asked to in one language or the other? Urdu, Hindi, English, Punjabi!

And then came the shattering moment of truth, Pappu uncle asked me to take of my kurta. And then he said, "Please take the thread off from your body and throw it."

I stood frozen in the water for a few minutes recouping from the reality, I never believed in the holy thread, but it had been a part of me for the last seventeen years and it had to be thrown away in a whisker! But, I had to take it off to be a part of Smitha's life. Everything from the childhood days flashed right in front of my eyes, there were tears which were hidden as my face was wet, and the droplets disguised the tears.

"Pleaje come here now" Pappu uncle asked me to come out of the water like a hot model in a bikini round. And then he placed the holy cross on my head and sprinkled the liquid from the bottle on me which ensured my acceptance for the religion. It did not matter if I actually accepted it or not, however, Pappu uncle's pay cheque got ensured.

The entire operation took not more than fifteen minutes, but, it did make me feel like in the middle of an exam which had maths, physics, chemistry, accounts and tax questions to be answered simultaneously!

Pappu uncle then showed some mercy, probably because I was a part of his force now, and said, "*Beta*, bhear your clothe quickly and change. It is bhery cold." And then I realized the secret of underwear and towel!

I wanted to ask Pappu uncle that why not he asked me to get new underwear as well along with kurta pajama! Is it that God does not bother about your basics? Is he also interested in the outer beauty? I smiled at my own questions, changed quickly, combed my hair and came out to say bye to Pappu uncle and Coopers, when Pappu Uncle threw the worst.

"*Beta*, This ij your certiphicate, pleaje sign thij. Read iph your name ij mensoned correctly! I bill process thij and gib it to Swami."

It read, "It is hereby declared that Rama Chandran Iyer, s/o Mr. Narayanan, has been bestowed with rights and duties of Christianity by the grace of our Lord Jesus. He will now be known as Rama Chandran Suzzanne!..............." And that was it, I was scandalized that not only my religion and life, I had lost my identity.

There you go Mr. Suzzanne, that ensures Smitha is yours!

20

Engagement

I decided not to flaunt my newly equipped surname, because, I was scared if people would start addressing me as Mr Suzanne! And a bouncer with such a name is like masturbating at the mirror! My horrendous stint at Mysore had come to an end, and I was moving to Gurgaon, the head office, where I would witness Tiger and all the serious looking men who obeyed his orders.

However, more than the Tiger and his disciples, I was sniggering at the possibility of staying at the Den again. Because, it would not only complicate relations but might trigger me to do murders. Therefore, to avoid being a murderer, I plotted a scenario which would make Mama say, "*Beta*, no need to stay here with us, better that you stay at the chummery."

Packing my bags with a screwed up impression, with memories of Shiva, I reached the airport thinking how drastically my life had changed in the past few months, but, I was content that I was able to do this much for Smitha, who otherwise had no courage but to sink this relationship!

I went straight to the den, where Mama welcomed the newly converted Christian boy with open arms and mutton, both of which I was repulsive to, and said, "*Beta*, now you are here, I hope that you will stay at one place for some time now. What sort of company is yours? They keep on transferring you here and there! And they don't pay so great as well."

I was slowly falling into a silent zone, where I had learnt to keep things within me, from an outrightly outspoken to someone who drank his thoughts was a journey with humps and bumps. I nodded to what Mama said and thought, "They are called stints and not transfers you dumb lady. And yes whatever I get paid will always be less if compared with Kelly and all those bastards you must have compared me with."

Instead, I said, "No Mama, I'll be here in Gurgaon for only four to five months and not more than that! Seriously, they keep on transferring me and pay is not that great! I completely agree with you, but what to do?"

"I have been asking you to apply in Papa's company, you don't do that. Please send your bio data to Papa, I am going to Saudi and I will speak to him." this was the only solution which Mama could suggest.

"No Mama, that is ok, I will get a good hike once my training stint is complete and I might get a permanent posting as well." I clarified and thought funnily, "No one sends bio data these days, it is CV or resume. Old fashioned!"

"So, I am leaving next week to Saudi to meet Papa and you would be staying here with Ranjan right?" Mama was quick in making her own decisions and quicker in imposing it on others.

And then came the plot which I had cultivated which would force Mama to speak what I wanted, "Mama, it is compulsory that I stay in the chummery, if I don't, I will not get the equivalent money component, but I have to pay tax on that, plus travelling from Delhi to Gurgaon is not really easy as the metro is yet to come. It will lead to lot of expenditure Mama" I said with lot of worry.

"And as it is you struggle to save." Even Mama's agreement had to take a dig at me!

"Yes, you are right." I agreed! "So, I'll move to the chummery tonight itself." few moments when I made decisions for myself!

"Ok, but you will come to see me off at the airport right?" I was confused if Mama requested or ordered, but I assumed it to be an order and said, "Of course Mama, what is there to ask?" (I am always open to throw the garbage out of the country!)

At the airport, Mama waited for me, when I had to screw up my lovely Sunday morning to travel by a strange mode of transport hardly found anywhere in the country. You have to chase the mode of transport, fight for the survival, kick a few, punch a few, bit of gymnastics, step on somebody's feet, a strong glare, and then stuff yourself in, when somebody would come and say, "Make some space." The strange mode of transport is "Call Centre Cabs" which ply between Delhi and Gurgaon, and over smart drivers make money by using the vacant vehicles for their advantage.

Mama was ferociously staring at me when I fought the crowd to mend my ways towards her! And said while catching some breath, "I am sorry Mama, got a little late. Transport is a mess here."

Mama said in hushed tone, "I know what a mess here is! Anyways, pick up this suitcase and put this on the trolley." the second part was powerful.

I picked up the suitcase and asked, "Where is Ranjan?" I understand the time selection of the question was undoubtedly provocative.

"Why do you need Ranjan? Can't you pick up the suitcase?" Mama was imperative!

"No Mama, I did not ask for that. I will pick up the suitcase, I was just looking for him." I clarified.

"He has gone to check the gate number." she said perkily and Ranjan emerged suddenly and snatched the trolley from me and said, "Bro, hang on, I'll take the trolley." and I looked at Mama who still had airs about something. Going abroad probably gets on to a few.

"So, Mama, when will you be back?" I asked casually to analyse how long Ranjan and me could breathe freely.

"We will come to Bangalore in March and…." She said and I intervened to say, "Oh that is superb, amazing. Then you can probably come down to my place and meet my parents as well."

"Hmmm. Guddu's cousin is getting married in Bangalore. The guy works in Australia, he is a CA." Mama told me the unwanted, she stressed on Australia! I knew what she meant!

"Ok, so you will be coming for the wedding. That is great!" I said without reacting much.

"Yeah, we are yet to get the tickets booked, I will speak to Papa and will let you know." she said as she entered the terminal. And at that moment, I wished if India and Saudi get into a war and all the traffic stops between the two forever.

Ranjan's eagerness to send Mama packing was elaborated when he held me by neck and started jumping up and down shouting, "Beer Beer Beer Beer!" and we drove straight to a wine shop which helped us stock up for the day!

Since Mama had thrown enough hints, I wanted to prepare for the best. And any preparation could have been just better had it not had either Mama's or Smitha's inputs. So, inevitable that I did not fly to Hyderabad!

"Baby, I am sure Mama and Papa have decided to get us engaged by March, Mama was telling me that she would be coming to Bangalore in March to attend some wedding." I told Smitha over a call.

"Yeah, even she was telling me that she has plans to go to Bangalore. Things will become really awesome! And Yay, finally we will marry. Muah!" Smitha was over joyed at the fact.

"So, I wanted to buy a ring which I could make you wear then. When should I come there?" I was romantically high, "We will select together right?" and the romance continued.

"Oh my baby! That is so cute, you can come this weekend." Smitha confirmed it too.

The weekend listed a big bash for me, where I would become poorer by a considerable margin! The flight tickets to Hyderabad and a ring obviously made up the bill, but, the ancillary materials accompanying the ring would be more annoying! I thought so, but the top of the world feeling to have finally won Smitha had encouraged me to cross all boundaries and do whatever it took to keep on making Smitha smile.

We looked for the best place, where Smitha could shop. It was important that Smitha understood how much I loved her, she kept on pointing what she wanted, and I kept on buying!

Shoes, perfumes, this dress, that dress, this jeans, that jeans, junk jewellery, good jewellery, perfumes and finally came the moment which I eagerly waited for when Smitha said, "Let's go and buy a ring baby!" Probably Smitha, on Mama's standing instruction checked my propensity to spend! And boy, I did not disappoint her. I had already spent close to fifty thousand on tickets and the unwanted shopping.

But this sealed the fate; I was buying a ring which I would slide into Smitha's fingers, which would connect the two souls, which would mean that Smitha would be mine forever, which would mean that I could die happily, which would mean that I was able to stick to my commitment, which would ensure my service towards her till world existed! A ring with so many implications had to be a special one! Something which would bring a smile on Smitha's face whenever she saw it.

A premium jewellery showroom was graced by our visit, where I wanted Smitha to spot her best and place her interest, and I would shoulder to complete it. After a series of rejections, half-hearted interests, pick and drop, elevators, escalators, stairs, finally the wagon stopped at an unconventional ring which I could not trace to any of the culture, not to any religion, and not to any fashion sense. But, Smitha had an unusual taste, and said, "Sweeties, I think I'll buy this one, check this out, this is really different." She pointed on the glass surface under which the ring was kept. Her eyes clearly lit up as seen on the image on the glass.

I could not understand what drew Smitha's interest into the ring, for me, it was the most irritating design I had ever seen. However, I believed in my ignorance towards the fashion and gave way for Smitha's interest. And when I looked for the sales girl who would sport the same smile which Dipti did on our day of joining, Smitha did what I was designated to.

"Baby, this is really costly, almost 75k, no no, let's go, we will buy something else." And Smitha started walking as the sales girl came towards us. I held Smitha by her elbow and got her back for two reasons,

First, it takes a kick on impractical male ego when her lady thinks him to be a pauper in front of another lady (sales girl in this case), second, this was Smitha's interest and I had done enough ass rubbing to be in a position to afford what she liked. I had a statement to make to her mom.

"No, come on, it's ok. We get married only once in our life, and we get engaged only in our life." I picked up a line from a Shahrukh Khan's film, good enough to impress Smitha! And continued, "If not you, whom will I spend for? Come on, try it." And turned towards Khushi, the sales girl! That is what the name badge read and I assumed it was her name.

Sales girl showed her entire teeth packet, and spiced up the cheesy lines mouthed by me, "Exactly Mam, you should be thankful to god that you got such a nice husband." and smiled further, when Smitha said, "We are not married yet."

Khushi said, "That is ok, you will sooner! But it is absolutely pleasure to have such a fiancé, I wish I had one like him, you are lucky mam." And I looked at Smitha's response to the unwanted admiration! I wanted Khushi to shut up as this might have triggered Smitha's anger towards her and doubt if I knew Khushi beforehand! However, it was necessary that Smitha realized the importance of a donkey like me which Khushi did easily.

Smitha tried the ring, and somehow, I felt that the strange looking ornament was specially designed keeping her finger in mind, it fit her perfectly without any alteration! I gave my card to Khushi to swipe it and debit my account by another 75k. And I looked at Smitha, who had her eyes fixed on another ring! And before she changed her mind, I said, "Khushi, can this be done quickly? We have to leave!" and Khushi replied, "Sure sir, just packing it." and handed over the packet to Smitha, card and counterfoil to me to sign and said, "There you go mam, wish you a happy married life!" and Smitha smiled.

Everything we bought that day other than the ring had to find its possession with Smitha, I had decided to carry the ring with me and bring it out on the day of engagement.

I was poor by one lakh fifty thousand by the time I returned to Delhi, but I knew I would not have to explain this as this was purely spent on those who questioned me. But, amidst all the high voltage romance and the excitement to get engaged, I forgot that I had gone poor before fixing the date of engagement. Therefore, the next step was to ask Mama that when were they planning to come down to Bangalore.

I had decided that I would not make international calls and would speak to Mama Papa only when they called up. When Mama called up once, I had to ask her, "Mama you said that you would be coming to Bangalore in March. It would be great if you could tell me the exact dates, so that I can fix this up at home and do necessary arrangements."

"*Beta*, the marriage is on March 9th. We will take a direct flight from here and reach Bangalore on 8th early morning." Mama said.

"Early morning? By 5 or something?" I confirmed.

"By 2.30 in the morning." she said.

"Ok that is fine; I'll come with Raghav to pick you up from the airport." I offered assistance.

"Also, *beta* arrange for a hotel as well." she ordered.

"Ok Mama, I'll take care of that." I said.

"One more thing, you keep yourself free on 9th and attend the wedding. We will get you introduced to our family." Mama said and I was satisfied that nothing would go wrong from there on. It was just a matter of time then.

"So Mama you will meet my parents on 8th? Do you want the meeting to be organized in a hotel or will you come to our home?" I asked for guidance.

"Of course at your home!" Mama said and took a soft shot, "We also need to see what kind of family is yours."

"Great Mama, I'll inform my family then." I said and disconnected.

So, 8th March was the day, and the way things had evolved, my parents hardly had any say! They just needed to be informed that the day of my engagement has been filed and they should stick to it.

"Amma, Smitha's parents are coming to Bangalore on 8th and they would like to meet you to fix up the wedding date and other details." I called up Amma and unveiled in a shameful manner.

"Oh! That is really great. Is Smitha coming along?" Mama asked a strange question. I could not understand it.

"Yes Amma, of course, she is coming." I said a bit hesitantly, still thinking what made her ask that.

Then answered myself, and said "Ok, you have not seen Smitha right? Don't worry, she is coming."

Amma gave me a grounding shock, "She has to come, and it is your engagement! How can you be such an idiot?"

"So, things will be organized at home itself? Will they be able to adjust here? Or if the venue is decided, please let us know!" Amma picked up sarcasm!

"No, Amma, please understand. I have already done enough running around to get Smitha's family on board. I have no energy left to get into another round of persuasion. I always thought that you support me in whatever I do, one last time, I need you to pull this one off. Please Amma. Please support!" This was the only level of persuasion and respect my mother commanded, and this was enough for her to get convinced.

"Ok, Relax Rama. We will do this. They are coming on 8th right? And you on 7th?" Amma had a plan it seems.

"Yeah but why are you asking like this?" I was curious.

"I will make some amazing delicacies, and we will decorate the home when you are here. Ok, happy now?" Amma smiled; it was evident from her speech.

"Love you Amma!" I said and disconnected.

So, I could fold my hands, broaden my shoulders, and hold my head high! And Smile at the sky and say, "Here I come" I had done a brilliant job by taking extreme, drastic and yet crucial steps to get this one working! I had to buy the decisions which were imposed on me, own them and finally sell them again to get everyone on the leveller. Smitha's family had been pocketed, and so was mine! It was a victory of sorts, even when I had lost a lot. It was up to Smitha and me now to sail the ship, face each other and enjoy the voyage.

I informed my boss, who had become a good friend in a month's time. Informed him not only about my engagement, but also about the heroics I had undertaken to make it true!

On 6th March, the Friday, when I was leaving the office to catch the flight, my boss said, "All the best man and have a safe flight!"

I packed my bag, ensured that I carried every small thing which was important including the certificate of conversion as well, the intimidation was showing on me as I checked the same bag repeatedly for the same thing. While I kept everything in the bag, I pocketed the ring in my jacket! I combed my hair multiple times! I shaved not once, not twice, but thrice not leaving a mm of hair on my face! I did not take bath, I dry cleaned myself!.

While I continued my acts of idiosyncrasy, Ranjan, who witnessed it, intervened to say, "Bro, it is not that Mama and Papa are going to see you for the first time. Plus, the big day is day after tomorrow; you will have to repeat this entire session day after. Stop being psyche about this. And Relax! Let's go. You are looking good and you know that, I know that and Smitha knows that as well!"

Now, you must be wondering if Ranjan and me were travelling together, here is a small surprise, he was asked not to attend the engagement as it had nothing in store for him supposedly. Buy that? Therefore, the brother in law decided to see me off at the airport if not anything else. So, he came down to the chummery to pick me up.

"Come on, take your tickets and lets go", he said while he picked my bag. And I followed him.

I did look extra clean, extra good and sounded extra sophisticated at the airport; my English automatically notched up a point higher. I realized that I was damn impressive when I was consciously moving. The hot chick who happened to sit next to me at the plane hit on me prolifically, which three years ago would have seen a positive response from me, but not anymore as I was headed to lock my love, my girl!

At Bangalore airport, Raghav picked me up. His grim face had written all over it that he was fucking burning from inside for what I had done! If his will allowed him, he would have thrown me out of the running car! But he kept on driving and I spoke at length, trying to justify my actions, and I only looked stupid! Raghav's only question threw me in a silent zone, "Are you sure that you will remain happy with this girl whose mom interferes more than she does? Relation in which mother's poke their nose unnecessarily doesn't work. Anyways, good that you brought it so far, now stick to it." And I began to think hard about it till we reached home, exchanging couple of smokes on the way.

Everyone tried to be normal at home, but they were bad actors, I was aware that I had sent a negative energy in the family, which left their minds animated, while their faces trying to be non-animated. I started to feel the formality I was subjected to for which I was largely responsible.

I was served water, when I would barge into the kitchen to dampen my throat!

I was served tea, when I would take off my shirt and shout, "Amma Chai!"

I remained seated without changing, when the first thing I would do is to change my costumes to boxers!

I sat on sofa, when I would spread myself on the bed.

I did not pick up the remote, when my hobby was to flip channels without stopping at one.

I could not help the detachment which began to evolve; drifting from the family of parents to the family of parents in law was not very soothing. Since I could feel the sense of disownment, it was eventually left to Smitha to be my backbone and take care of me. I had done enough to get this going, now it was Smitha's turn to subtly take me through the period of screws getting loosened.

Not only my family would gear up for the engagement, I decided that I have to lend a helping hand as much as possible to make the occasion a success.

7th March 2009

I could not help in the kitchen, but I could arrange for the kitchen operations. "Amma, please tell me what all is required from the market, I will go and buy it." Amma gave me a list with which I rushed to the market and ensured everything was put in the basket and payment be made from my pocket only. I did not know if Raghav would have appreciated such thoughts, but I did not want to take any chance.

Once back from the market and knowing what a cleanliness freak Mama was, I assured that I personally put an effort to clean the house, to put things in order even when they were in order, rearrange the sofa cushion, rearrange the bed cushion and rearrange everything which as per Amma's understanding were in order, but I knew Mama, I did not want her to give any bait for her to do anything which would make my parents go wary about this association. Amma could easily understand that I was just not myself and something continued to dribble me and said, "Do you think that house needs to be in order?" and looked at Geeta.

Geeta, by far was the most supportive in my decision! She was from a different school who believed that come what may, relations need to be lived and lived strongly! She put her heart and soul to make this one click, she said something to Raghav and both of them walked out of the home. During this period, I kept on looking at the tiles on the floor, Amma asked, "Now what is wrong with the tiles?" I guess Amma knew the answer, still, I made it a point to be expressive, "Amma there is nothing wrong with the tiles, but the gap between tiles, I mean the borders have got lot of dirt stuck in them."

Amma was quick to reply, "Clean it then."

"Should I use Acid?" I confirmed and Amma looked with an emotionless face, which meant, "Do whatever you want to! If possible, put some acid on your brain as well to clean it!"

I got a bucket from the bathroom with water, added detergent, and then added some Lizol and two caps of Domex! This recipe was splashed on the floor, and allowed the recipe to take its own path and move to the extreme corners. While the solution made its way through the tiles, I got a bottle of hydrochloric acid, made a hole on the cap, and sprayed it very artistically on the edges of the tiles. Mama was right to think that I was a part of housekeeping in my office.

Once the acid started boiling, small traces of mud and dust expanded and popped out. I always liked this sight as a kid, but doing it was a different emotion; then I arranged for a long copper wire from the store room to scratch the mud and dust out of the gaps. With 2 bed rooms, 1 kitchen and a massive living room, my knees were tested and so were my ankles and my toes. I continued to sit to make the copper wire do the talking, slipped a couple of times on the soap water, and burnt my finger with drops of acid, but as my nature goes, I did not leave a single stone unturned and cleaned the floors. And I wish I had taken a before and after picture, the same could have been an easy entrant to Domex, Lizol and other floor cleaners'commericals!

After I finished the housekeeping job, Raghav and Geeta walked in with some huge bags, which I opened in anxiety when Raghav said, "First go and take bath, you are smelling of some irritating chemicals. I feel like puking." I sensed a huge dose of sarcasm in that.

One had to praise Geeta's sense of aesthetics, I believed Mama possessed a terrific sense of order, but I was confident Geeta was going to give her a run for her money. It is an eternal fact that South Indians have the most messed up home, you give them a palace, and they will give you a pigeon house! What sort of interior designing advocates a mop, broom, underwear and dustbin at a balcony, what sort of interior designing encourages clothes hanging on the door, and a wooden bed accompanying a plastic chair set. Ask the Southies, they will tell you how!

But Geeta excelled in this field, non-typical of a southie! She got pots and flowers which remained in the car and the bag what she carried had curtains. Again typical of a woman, she opened the bag, spread the curtains as layers on her shoulders with a perfect colour combination and started discussing them with Amma. I looked at Raghav who hardly had any clue of what was going on and I recalled the day when I went shopping with Mama and Smitha to Sarojini Nagar market!

Raghav threw the car keys at me and said, "Go get the flowers and pots from the car." I kept on looking at him, because this was not the Raghav I knew, he would support me in every inch of my decisions, but, this was self-invited. It was expected and it was accepted.

After a long day of SUPW activities, I ensured that I had played myself in to be a part as used to be before. To lighten the grim atmosphere at home, I proposed for dinner and Geeta was the first one to take it to the next level by behaving like a child who had never tasted food outside. I understood her gesture, she want to solidify what was going liquid.

"Yeah, Yeah, we will go to Chandini Chowk" she jumped up and down shaking Amma's left hand a little wildly.

"Back to Delhi again?" I tried to crack a joke.

"You Loose! Chandini Chowk is a restaurant here. They serve good North Indian stuff." Raghav intervened without understanding the joke. Amid all the seriousness, he lost his sense of humour.

"So, that is open till late night, we can probably do the curtains now. What do you say Amma?" Geeta wanted to utilise the time in the best possible manner. Even though the question was directed at Amma, it ultimately boiled down to the men of the family to do all the juggling. It is only the idea of beautification which would strike women; they need men to execute them.

I removed all the old curtains, which were pretty as per my standards, threw them in the washing machine for future use. By that time, Geeta had pinned the curtains in a sequence, in the middle was a thin transparent liner, at the two sides were orange and red sheets, thus giving a picturesque view to the arrangement. This was exactly in line with what I had seen at Smitha's home, and I thought, "How all women can think alike!" when Geeta told Amma, "This kind of combination is quite popular now a days!" and I wondered, "What if someone wore a shirt like that?"

Once the royal look to the home was completed, the family proceeded for dinner; it was an unusual truth that it was always me who donned the driver's cap when the entire family went out. Could be for the fact that I was the one who taught Raghav to drive! But will this driver family relation exist forever when I buy a SUV lurked in my mind as a thick question mark when the engine got ignited.

The restaurant lured me to its fullest, and my imagination unrolled. The legacy of kebabs to the beauty of tandoor, the swirl of Mughals to the richness of Punjab! I wondered how a mouth-watering tandoori chicken would taste there with a green chutney and how delicious would be butter naans with chicken tikkas! I looked at Geeta and asked, "Have you guys been here before?" speculating by their faces that they knew how yummy non veg was served there! Raghav said, "Yes, only me and Geeta!" which meant "Yes, we have eaten non veg here and it is awesome and we are sorry that you will be deprived of it today as Amma and Appa are with us."

I forewent the fortunate chicken and said, "I will savour myself with veg today, which should be equally good." When it was vegetarian, I allowed everyone except me to decide what one would eat! And when it was non vegetarian, it would be Smitha who would decide what we should eat! (So, when did I decide what would I eat? It did not make a difference to anyone!)

For starters, chicken tikka was replaced by paneer tikka, chicken manchurian was replaced by gobi manchurian!

For beverages, whisky and soda was replaced by lemon soda.

For main course, butter chicken was replaced by shahi paneer, dal remained as dal, keema parantha was replaced by butter garlic naan, chicken fried rice was replaced by veg pulao!

The above replacements remained successful to entertain my taste buds and lighten the mood of the anger ridden family members. While the group enjoyed the dinner, Geeta reminded everyone, "What time you guys have to reach the airport?" and I looked at Raghav whose face said, "Why do you want to drag me into this?" but he actually said, "2.30 we have to be there I guess! What Rama?" and I acted absolutely unaware and said, "Yeah, yes, right, correct!" and I looked nothing but stupid.

"So, let's wrap up fast, it is already 11, you guys will have to drop us back and then go to the airport." Geeta was the most sensible, at least on that day!

"And this new airport, my god, is so far, almost takes a couple of hours." I added and everyone looked at me. I did not know why.

We wrapped up everything and I ensured that the bill was directed to me, therefore, I occupied the aisle seat, facing the counter, "Here is your cheque sir!" I looked at the waiter and it reminded me of my bouncing days.

I placed my card in the diary, which would have a bill, and gave it back to the waiter, when Raghav asked, "How much is the bill?", and before I could answer, Geeta hammered a brilliant one, "Why do you want to know? Rama is treating us, you enjoy! It is probably for the first time he has treated us after getting a job."

Waiter returned with the counter copy and card, and I said, "Let's go!" after signing the merchant copy.

8th March 2009

It was 12 by the time we dropped everyone at home, without waiting for a second, we turned around, and headed to the airport! The relation between me and Raghav had taken a serious beating, which was reduced to only sharing a smoke. The erstwhile communication would include everything from cricket to politics to movies to the hottest chick in the community.

I tried to understand what crime I had done to be at the receiving end. I thought of sharing it with Om by messaging him, but realized, that it had been more than 6 months I spoke to him. Checked the option of sharing it with Sri, whom I spoke to almost a year back. And I clearly remembered that it were they who called up to initiate the communication, but I was engulfed so much with Smitha, that I had lost my friends in the process. They also left messages on Facebook, but I did not remember what made me not reply to them. Probably, what I was doing to be a part of Smitha was embarrassing that it was proscribed to even share that with best friends.

I did not want to lose Raghav, I loved him, he was my hero and my idol. I had grown up all my life copying his style, copying what he ate, copying the deodorants he used! The best was my signature which was derived from his and it did not look much different. And I started clarifying to Raghav, "This is something which I have fallen into, it has got nothing to do with Smitha, she is very sweet and supports me in every bit of it. It is only that her mother is creating problems, and since Smitha does not have guts to stand up against her, I am taking the responsibility of pulling it off. Her mom has tried enough to create hindrances, but I have crossed all of them to bring it so far. You will never understand the trauma, the efforts I have gone through, I don't want to complain, but I don't want to be a pain as well to anybody. It feels immense shame to stand up in front of the mirror; you have been there always, even when Manni and Sunny used to pull my leg, you used to beat them up! Please, please Raghav! I don't want to lose anyone of you, so, please stop behaving the way you guys have been."

And I lit up a smoke. (Manni and Sunny were our neighbours in Delhi who called us Bengalis).

Raghav patted my back and said, "Chill, we will do this! Geeta has been telling me to support you." and he snatched the fag from me, tapped the ash, took a drag, and asked, "Have you booked their hotel?" and smiled.

"Yes" I said and looked at my watch, it was 2.40, and I said, "I think the flight has arrived. Let's go to the gate."

I saw Mama Papa, with their patented king size suitcases! I wanted to know the idea behind such massive carrying equipment, Raghav looked surprised as well and I hushed in his ears and said, "Ignore" and he smiled.

What followed was non understandable by a normal human brain, it seemed that the world had changed and so had people! Mama not only hugged me, she pounced on Raghav as well, and Papa shook hands with me and shook both hands with Raghav.

This entire act of affection sent Raghav on a track against me, he looked at me thinking that all the stories I had built about Smitha's family was fake; they were so good, so respectful that they even bothered to show that to Raghav! Raghav became a good boy, a sudden transformation from an anti Smitha campaign to pro Smitha's parents' campaign.

"Aunty, I have an Alto, and I think all of us will not be able to accommodate in one car with the luggage, so, please wait here till I arrange a taxi. Rama and Mama can come in the cab, and I and you will go in my car sir, if that is ok?" Raghav unleashed a series of manners and sophisticated talk. I was going bonkers!

I was thrown in a Mahindra Logan with Mama, Papa joined Raghav; both of them happened to discuss some serious topics like world politics! The cab driver followed Raghav's car straight to Basvanagudi where the wedding was scheduled.

"Aunty, I hope you like the hotel, this was the best I could find which was close to the venue." Raghav lied blatantly, Papa continued to fill in the details, and I held Raghav by his shoulder and took him out of the reception, when Mama asked, "What happened?"

My presence of mind said, "Nothing, we forgot to lock the car, will be back in like two minutes." and we rushed out.

"What the fuck? When did you book the hotel for them? Dude, it was me who booked it for them from Delhi! And now you are asking them as if it was you who booked it. What are you up to?" I did not understand Raghav's intentions.

"You wanted me to stand by you and I am trying my best to impress them. So, leave it on me, you have done what you had to!" he said and messed up my hair with his palm and said, "Let's go!"

The moment Mama entered the hotel room; she asked Papa, "Swami, can you check the toilet?" and my brother looked horrified, to which Mama said, "I can't stay at a place where the toilet is not clean." with pride!

Raghav's reply on any other day, "Do you plan to sleep in the toilet or is that if the toilet is not clean, you will check out? Brilliant, what about the money you have already paid, if that was the case, you should have checked the toilets before checking in!"

But that day he said, "Absolutely correct aunty, cleaner the toilet, cleaner is the place! Perfect" and he stopped Papa, "Uncle, you please sit, I'll check!" and he opened the toilet door and said, "See aunty, it is very clean" and Mama smiled..

By the time things got settled down, it was 5 am, when Raghav said, "We will order for some tea now aunty, and then we will leave to pick Smitha from the bus stop, why don't we call her and find out where has she reached?" (Smitha was coming by bus from Hyderabad to Bangalore)

Raghav turned to me and said, "Call her and find out where she has reached."

"Hi, where have you reached?" I called up Smitha.

"Don't know, looks like Bangalore airport, driver says that we would reach in an hour's time probably." Smitha said.

"Ok" I said and disconnected and informed everyone, "She will reach the bus stop in an hour."

"It is not really safe early in the morning; we should not allow her to wait for us at the bus stand. I shall arrange tea for you and we will leave to pick Smitha. I am sure that is ok aunty?" Raghav continued his act of impressions!

Mama could not say no to Raghav's proposal, we arranged tea for them and headed to the bus stand. In fact, we were able to smoke before Smitha arrived. Smitha hugged me and shook hands with Raghav and said, "Hello *Bhaiya*!" Three of us moved towards the car, while I carried another suitcase, which was slightly smaller.

It was 6.30, when we reached hotel again, Smitha hugged Mama vigorously and Raghav was stunned, I looked at him and whispered, "They are like that only. Ignore!"

I remember that in the past forty eight hours, I had slept only for six hours, my eyes were red, they were swollen and pimples created havoc on my face, stomach disturbance followed as well! The effects of lack of sleep were visible on Raghav's face as well, which said, "Give me a plain surface to lie down, I'll doze off and wake up tomorrow."

I said, "Mama, I think we should leave now. It is time that you also take some rest. And we will also go home and sleep." but Mama disagreed, "No, no *beta*, you will have to have breakfast with us."

Before I turned down the offer because of no tooth brush, Raghav said, "Sure aunty, there can be nothing better than this to start a Sunday!" and called up the room service, ordering idli, vada, and dosa!

It was 8 when we finished breakfast and were loaded with sleep; still we made a valiant effort to move our ass to the car. But, the sleep was not enormous to let Raghav forget his last weapon in his armoury of manners, "Aunty and Uncle, on behalf my entire family, Amma, Appa and Geeta, I invite you to come to our place this afternoon! Thank you!" and he folded hands.

Mama smiled, Papa smiled and so did Smitha, we also smiled and drove the car straight home, and without waiting for a second, crashed into the bed! Bangalore's snarled traffic took us more than an hour to reach home.

And before we could complete our share of sleep. the noise of the vessels, the chopping of the vegetables, the batter making, the whistle of the cooker broke into our minds and we got up. Raghav shouted, "Geeta, what is the time?" (This was Raghav's peculiar quality; as kids, when Appa, like any other South Indian daddy, would wake us up at 4.30 in the morning to study, Raghav would still slip his limbs into the quilt, would hit me with his elbow and ask me to flip pages for him! Why couldn't he pick up the phone lying next to him and see the time? What was the need to make Geeta run around for his fancies?)

"Its 12, you guys should get up now and help us!" Geeta answered his query and sent one for him to obey. He quickly came out of the bed and went to the wash basin to pick up his tooth brush. I kept on looking at him and told myself, "Dude, how wrong are you in obeying Smitha's orders? Everyone does that, I am not unique, and it is just the degree which varies!" and I smiled to come out of bed to take out my tooth brush as well.

After sipping on the tea, munching on the biscuits, I could not stop myself from entering the kitchen and examine the situation, which, of course Amma and Geeta were best at! After dropping the tea tumbler in the kitchen sink, I turned to open the lid of the vessel kept on stove. I used my index finger's nail to push the lid, the steam made its way out to deny any vision as it got spread on my glasses. I cleaned my glass and then used my sense of smell instead of vision to appreciate the boiling sambhar! No one could beat Amma in making sambhar; she held a doctorate on sambhar!

The other burner was at Geeta's behest which processed kesri which is halwa for North Indians! "Oh, great job Geeta" I said!

"Amma's instructions!" Geeta confirmed.

"What else do we have in the menu?" I asked and Geeta took guard to answer.

"We have daal vada, medu vada, onion chutney, coconut chutney, sambhar, appam and kesri." and she looked for appreciation!

"Awesome, can I get to taste?" I requested and Amma intervened, "Yes, take some sambhar; we will make vadas half an hour before they come so that they could be served hot!" I acted on Amma's orders, passed on some sambhar to a bowl to enjoy when Geeta added, "Take kesri as well, my preparation." and I smiled at the small things women compete for! Kesri vs Sambhar!

House was perfect, curtains were magical, and the show pieces shined to the brightest, glass surfaces looked thoroughly transparent! I was shaved neatly, dressed well in a T shirt and jeans, Appa wore a nice clean veshti (Dhoti for North Indians, which they think is the only attire worn in South India) and a grey shirt, Raghav wore a kurta and jeans, Geeta decked herself up in a blue sari which I gifted on her last anniversary, Amma pulled out her best Kanjivaram to flaunt.

I was roughly one hour away from sliding the ring on Smitha's finger; I eagerly waited for that moment. It was 2.30. They were expected by 3.

Amma and Geeta took charge of the kitchen, vadas were due! I thought of calling Smitha to find out where they had reached.

The call was the first in the chain reaction, which would turn out to be powerful than the one happening in nuclear reactors.

"Hi, have you started from the hotel?" I confirmed.

"No, I am not coming." Smitha said casually, as if I knew everything about it.

"What? Are you nuts?" I began to lose my temper, I had to, and there was nothing which would boost me to hold my patience, I continued, "Where did this come from? Was this planned? You can't be serious! I mean that we went shopping together, we bought a ring as well, who will wear it now? What the fuck? Where is Mama?" I began to disintegrate.

"Listen, I cannot do anything, Mama asked me not to come." Smitha began to justify the unjustified.

"Please give the phone to Mama, What are you guys up to?" I was screaming, and did not realize that it drew Raghav.

"Mama Papa have already left to your place, I am alone at the hotel." Smitha said emotionlessly.

I disconnected and dialled Mama's number, my hands trembled and Raghav was artistic in holding my trembling hands, snatched the phone from me and disconnected, asked, "What happened?"

I looked down straight on the road from our third floor balcony, felt like jumping, then stammered to say, "Smitha is not coming!", closed my eyes tightly and bowed my head down and a tear dropped on the floor which was washed with acid!

"What will I tell Amma? I am dead" I banged my palm on my forehead, kept one hand on my waist and looked on!

Raghav, kept his hand on my shoulder, slipped quickly into big brother's responsible shoes and said, "Now call, let Amma speak, relax, you are not alone, we all are with you!" he held me by my waist, rubbed his hand on my back to console me, took me straight to Amma, and narrated everything to her in one go.

I dialled Mama's number, and gave the phone to Amma! For the first time, two headstrong women, from different schools of thought, with diagonal outlook towards life were going to lock horns, and I was expecting only and only fireworks.

"Hello! Is that Smitha's mother?" Amma said in a manner in which I never saw her, she was animating to be really sweet.

"Yes." I heard Mama, the speaker was on.

"This is Rama's mother. How are you doing?" Amma asked, and everyone was glued to the phone like it was a cricket commentary!

"Yes, tell me." Mama sounded absolutely out of etiquettes, she conducted herself as a lady of the land, but that attitude was fine with me, not with my mother. Amma rejected the impolite behaviour and continued.

"Where you people have reached?" Amma asked with concern, genuine or not, I did not know!

"Don't know where are we!" came another rude one from Mama, Amma chose not to respond to this either. I felt like a batsman at 99 on the non-striker end seeing the number eleven playing through the entire over of fast bowling!

"Rama told me that Smitha is not coming." Amma decided not to please the rude lady and talked business!

"Yes, she is not coming!" Mama sounded as if she was doing a favour, Amma allowed this one to let go as well! And looked at me, Geeta held Amma's wrist, a sign of asking somebody to calm down.

One thing I noticed while Mama spoke was that I could not hear any noise of traffic in the background; I began to speculate that if they were actually travelling! "Kill the nonsense, can't get worse now!" I told myself!

"What happened? Why is she not coming? Is she not well?" Amma displayed her multiple questions asking abilities, yet again!

"Nothing, actually we don't go on displaying our daughter before marriage, in fact, it is not good that we bring our daughter to your place! Not pleasing you see!" Mama was at her illogical best, Amma was at her losing best! Was she? No, she filed another suggestion.

"If that was the case, then we should have met at some hotel or a restaurant over a lunch." Amma struck prudence.

"No, that is fine. But why are you so hell bent to see Smitha? Let me tell you clearly, she is far better than your son on every scale; you don't have to really check her! Your son has chosen her, so, we will not let you judge our daughter. It was his call." Mama displayed three personalities in one go, "Stupidity, Arrogance, and Sneakiness" which were enough for my mother to turn the heat on!

I lost my temper, and was about to burst my anger, "What the………" and Raghav closed my mouth and dragged me out of there, and said, "Gone crazy? Hang on, Amma will handle this. You are messing it up!"

We stood at a distance, but could hear the ladies talk. Mama said, "So, there is no point we get Smitha to your place."

"How can you talk like that? You have examined Rama in every manner; I am just saying that all of us want to see your daughter. Where does this scanning and judging come from? He has even stayed with you for 4 months; you have checked him to your satisfaction, and there is nothing wrong if we want to see your daughter! We have all the rights to see whom our son in planning to marry. Plus, why are you pressing on the fact that your daughter is better than Rama on every scale, if that was the case why did you give him a go ahead? This is insane!" Amma made pure sense, I closed my eyes in horror as this was the dynamite on all the hard work I did.

"Anyhow, let us not discuss this over the phone, we will discuss once you are here, please call Raghav or Rama, they will come to pick you up at the HAL, old airport entrance!" Amma shifted gears to controlled emotions and got this one to roll back into her court and disconnected.

The atmosphere turned unattractive, I did not want to be a part of it, and remained shattered on sofa, while Geeta held my hand and sat next to me. Raghav waited for their call, Appa looked silently dejected, Amma looked silently fuming!

It was 3.30, nobody had called, and therefore, Raghav decided to call Mama and find their whereabouts, Mama's phone was switched off! He called her repeatedly, the phone continued to be off. The switched off phone was not only disturbing, but raised doubts on their credibility. Raghav asked for Smitha's number, and called her repeatedly, she would not answer the call either.

The kesri, the sambhar, the vadas and the chutney smiled at their fate, they were not to be eaten that day! It was 4, when Raghav's call was answered by Smitha, who said, "Hello Bhaiya!"

"Hello Smitha! Where are your parents? They have not reached here." Raghav sounded firm, and concerned and put the phone on speaker, he did not want to hide the proceedings of my crest falling to be hidden!

"Yes *Bhaiya*, they have come back, their driver was not able to find the Old Airport Road!" Smitha lied shamelessly, or was she forced to lie shamelessly? Highly improbable that a driver of an established radio cab of Bangalore did not know where the Old airport was! Was he dropping people at the Railway Station who wanted to go the Airport? It had been only five months the new airport became operational in Bangalore! It was the duty of the driver to know the old airport road! Did Mama force the driver to forget his duties? Was my speculation around no noise of traffic holding good? Whatever it was, my efforts were being washed away!

"Please give the phone to your Mama." Raghav said.

And Raghav gave the phone to Amma, kick starting another round of arguments, which I expected to climb a point higher! "You should have called Raghav; he would have guided the driver to the place! Hope you are not angry, let us not spoil this, we have to think about our kids." Amma was resolute, and I was embarrassed. My mother was going down for no reason.

"But, we are highly disappointed with you people." Mama said, I told Raghav in exasperation, "Who the hell asked her? Who the fuck is she? Screw her if she is disappointed? Are we sitting here to please her?" Raghav looked at me sternly.

"Why disappointed? What happened?" Amma gave Mama a chance to go full monty with her thoughts! Mama grabbed it! While I continued to crib in Raghav's ears, "How could they not come to old airport? They must be kidding, they are liars!" Raghav gave another stern look.

Mama said, "As guests, we expected Rama to come and pick us up from the hotel, albeit, he just gave us the address and expected us to come to your home? This is not the way you treat guests."

I cribbed further in Raghav's ears, "Dude, What she expects now? We picked her up from the airport, dropped them at the hotel, acted drivers for Smitha as well, and killed our sleep! Now, she is complaining for a pick up from the hotel? How much so ever you do, this lady is always left for wanting more."

Amma answered Mama's disappointment with sheer display of logic, "Oh I am really sorry about that, but you have to be fair towards Rama; both the brothers gave up their sleep to make you comfortable the entire night, reached home by 9.30 and have slept only for two hours. Also, since you were to reach here by 3, it would have required you to leave hotel by 1.30 given Bangalore's crowded traffic, for that it would have required Rama to leave from here by 12 at least! Basvanagudi is good twenty to twenty five kilometres from HAL. Also, Rama has stayed very less in Bangalore; he does not know the places and roads very well. So, it would have required Raghav to accompany him! He is quite elder than him, you will have to respect that fact. Therefore, instead of so many people running here and there, it was sensible that you reached old airport and Raghav would have picked you from there. However, I am really sorry if you felt bad. Should I send Rama now to pick you up?"

There were multiple emotions running through my numb head, I cribbed further in Raghav's ears, "I am telling you, they did not leave hotel at all, that is the reason they did not pick up the phone. What kind of people!" I was losing hope, Raghav kept his hand on my shoulder. And I said, "I'll screw them up, Let's go!" I vented out all the frustration I developed.

Raghav said, "Shut up" and I said, "What shut up?" and we looked at Amma again who continued to talk to Mama.

Mama said, "No, not needed, we have Janavasam in the evening, so, we will not be available." (Janavasam is a function where groom is taken through the street in a procession on the eve of the wedding, in a nutshell; the function is equivalent to North Indian Baraats!)

Amma replied, "Oh yes! Congratulations for the wedding! How are the preparations?" I thought why Amma discussed somebody else's wedding when mine was at stake!

"Everything is fine." Mama sounded dry! I thought that Mama should have had enough etiquette to take that as an opportunity to invite my parents for the wedding! But, I had forgotten that Mama had landed in Bangalore with the sole mission of demolishing this relationship and demolish me. I was bringing disgrace to myself in front of my family.

"Fine, Janavasam will get over by 9.30 right? We will come to your hotel at 10 in the night? I think that should be fine!" Amma's strategy changed to throw ourselves on them and get Smitha by any means, what if it required my parents to forego their respect? I had already sold it off cheaply, was there anything left which my family had to forego?

Mama's another haughty answer, "Your call. Please call before you come!" and she disconnected.

I asked Raghav, "Why do we need to call them before we go there? Will they lock their hotel room and run somewhere else?"

Raghav smiled and said, "Easy Rama easy! These things happen." and then turned towards Amma, Geeta and Appa to present his analysis of the entire situation, "They have come to Bangalore only to attend the wedding, they have no intentions of getting Smitha married to Rama! I had doubts on this when I came to know that Ranjan was not coming. How is it possible that a brother does not come for his sister's engagement?" and he looked at me. I was shell shocked, and he just blinked his eyes, which meant that more was to come. "Smitha's mom tried everything to get rid of Rama, they kept on keeping conditions which just became tougher day by day, and he agreed for everything, also on track of achieving them. Any other guy, would have not agreed to such conditions and things would have got over earlier itself. But, he worked hard and got this so far, and they could not find reasons to say no. So, the ultimate thing they did is to disrespect you and complicate things, and now, if we say that we will not agree to this relation, we will do what Mama expects us to do and that would be victory for her and loss for all the efforts Rama had put in. He will be destroyed, so, we have to get Smitha, for Rama!" and he looked at me, I smiled with a maudlin face.

The next four hours were the trickiest in the recent past, everyone in the family sat at their respective places without changing clothes waiting for the needle to make rounds on the clock's surface! Sunday evenings were generally a fair like atmosphere at my home, friends drop in, TV watching, tea, biscuits etc.! But even though the best of the delights were available for our taste buds in the form of vadas and kesri, we chose to mourn that evening. Raghav came as a respite and took me out of home for a smoke.

All five of us got ourselves stuffed into the Alto and drove to Basvanagudi in the night! The drive took us only half of the time it took in the morning, I was burning from within trying to figure out that what went wrong and how should I confront them when I reach the hotel. We reached hotel by 11.

Papa opened the door, and Appa handed over the sweet box we bought on the way to the hotel. The best Mysore Pagh from Adyar Ananda Bhavan! Appa was in some sort of hurry to transfer the weight he carried. The hotel room looked like a high tension zone where the sensitive security measures for the country were discussed; Mama sat on one corner of the bed with a swollen face, Smitha sat on another corner with a mourning face. I wondered if that was the way to greet someone who talked high about respect towards guests.

Mama and Smitha did not even bother to get up and wish my family. Their asses remained glued to the bed, such acts were a clear signs of committing suicide and creating unnecessary trouble! Geeta knew the antics well, she eased the tension by smiling big, went straight to Mama to hug her and then went to Smitha to hug and kiss her. My eyes remained fixed at the two demeaning ladies to see how they responded, while Mama did not even bend forward to hug Geeta, Smitha did a confused job.

Papa, who came from sensible genes, gave his chair to my father to sit. At least, he could realise that my parents were very elder than both of them, and such arrogance on the part of Mama was absolutely disgusting. He pulled another chair and asked Raghav to sit, which Raghav denied and asked Papa to sit and not bother about youngsters in the room. Geeta forcefully placed herself next to Mama, a tricky call; she wanted to pass on the positive energy she carried. Amma sat on another corner, away from everyone, and least bothered about everyone, with an "I care a damn" look! Raghav and I found solace against the wall!

After Geeta's effort to ease out the pressure, the room again slipped into a silent mode, where everyone looked at each other's faces looking to begin some topic of discussion. I was firm in my mind that I had to ask them about the whole story around driver's ignorance on old airport road! So, I began, "Papa, can you tell me the cab service provider's name? We will sue them for having drivers who don't even know the routes."

Papa stumbled and gathered thoughts, because he had to cook up an answer; I was sure that they never left the hotel, "No, it was a private taxi arranged by my brother whose daughter is getting married. So, I don't have the details."

Then I turned towards Mama and said, "Mama, you could have told me that you wanted me to pick you up. You give so many orders, could have given one more!" I threw sarcasm, without getting bothered about the consequences!

"Why is it that everything needs to be told to you?" Mama shot back, and then pitched in Amma for defence, "That is ok; now let's discuss what we have come here for!" Amma meant business! Did it work?

Such delicate situations needed antics of Geeta, who was polished in her approach and had the ability to sport a cosmetic smile, good enough to calm down others. Amma's strict looks would only charge up the situation.

"When do you want to fix the marriage?" Amma spoke as if she was conducting an army interview.

"We were thinking December! But now, we will have to rethink!" Mama gave it back to Amma.

I stood frozen; my life could not have been so ruthless to me! I had worked day and night to construct the relationship, it was not cultivated only with love, my sweat and blood had gone deep into it. The ceiling came crashing down on my head, and I got buried under the ground. It was a plain black out and I looked for a small ray of hope. But it was a dead end! The tunnel was blocked!

"Rethink? Mama, what rethink? You said that you will get me married to Smitha in December." I opened up, and decided not to throw attitude anymore, as Smitha was the objective I lived for! She meant life to me! How could they expect me to breathe if my life was taken away?

Raghav realized that the situation was worsening due to pure ego clash between Amma and Mama, "Excuse me everyone, let us not decide our judgement basis for Rama and Smitha. We need to know what they want. We are unnecessarily creating problems for them! So, let them speak!" Raghav reminded me of Sri!

And before Smitha could say anything, I somehow sensed that her words and actions were already influenced by Mama. Therefore, to confirm and to clarify, I said, "Can I speak to Smitha alone?" and looked at Papa.

He said, "Yes, sure!"

I took Smitha to the balcony and went down on my knees the moment the balcony door got closed, and pleaded, "Please Smitha, please, can you tell me what is happening? Why is everyone behaving this way? What is wrong with Mama? I will not be able to face my family; I have come very far, I am converted, only you can take me from here! Please!"

Smitha heard only one line from my request, "What is wrong with Mama? What is wrong with your family? All of you have stormed into the hotel room and behaving like goons! How dare you ask my dad for the driver's details? Did you see the way you spoke to him? My parents are not answerable to your cheap behaviour? Why are you going gaga about old airport road? Is it the Parliament House? Driver could not find it, that is it! And generally you don't speak much in front of my Mama, where did you get the guts from today? Stop acting like a hero just because your family is here."

Smitha's answer took the discussion to a new direction, we digressed, "No, but I still can't digest that driver could not find the place, I feel Mama Papa did not leave for our home at all. And what do you expect? I sit and watch all of them raping the hard work I have put in, I need to speak."

Smitha lost temper and said, "Yes, they did not leave. Fine and we thought that since we did not come to your place, you and your family would be shameful enough to understand that we have no interest currently! But you have come with entire family here. I don't know why the hell you people are trying to get close?"

For the first time, Smitha cited the monetary difference between our families.

The blood gushed on to my head and I held Smitha by her arm and said, "What? No interest? But why the fuck your parents did not call up and tell this to my parents, rather they kept on lying, driver's ignorance and my misbehaviour? Do they themselves know how to behave? And where does this come from now? We had decided everything right? See I have the ring also." my voice began to shiver as I showed the ring to Smitha! And the first drop of tear rolled down.

Smitha was unmoved, "Now, don't create a scene here. See, basically, the amount of insult you brought to my parents by questioning them openly, challenging them, I think this needs to be rethought! Anyhow, let's go inside and wipe your tears." Smitha, without waiting for my consent, opened the door and went inside. I followed suit.

My eyes met Raghav's eyes which sensed that the devastation had occurred, and I confirmed with a waggle of my head. It was left to the formalities only from Smitha, who suddenly sported a smile. She always behaved like an idiot in chaotic situations, what was there to smile?

"See, actually, I don't want to get married now, at least for next two years! I spoke to my grandparents and told them about the same. I have written my GMAT and going for my PhD to Australia. In fact, I gave one attempt." Smitha revealed the secret! Did Smitha lie? I did not know!

I had transformed from mad to maniac, and asked, "GMAT? PhD? Attempt? You did not tell me before?"

"The score was not good enough to tell you! And there was nothing to tell you, I am not going to Australia, I have to give exams again. So, what was there to tell you?" Smitha answered conceitedly disrespecting my presence in her life. I looked like a complete idiot; Amma, Appa, Raghav and Geeta, they all fixed their eyes at me. Every eye had the same question, "Is this your choice? Is this what you have done so much for?" but Amma could not tolerate the humiliation her son was getting subjected to.

"Nothing to tell him? You guys are making marriage plans, and you have taken such a big decision and you are saying there was nothing to tell him! If that was the deciding factor, then why did you wait for this day to speak up? Why did you ask him to travel all the way from there to here? This could have been disclosed over the phone as well? You can't take such decisions alone when that affects my son as well." Amma spoke with lot of emotions.

And I had gone emotionless like an ice, absolutely cold and shattered! Mama pounced on to reply, "Yeah That is what, even we don't want him to keep on waiting for two years. In this period, if he comes across some other good girl, please go ahead! Please don't wait!" This could have been the most shameless reply from Mama.

Such rash reply from Mama was the thumping point for Amma to make over from a well behaved woman to someone who breathed fire, "What nonsense are you talking about? You got him converted, you made him go through all the humiliation, and you have complicated his life! And now you are saying that he should change his mind! I have not seen people like you! It is an insult for us to be present in this room with people like you!" Amma got up to move, and asked Appa, Geeta, Raghav and me to join, "Let's go!"

"Ok, we don't want to keep any relation either with people like you." Mama shouted as we walked out of the door. I was the last to step out of the door. And I turned back to take one glimpse of Smitha, whom I probably saw for the last time.

While we walked on the corridor towards the lift, my heart began to sink, my body began to freeze, my heart beat began to terminate, and my eyes began to shed tears, and my knees began to bend, my back began to quiver, and I broke down! I was on my knees and started crying!

Geeta could not see the sight, and so could Raghav, he pulled me to get up and said, "Let's go home first" while I continued to cry and showed the ring to Raghav who looked plainly into my eyes making an effort to relate with the pain I reeled under.

21

Downfall

How is it possible that an eighty five kg body which was six feet tall, stored liquid worth a dam! The second form of matter stored in my body, found only one way out, through my eyes. After returning from the hotel, everyone went on to their respective beds. Amma was fuming at me, she would not talk! Appa was a free bird, he hardly cared about it, Raghav did not know how to react, and he would surf something on his laptop even when the internet was not on, Geeta sat by me, when I looked outside the window in the dark.

Once I dampened the windows slab, I got up from there to the kitchen balcony to cry in a different angle. After that I went to the toilet, locked myself, and then cried at a different frequency. After flooding the toilet, I sat on the sofa in the living room, kept on looking at my image on the centre table glass till the time it got faded with the water in my eyes.

I did not know when I went off to sleep; my sleep was broken with the sound of the vessels which had sambhar and kesri. I got up with a heavy head, courtesy all night tear shedding exercise, all to witness that kesri was being handed over to the maid, and the stale sambhar was being drained in the sink! I felt that I was kesri and my relationship with Smitha was the luckless sambhar.

No one discussed much about the fireworks of the previous night, and I did not bother to discuss it either; I developed a strong feeling that everyone in this world including Smitha conspired to derail the relation, I thought that was the way, packed my bag and headed back to Gurgaon wondering all the way what was the critical point which turned everything on its head.

A strong hammer and a blowing trumpet kept on hitting my head, multiple thoughts multiplied vigorously, without allowing me to stop at one place. I reached chummery in the evening, threw my bag at the peak of my anger and went to the living room.

With body stoned at one place, I fixed my eyes on the TV which played some Bengali channel. I did not realize the comedy I subjected myself to till the time Tirthankar shook me up from the soup. I faintly heard what he shouted, "Party, Party" and I was driven back to my senses.

I looked at him with a dejected face, wondering if he deserved a slap or not. I told him emotionlessly, "Nothing happened, it was called off!" and I threw my Bengali roommate into a stunned silence, I wanted to tell him, "My engagement has been dropped, not Sourav Ganguly from the team."

He did not bother to ask further, typical of MBAs, who don't brag about the emotional quotients, it was always better to leave alone emotionally down people! I thought so, but Tirthankar had plans. He was absolutely assured that things would never work out for me and Smitha; therefore, it was essential for me to open up.

He went to his room and returned with a bottle of whisky, and said, "Wanna booze? You will feel better.", and I replied, "Yes, Break up or no break up, I always feel better with booze." I did manage a tiny joke in the middle of sad affairs, but Tirthankar could only display a tensed smile, bothered about my mental state.

I kept on boozing, till the last drop of alcohol, even when Tirthankar denied me alcohol after a couple of drinks; I snatched from him to draw off the bottle. And it was followed by something which is always discouraging after the alcohol.

With my head getting labelled as the epitome of frustration, and my heart becoming the centre of anger, for what I did had become irrevocable; alcohol only managed to magnify the sentiments I lived with. And I called up Smitha under that dreadful influence.

Smitha, who for any other day, would have snubbed my calls after such a disaster decided to answer my call without any delay; she was probably as hurt as I was, and waited for my call. But addendum to the mistake I had done of calling her up after getting drunk, Smitha screwed up by resorting to rudeness.

"What? What is there to call now? Why did you call?" Smitha launched a missile attack!

And the alcohol cantered in me had to retaliate with a full blown air attack, "Why the fuck you are acting weird? Is it only my fault that things did not work out? In fact, it was you who had called it off, it was you who secretly planned for GMAT and Australia, it was you who had been living with a plan for some time to go and die abroad."

"I called it off because I have some aspirations, that is about it, wait for two years if you can." Smitha continued to argue.

"You know that I could have waited for you throughout my life, I am not disturbed by what Mama said, it hardly matters to me because that is how I know her, but you said that you had no interest currently and still we were trying to get close to you." I threw something for Smitha to think.

"See, again, you are taking shots at Mama, and this is what you did yesterday with my parents. Let me make it very clear, I can't tolerate any nonsense and any misbehaviour towards my parents. So, better mind your language." Smitha got angry again, she did not like the taste of her own medicine.

"Oh is it? I have been taking the same nonsense and same misbehaviour for the last one year, and when I complained, I was always rebuked. Did you ever realise what your parents and you did was also not correct? And coming back to your aspirations point, where did that come from? Your ambitions and your aspirations are more important than this relationship. You also said once that come what may, I will marry you baby! Is that you are a liar? How can you just go back on your words?" I was losing it; alcohol gave me the required courage.

"Yes, my aspirations are important. Don't blame me, Mama and I have always asked you to apply for a job abroad, you never listened to us! Why are you acting like a cry baby? You were given your share of chances, but you never grabbed them. I can't rot in this stinking country forever." Smitha spoke like a businessman.

"What the fuck? You are such a bitch that you were with me only due to certain motives? College because of CGPA, after college because I was earning well and you expected a future abroad! You were aware that nobody else will give way to your Mama's stupidity, therefore, you persisted with me! I am sure this entire plot is based out of Kelly's fancies towards you. You used me and when you could not see any more advantage, you threw me. You whore!" my language degraded.

"That is what you are, as long as I was with you, you claimed to respect me, but all that was drama, see how has your language changed in a day. I was right about you, you have not changed from the time you hit me. All right, fine, yes, my needs have changed, and so, I don't need you anymore. Fuck off!" Smitha ripped my heart apart.

I was the volcano ready to burst and I did, I murdered every small link which we shared, "Ok, you bitch, you slut, that is so easy for you. You sleep with some someone to fetch benefits, and then get ready to marry somebody else to have far bigger benefits! What kind of woman you are? Ok, but, I am no idiot to be fooled like this, I want you to pay me for whatever I did for you." I was nothing sort of a ruthless businessman as well!

"Oh, there you go, you have been keeping a count of what all you did. That goes to show how cheap you are!" Smitha spoke as if she discovered the truth of national importance.

"Ok, I am cheap, agreed, can you pay me back? I spent close to a lakh on you including the fridge, the cooler, the recent shopping and all those gifts." I put the first nail in my coffin.

"And yes, do send back my credit card as well!" I continued without realizing that I was putting an all-time end to my relationship, "I will have to check how much is due on my card, I don't know what all did you spend at!"

"Ok, I will send everything, message me your account details and address. But one thing is for sure, you are just a big loser, who is absolutely drunk with himself, and you will ruin yourself with this kind of attitude. Forget me, I will marry somebody else, will send you the card." and Smitha disconnected.

Her last line ruptured me, and I wondered how it would be if Smitha made love with someone else! My nervous system got into error full mode, and I stepped out to get another bottle of whisky, when Tirthankar stopped me. But I did not listen.

The day marked the downfall of me, in every manner possible to a man after his evolution! So steep was the downfall that before I gathered methods to control it, I was neck deep into the hell. Health, wealth and mind, I began to lose them all! Only a miracle could have saved me from slipping into a dominion of complete shame, extreme exasperation and undisputed melancholy. But miracles were only done by God, and I had disowned him long back!

Smitha managed to only send the credit card; I did not send her the account details to repay the money I demanded. Still, I had piled up good amount of money, thanks to the nagging nature of Smitha and her creator. But the objective for which the money was saved was dead and buried. I always dreamt of buying a car from my own money and unwind myself on the road. Within a week of getting dumped, I approached Safdarjung Hyundai, asked for the quotation of i10, and without bothering to negotiate or wait for better deals, I signed the cheque, fixed the date of delivery, and got the car a week later. The hit of 4 lakhs was not felt, as I had accumulated enough money to entertain such nonsensical activities. After the night of fireworks, all communications were lost with my parents, only Raghav and Geeta spoke to me, yet, I dared to call Amma and Appa to take the delivery of the car with me!.

"Amma, I am buying a car, please come to Gurgaon to take the delivery! I am booking your air tickets and sending it to Raghav. Please come!" I said.

Amma replied dryly, "So, you have decided this as well without asking us. Ok, we will come but please book our return tickets for the same day."

I chose not to please Amma, if that was the way she wanted to respond to my only achievement after I got the job, I decided not to disturb her response, and therefore, booked their return ticket on the same day!

Amma and Appa reached Delhi airport on the delivery day of the car, I picked them up from the airport and took them straight to the car showroom, where the male version of Khushi, waited for us to greet and handover the keys. He smiled relentlessly, whereas Amma began to fume looking at the colour of the car. "Why did you buy a black car? Black is such an inauspicious colour. You never listen to us, and that is the reason you have landed yourself in such a mess today." Amma complained.

"What is with the colour? Black colour in hatchbacks are cheaper, I saved good twenty to thirty thousand. Now, don't argue, please take the keys." I gave it back to Amma. Amma turned down the offer, instead, Appa took the keys and Khushi's male version thought that my dad knew to drive and opened the driver's door for him and Appa sat on the driver's seat looking completely blank, when I intervened to enlighten Mr Khushi, "He does not know how to drive, so, you help him start the ignition."

Mr. Khushi, with his million dollar smile handed over the relevant documents to Amma, opened the door for her, and said, "Mam, please sit, and congratulations!" and then he opened the door for my father, and asked him to step out, then again opened the door for my father to sit. And we drove to chummery.

My mother chose silence over words during her short stay at the chummery, it was sure that she would not have eaten lunch if I did not arrange for it. She went off to sleep, and got up on time to leave for the airport. I did not take much pain to peep into what was running in my mother's mind, but it came as only a sign of disappointment and disownment from Amma. I was broken, the fear of losing parents and the depression of losing Smitha continued to maul me.

I dropped parents at the airport, and drove straight to Puneet's office! Puneet had been a friend since childhood, someone who silently knew everything about me, someone who would patiently listen to me, someone who would see me smoking but would not smoke, someone who would sit with me while I boozed but he would not booze, someone who always dreamt of going to Amritsar in the car which I bought; In short, someone who remained all throughout the pandemonium, waiting for me to get it right.

The abandoning by Smitha followed by the same from parents had left me dejected; for me, the sole purpose of living had vanished, negativity had engulfed me to an extent that I stopped trusting anyone! Relations with others started to rip apart as well; the only companionship existed with Puneet and high voltage alcoholism!

A week later I bought the car, on a Friday night, I drove to Puneet's office, and asked him to join me to Jim Corbett National Park, looking at my state, Puneet tried hard to convince me to call off the trip, "Dude, you must be kidding me! Jim Corbett? Is it some kind of a joke?"

But, I would not budge and said, "You are coming or not? If no, then I will go alone."

Puneet tried another one to hold me back, "But dude, where are the clothes? I am in formals, and it is 11 right now! Where do we get the clothes now?"

"You fucker! Don't act like a woman! We will buy something on the way; we will reach Jim Corbett by morning. Now get in, fast!" I developed zero listening abilities and opened the door for him to get in.

Puneet joined me and called up his parents to inform them about his whereabouts. Such was my impression at his place, that even if he went to a brothel with me, his parents would agree.

Puneet said, "Let me drive. You are drunk." and I replied like a perfect drunkard, "Fuck off! I'll drive. Relax, you will be safe." and I pressed the accelerator giving no hope of safety to Puneet, who somehow managed to put his seat belt.

"We have to reach by 7 in the morning." I had no logical calculation behind that statement but Puneet knew why, "You need reasons to drive fast." and I did not prove him wrong. Clutch, gear and zoom, we were nicely doing hundred plus, when Puneet reminded me, "Dude, why are you raping your new car? Slow down." and I pressed the accelerator further and braked suddenly and left the highway for the mud turf.

"Why did we stop here?" Puneet asked while taking his trousers off to ensure his comfort in boxers. And I answered him by opening the rear door, which left him disgustingly enraged. A bottle of whisky, a paper glass, a coke found their way out of the door, a newspaper was spread on the lifted bonnet, a fully packed tandoori chicken was thrown for Puneet, and I gargled with whisky.

"You are insane, what is that you want to prove? You are not the first one to have had a break up. You bought a car, that was good, but the way you are using your car right now, that is fucking crazy! You go to work on time every day, but what you do every day before work will only land you in trouble. Can you tell me what is this all about going to Jim Corbett right now? I don't discourage adventure, but this is suicide." Puneet was more worried than ever. While he spoke, I continued to booze and opened the foil to pick up a chicken leg and took a bite, with least interest in what he spoke.

He waggled with disappointment, and thought that eating chicken was a better option than becoming a not to be heard. Once the chicken was cleaned up, Puneet got into the driver's seat and said, "Sit here, I will drive." and held the steering wheel firmly indicating his firm intentions. But there was a deal which he had to approve of, "I will booze and you drive. Drive slowly, else the drink will fall."

This idea was the best given the kind of circumstances Puneet got himself into, he said, "Fine, then only a couple of drinks, and then you will not booze!" and I was quick to counter, "Fine, then I will drive. So either let me booze, or let me drive."

All he could mutter was "Screw you" and got the car on the high way and drove like a good boy, while I continued to gulp down alcohol like water!

Puneet kept on speaking, which I could hardly understand, and I kept on boozing. We crossed Moradabad, and the sun was cracking at the dawn, when I got my head hanging out of the window and began to puke. The body of the new black car was artistically upgraded by amoebic plots of vomit. The driver realized this a bit late and braked to get me out of the car, while he did that, a car came and braked right in front of us. A big guy stepped out and held Puneet by his collar and slapped me.

Struggling to stand me fell down on the ground and puked further, when the big man shouted, "He has been puking, and everything flew to my vehicle. I was following you." he pointed towards his car which had marks of puke on the windshield which originated from my inner self.

"Your mistake! Why were you following us?" I replied confidently, which forced the big guy to advance towards me, when Puneet held him and said, "Sorry, really sorry. Please, he is into some problem. Please!" and the big guy spared us, yet I shouted, "Hey, you come here, I will show you. You wanted to fight?" and stumbled with vomit all over my shirt.

Puneet held me and made me sit on the rear seat and said, "Shut up and sleep now." He took off my shirt and put it in the dickey, allowing to shrink myself to slumber.

When my eyes opened, it was a tall ceiling and a fan rotated like asking me questions! I got up to see Puneet enjoying his tea. The steaming tea attracted me; I did not wait for a moment, jumped out to snatch the tea from Puneet. "Where are we?" and I took a sip.

"Why are you so wild? There is tea in the flask as well; you could have taken from there. Dumb ass" he said while cleaning the tea which fell on the chair.

"Fuck you! Where are we?" I was not able to figure out what that room was!

"We are at Jim Corbett! You kept on sleeping. And there is your shirt. You puked asshole!" Puneet pointed towards the shirt hanging outside, and I said, "Thanks, you washed it." and I got out of the room and went straight to the car, and said, "Give me the keys." which Puneet threw at me.

With tea in one hand, I tussled to open the door of the car, and returned with a packet, which Puneet tried to snatch from me. "Back off, this is not for babies!" I alerted him, to which he replied, "What are they? Sanitary napkins? Have you got periods?" I kicked him and we laughed, while I placed the packet on the bed neatly.

I opened the packet and I did Ranjan, probably a step ahead of Ranjan and Puneet looked on suspiciously, when I ordered, "Close the door!", he obeyed by getting up slowly looking at the packet. And he went towards the door, and closed it.

"What the hell is that? Don't tell me you are going to make joints here!" Puneet asked for unnecessary confirmation!

"Not only joints, I have got mushrooms as well, and a couple of ecstasy pills." I behaved like a kid who boasts of not only splinters, but other bombs which he would buy on Diwali!

Puneet closed his eyes in horror, bit his teeth, and murmured a little before unleashing a dose of aggression, "No, you are not going to do this. No way! I will call your parents. What has gone wrong with you man?"

"Fuck you! I have been doing this in college as well, were you there then? Just that I am taking it to the next level! And you are not going to call anyone, please. Please, a bit of fun, that is it!" I started persuading Puneet, but I did not care for his approval, and I began to roll the first joint. And I got all my skills picked up from college days to roll joints. And my dear friend continued to look on with an awed face.

Exhaling the dark smoke, I pounced on the paranthas ordered by Puneet for breakfast. Going from bad to worse was the trend those days; I littered food all over the place, and with shabby hands continued to drag the poison! Puneet did not like that sight, given that he came from a sophisticated Punjabi family, and therefore passed on the tissue papers to me which was instantly turned down by me.

The grass I carried could churn out three cigarettes, which I cleaned up, and climbed to heaven again, and as a liberated man, I spread myself on the bed and told Puneet, "We will go out in the evening, till then can you get some booze. And order some food as well." and I crashed.

With dead grass sending my head into a vibration mode, a fearsome force was needed to grace the effects rolled out by joints. And nothing would have been capable enough than the fast flowing Kosi river, the water with strong currents was the only attraction in a god's gift to mankind, Puneet was vocal in expressing the same, "Dude, Are we going to cross the river? Is this the only thing you would do? What about safari and all? We have come so far and will we not go to the jungle? No, that is not fair!"

"I don't want to go anywhere else, only water, I will cross it thrice. Let's speak to the guy and do it." we both walked, with me dragging cigarette after cigarette.

The boy who helped us cross the river was the symbol of fitness, tied one end of the rope to a big rock and jumped into the water, disappeared and emerged after a minute at the other bank with ease, tied the other end as well to a big rock. With safety equipment on, Puneet set out to cross the river, not as easily as that boy could do, but he did come back without puffing for the fact he never allowed alcohol or tobacco to entertain his body.

With confidence overflowing from my body, I stubbed the fag, and stepped into the water. Barely a few steps into the ruthlessly flowing liquid which did not allow firming of my feet, I slipped and hit a huge rock under the water.

I submerged into the water, sending Puneet and that boy into a tizzy, who dragged me out of the water! I turned back quickly to see that the water which was purely blue flowed with traces of redness; then only I realized that I bled profusely from my head. To hold back the bleeding from causing unconsciousness, that boy ran to get a big cloth, folded it and gave it to me to press it against the wound.

The boy helped me to walk to the hotel, while Puneet ran ahead to get the car. At the clinic, I got five stitches and was asked to take certain medicines and rest. I told Puneet, "Let's go back to Gurgaon now, it is 5 right now, we will reach by 1 in the night." And my friend smiled.

As the impact of joints started to wither off, I started to feel the pain and so, popped in a mushroom I carried with me, without letting Puneet know and went to sleep again while Puneet drove us to Gurgaon. At around 10 in the night, I got up to feel better and offered assistance to Puneet who was deprived of sleep.

He agreed and I began to drive decently, however, driving fast was a part of my character! Straight strips welcomed us as we crossed UP border, driving incessantly on a high speed, we overtook trucks with ease. Though the head injury hindered my abilities to drive, yet, I fought to ensure the continuity.

"Blow Horn" was written at the rear of a truck, which I tried hard to overtake, but the truck denied us any space. Therefore, I adhered to the message at the rear of the truck, and honked like someone out of his mind. I chased the truck for good two kilometres, but was not able to defeat it! The traces of mushroom, tickled the anxious hormones, and I chose to overtake from left, highly against the traffic rules. But, who was following any of the rules from any book? Me?

I went down to the third gear, slowed down a little, got the car distanced from the truck, switched on the left indicator and shifted lanes. I geared up again, accelerate and continued to honk. The truck began to honk as well and it was out of my comprehension, got irritated and I looked up for verification only to see the driver's assistant hanging himself with one hand signalling me to stop.

The entire circus from the driver's assistant was an effort to avert a major accident; the lane which I picked had an extra-long trailer carrying iron rods, the part of which hanged outside the trailer! However, the assistant was late in his effort, as I could not spot the same trailer, and was really close.

I closed my eyes, in a second recalled the way I had lived, looked at Puneet who continued to sleep and just when I accepted that was the end of the life, the driver of the truck which I tried to overtake came as a messiah and skilled his truck to take the divider and made way, only enough for the car to sneak through! I grasped that as an opportunity to save this life, and zipped between the two trucks, losing the left side mirror which rubbed against the trailer. The noise of trucks, mirror cracking and horns were able to wake up Puneet.

He shouted, "What the fuck! Stop the car, I say stop the car." and I still recovering from the death, and obeyed his orders. With trembling hands, and a sweating forehead, I drove to the corner of the highway. And we got down from the car looking for all possible damages. As we examined the vehicle, the truck which I tried to overtake stopped in front of us, and got down the messiah driver, and held me by the collar, slapped me and abused me.

It was crime to argue with the driver, we owed our lives to him for the risk he had taken by getting on the divider which could have resulted fatality for him. Holding his hand, I hugged him, and told him that the injury denied clear vision. Puneet thanked him further and apologized which cooled the driver down, who opted to drive again.

As the truck left, Puneet turned to me and said, "Your life is balanced, you got a slap while going, you got a slap while returning" and he laughed alone, he realized that the joke was mistimed, and asked, "What happened? I asked you to drive slowly."

Similarities were striking between car and me, both of us looked fucked up, the agony with which I had lived for almost a month had begun to show its lasting effects. I kicked the tyre violently and banged the bonnet with my fist. Puneet stopped me to console, "Its ok, if you have a car, you will drive it and if you drive, accidents will happen. It is ok. Drive sensibly now."

"What sensibly? Do I look sensible in any which way? I am smoking heavily, I am drinking heavily, I have resorted to drugs, sensibly is an endangered word in my life, soon it will be extinct. Screw me to have got myself into this!" I cursed myself, and claimed thorough frustration!

"But is that the break up with Smitha still troubling you?" Puneet asked, and I looked at Puneet fuming over what he asked.

"Wow, very intelligent! Finally you were able to decipher the root cause of my weird behaviour. I know I am weird these days. I have stopped sleeping; only time I sleep is when I am drunk or done joints. Still, I get up at 5 in the morning, and first thing I do is to make a drink for myself. I drink almost a quarter every morning before setting off for work. The day they come to know, I'll be terminated. Plus, they just need a reason to throw me out, given the brilliant performance record

I have!" my face glowered. And Puneet recognized for the very first time the pain I lived with.

The vehicles zoomed in the background, and I continued while lighting up a cigarette, "It has been almost a month that I have spoken to Smitha, she does not answer my calls at all. Tell me what I should do!"

Puneet listened to me carefully and started cultivating a plan, "Do you still want to marry her after whatever has happened?" he asked and I replied, "I always wanted to marry her and I know whatever has happened, she was not to be blamed."

At 11 in the night, somewhere in the Northern India, under a heavy duty fog, with dippers on, a shocker hit Puneet who confirmed, "But asshole, if that was the case, then why did you get into a brawl with her? Who asked you to abuse her? You even asked for money and all. Now, how can you expect her to speak to you? Forget about getting married!"

"I abused you so many times, remember our cricket playing days?" I said and it brought a smile to our faces, for a moment though! And we decided to drive again, Puneet jumped into the driver's seat, as he had almost died few minutes ago.

I lit up a cigarette, while Puneet drove, and I said, "So, what if I abused her? Just one wrong day cannot take away the amount of efforts I have put all these years. I always think of getting out of it. But the moment I imagine Smitha with somebody else, it is horrifying! What do I do? Can you help?"

Something should have stopped me from asking Puneet to help as his help would not limit to a suggestion or an advice, he would take personal interest and assume it be a task which he has been entrusted with to complete. And with any positive talk looking like a mystical ray of hope, I was for sure going to adhere to Puneet's suggestion, forgetting the fact that Puneet had adhered to my suggestions since childhood.

"Ok, you told me once that she is fed up of this selling profile. And she finds it tough to meet her targets as well!" Puneet began to understand the complexity to throw the plan which he seemed to have cultivated for some time.

"Yes, so what?" I asked.

"Why don't you arrange a job for her in your company? I mean your boss is a good friend, why don't you ask him?" the unwinding began.

"But fucker, my job itself is in doldrums. My management trainee stint has been extended, which means that I am the worst performer. Why would my boss agree for someone whom I recommend? And there has to be a strong requirement, they will not take anybody. I spoke once about this to him and he did not respond well. So, tell me something else!" the discussion took off!

Puneet never knew me as a worst performer, hence delayed the acceptance of what was told to him, and responded with an alternative, "So, you have already forwarded her CV in your company and you think that she will not be selected given the background and the profile she has been handling currently?" I thought what was the need of rephrasing everything!

"Yeah right. What are you thinking?" I sensed something running in his head.

"We are not actually going to get a job for her in your company; we can stage a telephonic interview which would show that you have pushed for her even after the break up! Who knows? She might speak to you!" Was I going to accept the foolishness?

Yes, I did, "You call her up for the interview. I'll give you a script and read it out and drag it for some time. Let's say over a week. I'll try getting close with her again during that period." and he agreed and we zipped towards Delhi as I popped in another mushroom and Puneet said, "Don't get addicted."

Puneet lived up to his characteristic and dogged to make Smitha speak to me, few moments, he had to be reminded that Smitha was not actually going to be selected!

As we reached Gurgaon, we checked in to the chummery, stretched our legs out, bent our fingers, and I said, "Dude, get a glass. I'll make a drink for myself and go off to sleep, speak to Smitha in the morning."

An extremely charged up Puneet, firmed to make it work for me, woke me up with a cup of coffee and the medicines, "Get up, it is 9, here is your coffee, and I have put eggs to boil, give me Smitha's number. I will speak to her." and I asked him, "What is the connection between eggs, Smitha, medicines and coffee?"

I mouthed her number, it was embedded in me, and took a sip of coffee, and said, "Tell her that you are Mr. Anurag Chaturvedi from my company and this is with reference to the CV received by you from Rama Chandran, which is me! The profile is for a business analyst. Ask her for a suitable time to speak to her. Don't drag it too much for now. We will call her later during the day."

Puneet listened to everything carefully, and developed thoughts to spice up the entire conversation which was clearly evident from his face and nail biting actions and asked, "Who is Anurag Chaturvedi?"

"How does it matter?" I hit back. "Idiot"!

Once the breakfast was over, Puneet took out his phone, took a deep breath and sent out the first call to Smitha which was the first mistake in the entire process.

Confidence vanished in a whisker from Puneet, and the money was placed on him illogically. Puneet forgot everything, the name of fictitious character, the profile she applied for, enough for me to sit on the sofa holding my head. I looked up.

Puneet said, "Hello, Good morning mam!"

"Who says Mam? Do they call you sir when they call you up for interviews?" I hushed.

"Is that Smitha Swaminathan?" he asked.

"First mam and now Smitha? Did she lose temper? You are messing it up!" I thought.

"Mam, Mr Rama Chandran gave your CV to me?" Puneet continued.

"Bastard, did I come and give it to you in person? What are you doing?" I held Puneet by his neck.

"I am actually Anurag Bhardwaj from Donne, we have selected your profile for business analytics." Puneet disclosed the blunder!

"Bhardwaj or Chaturvedi? Analytics or Analyst?" I murmured.

"What should be the best time to speak to you?" Puneet asked.

"The best time has been made the worst time by you." I thought.

"Ok. Thanks. We will call you at 3.30 today." Puneet signed off.

"Did you take an appointment to sell credit cards?" I shouted.

My obviously jacked up brain and Puneet's overly dragged emotional effort forgot something which Smitha chose to remind us, or did someone remind Smitha that it was her duty to do that? Second Puneet disconnected, Smitha fulfilled her duty by calling me up.

"Why the hell you don't leave me alone? Do you think that you will get away with all the cheap tactics you resort to?" Smitha was at onslaught.

I replied, "Hi, It has been so long that we have spoken. How are you?" and my lips trembled. Puneet held my shoulder expecting appreciation.

Smitha went into an unexpected pause, and spoke again, "Just shut up! Today is Sunday, and who calls for an interview on a Sunday? I could make out that it was you or one of your equally good for nothing loser friends who called up and acted to fix an interview." her voice echoed.

I looked at Puneet and bit my teeth and lips, while Puneet looked blank. I concentrated on the call again, "Is your phone on speaker? Who is with you? I can hear someone prompting in the background."

"There is no one! And why are you policing unnecessarily? Who are you? Just stay away from me!" Smitha was ferocious.

"I am sorry I played this trick, but I had no other way to speak to you. I have been dying without you." tears began to roll down.

"Is that Cecilia with you?" I confirmed but I doubted some male prompting Smitha for the way I knew Smitha, she was the queen of dumbs who would have never figured out that it was a trick I plotted.

"But please speak to me, I can't live this way." I said, and Smitha cut me short, "Shut up and don't call me again." and the call was forcefully dropped!

Puneet offered explanation which I never demanded for, "I am sorry; I got scared and lost all the confidence. This was the last chance you had to speak to her, but I screwed it up."

Desperately wanting to abuse him, I said, "That is ok. My life is screwed up, you can't make it worse. At least your intentions were good. Chill! Booze?"

Puneet answered loudly, "No way, and you will not booze either!" and I took out my phone to place an order.

"Hello uncle, Rama from Oakwood B 79. Please take my order. One tandoori chicken, one malai tikka, one butter chicken, one chicken biryani, five butter naans and a bottle of teachers and a coke. How much uncle?" I did that flamboyantly!

"Thirty three thousand six hundred and seventy? Fine, your guy will come with the swiping machine right? I'll pay here. Thanks!" I said and disconnected and Puneet grabbed the opportunity to step into the shoes of a hypothetical dad and explained, "Dude, you should not be spending this way! What was the point in ordering so much? Who will eat? It would be waste."

"Shut up and enjoy. I will eat now; I will eat in the night. And I am earning well, plus credit card is also there." I rejected his advice.

Puneet was an inch away from fainting, but got better to argue, "You are screwing up yourself. Who uses credit card? Are you nuts? Do you know that you will just get addicted and will find yourself in a circle and will never be able to come out of it? thirty six hundred thrown away just like that, that is like five to six percentage of what your earn and if this is the way you keep on spending, you will be neck deep in debt!"

By the time Puneet ended up speaking, my interest diverted from chicken laden ordered food to rolling of the joints! Puneet looked at me from the distance, understood again that he was not to be heard! And he switched on the TV before asking, "How much stock do you have? I mean grass."

After a few minutes of silence, he spoke again to mend things for me, "Why don't you go to Hyderabad to meet her?" and I made a strong reply to abandon Puneet's suggestions anymore for the day, "Fucker, that is what I have done for the last one year."

The chicken and the alcohol was delivered, which I hogged on till late in the evening, and when the alcohol joint hands with grass to engulf my head, I began to think hard about what Puneet said, "Why don't you go to Hyderabad to meet her?" but an approval from the boss was mandatory.

Next day at 5 in the morning, while I made my usual drink before getting ready for work, I woke up Puneet who salivated and said, "Listen I am planning to go to Hyderabad today, you drop me at the airport and take the car to your home and then to work. First I'll go to office and tell my boss about the injury."

"But tickets?" Puneet asked. Was he swimming in the pool of out datedness?

"Internet? Online booking? Heard of these?" I said and opened my laptop and booked a ticket for a flight leaving at 12 from Delhi.

Unusually, I reached office bang on time, and started fiddling around with my computer, when my boss walked in, and in an utter astonishment, said, "Where the hell did you get hurt? And why did you come to office today? Go back home and recover fast before joining work. Come on go now." I hid the sense of smile as things just fell in place without uttering a word; my stars were nice to me after a prolonged gap. Were they?

As I stepped out of office, I called up Puneet, who smartly waited outside the office, and drove me straight to the airport, handed over the bag which he packed for me, hugged me, held my shoulder tightly, and said the unexpected, "First thing, get your dressing done as you reach Hyderabad." and hugged me.

In the plane, I wished it to fly faster than it did, helping me to reach Hyderabad earlier, but the pilot was not my friend, and what if there were trailers with iron rods in the mid-air?

I did not obey Puneet's instructions about getting dressed, and went to Smitha's office, it was 5 in the evening and I expected Smitha to be at work. I messaged her, "Hi, waiting outside your office. Can we meet?"

Smitha did not respond, and I messaged again after a small waiting time, "Please! At least reply. I am outside your office, please meet me!"

Smitha sent out Thomas, whom I thought to be gutsy enough to counter me after the drubbing he got from me. He stretched his hand out to me, I shook it and looked over his shoulder too see if Smitha followed him. Thomas said, "Look dude, there is nothing left between you and her. She does not want to meet you. She does not want a scene to be created here. So, please go!"

I chose not to respond to polite Thomas, as I had nothing to speak with him. If Smitha had sent him to avoid me, I had to speak to Smitha only! Therefore, I walked out of her office and went to the coffee shop opposite to her office to keep an eye on when she leaves.

The same devilish black santro was driven out of the office basement; I could see Smitha from the distance who was beaming! They probably discussed, "Good job, you were able to shoo him away!" I hired an auto rickshaw and went to her residence, only to realise that I had reached earlier than her and the only option was to wait. The two hours wait brought me to a state of wrongly assumed disgust; I welcomed the Santro once again, which braked in front of Smitha's home, and I appeared to stand in front of Smitha who looked dumbstruck.

"Hi, I wanted to speak to you. Please! I have come so far." I said. The hunger, the injury, the pain, the tiredness and the willingness were to create a magic and they did create a magic! I saw the pain in Smitha's eyes after a long time, she mustered courage to be caring, "Hi, where did you hurt yourself?"

That was enough for my bombarded brain to loosen up, and I smiled. The smile made Smitha believe that she had given me wrong signals, and the presence of Thomas fuelled that belief, and therefore, the makeover happened. Smitha said, "Listen, you are acting stupid, there is nothing left between us. Why do you have to do all this and make me feel that I am doing some sin, some crime? Please go! Else I will have to call the police."

"Police? This is not how I know you! Someone is influencing you." I said, looked at Thomas and Smitha responded quickly, "I did not know you like this either! Please go back!" she made way for herself and walked upstairs and Thomas also followed her, he ensured to maintain distance from me. My teary eyes followed her, my heart was burning, the heat engulfed my ears and my nostrils breathed high degree air.

Sitting at a stone opposite Smitha's flat, my painful eyes were fixed at Smitha's window and I drew imaginary figures of Thomas and Smitha making love. Such thoughts were equivalent to the stabs with a dagger right on my heart. It took good two hours for Thomas to come down, and I confronted him.

Thomas was frozen, he expected another thrashing, but played articulation, "Listen brother, you can speak to Smitha and sort it out with her. I don't want to mess with you. You are already hurt, there is no point we fight. So, please let me go." I made way for Thomas, before telling him, "I'll fuck your happiness, slit your dick and hang it in front of your office, if I see you here with Smitha. Now go." As Thomas drove away, Smitha messaged me, "Listen, and never ever show your face to me anymore, if you keep on stalking, I am afraid I will have to lodge a complaint. And you will never ever mess up with Thomas. Be mindful! Get lost and I don't want to see you there in front of my flat! Now go."

I looked up and Smitha switched off the lights. She probably watched me from the window and waited for me to complete reading the message. I recalled the days when I was the king of the flat, and lived there happily. Time had changed and I was standing uninvited outside the same flat with someone else walking in and out freely.

The dagger which was at the surface was pushed in further, I kept reeling, called for an auto, boarded it with tears loaded in my eyes. Since I was aware of the points where grass was available in Hyderabad, I asked the auto driver to drive me straight to one of those spots and managed to get grass which was good enough to make one joint. The auto driver looked at me suspiciously when I unfilled the tobacco from a cigarette to load it with grass, and said, "Sir, Ye nako Auto mein!"

"Quiet. I'll give you hundred rupees extra! Go to airport!" I dismissed his appeal and dragged the hell out of the fag. Since I did not visit the doctor, the dressing had worn out and my wound was visible and looked dangerously ugly.

I remained stoned at the airport's McDonalds throughout the night and then boarded the flight in the morning. Few moments before the take-off, I messaged Smitha, "I will come back to you. You will come back to me. And that bastard Thomas will have to pay for it if I see him again around you! Tell him to stay away if you want him to be alive."

As I switched on the phone and boarded a cab for the chummery, an international number flashed on my screen. I had not applied for a job anywhere, then who was it?

"Hello!" I said.

"Why don't you let my daughter stay in peace?" It was Papa. My first vocal encounter with Papa was underway.

"Hello Papa, how are you?" I offered manners!

"Leave all that!" he chose not to answer my question, albeit, shot his question, "Did you go to Hyderabad yesterday?"

"Yes" I admitted.

"She told me that you have been threatening her and Thomas?" he confirmed.

"But Papa…" I offered an explanation but speech was disapproved for me when Smitha's parents spoke.

"Shut up and listen to me. Next time you disturb my daughter or threaten her, I will have to lodge a complaint with the embassy that someone has been troubling my daughter and she needs security. Then don't blame me if you are jailed. Get that straight into your head." the aggression was evident and he disconnected.

I fought with my loneliness and pain at the chummery, and could not resist the eagerness to booze. Since the car was with Puneet, I chose to walk down to Buzz, one of the most electrifying pubs in Gurgaon! I was the first one to enter the pub that evening and gulped beer after beer, and turned out to be the last one to leave the pub. The bouncer helped me to walk out and left me at the elevator allowing me to make my own way. What I did after that was not walking, I navigated my body towards the chummery when a police gypsy rounded me up. I stretched my eyes to confirm if that was a real police or not. And the next moment I thought if that was sent by Smitha's dad!

Before I thought further, a constable stepped out and came towards me, and before he could act, I distanced myself from him and said, "What happened? I have not done anything? I am walking back to my home." and I wobbled and my wound exposed.

Listening to my fluent English, constable backed out and stepped in their boss from the front seat, and said, "What is your name? We are not doing anything with you, just get into the jeep!"

"Why should I get into the jeep? What have I done?" I was scared of getting jailed.

"Nothing. You are drunk." he said.

"So what? I am not driving, I am just going back to my home." I offered an explanation.

"Just turn around and see where you are!" he said and held my arm to help me turn and showed that I was walking right in the middle of the highway with cars honking from front and behind. I did not know where my off stump was!

"Oh sorry! I am sorry. I will take care." I said and hopped onto the footpath, when the senior officer said, "Let us know where you stay. We will drop you. Get into the jeep, your safety is important to us. Someone can rob you as well."

I was left with my tongue wagging as I had never seen cops like him, well behaved and polished, "I stay nearby, Oakwood."

Oakwood was the house of millionaires and billionaires of Gurgaon, and the senior officer mistook me to be one, and offered me further help, "Sure sir, we will drop you and opened the jeep for me and I pushed myself in."

The jeep dropped me right under my flat, and I became a point of discussion for many who might have witnessed me getting offloaded from a police jeep. No one wanted to know the reasons; police jeep and a drunken guy were enough for everyone to cook stories which fascinated them. What I thought was assistance, turned out to be agony of the highest order.

Police and jail after conversion and commitment was symbolic of putting a hot iron rod into my ass and then bringing it out from my mouth. Post such consequences; there was no connection which I could afford, no communication which I could initiate and no concrete action which I could take. But, the detachment with Smitha had left a deep scar on me. How much so ever I tried to avoid her thoughts, the very thought of she being with somebody else would force me into a volley of alcohol!

There was no doubt in labelling me as a pure alcoholic; the only times I did not move with alcohol in my body was during office hours and that too was highly questionable. Days turned into weeks, weeks tuned into months, but I turned only from bad to worse! Attributing it to the abandonment by Smitha was only an excuse, I was weak and getting addicted; that was the truth!

My past could have easily become an after picture, whereas my present could have easily become a before picture; like the ones in fitness clubs. Excess of grass had eroded my vision, excess of chicken had enhanced the fat content, and excess of alcohol had raped my liver and excess of car trips increased my fuel bills. And excess of all them had left me gasping for money.

My bank balances took a nose dive, and my savings crashed, and as they say, "For everything else, there is a master card" I lived that anthem by blindly using credit card for every occasion like I forgot the difference between a credit card and debit card. The outstanding balances climbed up on me leaving me to look for avenues to settle the bills. I continued to pay the minimum amount due, but my outstanding balances which hovered above a lakh ceased to come down.

The pressure got the better of me, and the only source which I thought would help me come out of that was a personal loan, one kind of liability written off to another form of liability.

I recalled Puneet's words, "I will find myself in a circle and will never be able to come out of it!" I informed my decision of personal loan to Puneet, who lost temper and said, "More than a lakh outstanding on your card, I told you to be careful but you did not listen to me. Ask Raghav *bhaiya* to help." and I told Puneet, "I did not ask for suggestions, I informed you. Thanks!" My equation with Puneet was wobbling as well, but he did not withdraw himself.

I applied for a personal loan, got it in forty eight hours, my bank balance shot up all of a sudden, I diverted all the money to settle the outstanding balance on my card, and my bank balance crashed again. I was rich for a few hours, but my addiction for alcohol and grass, and the vacuum created by Smitha remained permanent.

I breathed easy as I stopped parting with a good deal of my salary for credit card bills, however, the new liability managed to take that share. On a Friday night, 14th of August, my flamboyant side stocked up alcohol and spirits in all forms as the Saturday was going to be a dry day. For a change Puneet also boozed that day, Tirthankar joined the party as well. And if Puneet managed to gulp a few drinks down, it was mandatory that I tanked on the beverages ruthlessly.

My alcohol ridden memory forgot that excess of alcohol can even cause deaths, even if one did not drive. Everyone limited their alcohol intake, but I continued the session singlehandedly till the dawn when the repercussions of relentless alcoholism started showing on me. It was not only for that night, but was getting constructed for some time.

I opened my eyes in a well lit room, which I thought was a hospital, with pretty Kerala nurses making rounds. Puneet stood beside me, spoke something to the doctor, when I said, "What happened? Why am I here?"

The doctor walked out, and Puneet said, "You are screwed up buddy, your bank balances are zero and you are a declared alcoholic! There is so much of alcohol in your body that there is some reaction which has happened. While we got up in the morning, you laid fainted on the sofa with surf like water oozing from your sexy lips. Some poisoning, they have cleaned up your stomach. You will have to be in hospital for 2 more days. I have called up *Bhaiya* as well and informed him. You did not have enough money in your account. *Bhaiya* has wired money. I'll call him up again and you speak to him."

I closed my eyes and a tear rolled down my cheeks, I wished if Smitha sat by me and held my hand. I asked Puneet, "Did you inform Smitha?" who made a strong fist, claiming frustration, and said, "Still Smitha? I will call the doctor and ask him to kill you. Come on Rama; don't tell me you have got yourself into this state only to get Smitha informed about this. Sheer nonsense! Think about your family." Puneet walked away and made a call which was for sure to Raghav. He said something over the call and handed over the phone to me.

The big brother made a statement, contradictory to his previous ones, "Puneet told me everything, and I don't think Smitha will ever marry you! And think that even if she married you, the amount of interference her Mom has, do you think that you would have remained happy ever? Boy, being in love should ease you, relieve you, comfort you and not torture you. If Smitha loved you, she should have acted as a shock absorber instead of asking you to do everything which her Mom asked you to. You would have never remained happy with her. Please forget her. You have Puneet right now with you and it is me who is calling you right now. There is no Smitha and not her family either. Amma is also worried; she wants to speak to you. Hang on, I will give the phone to her."

"Hello! Rama, I am coming there, Raghav has booked my ticket. Don't worry. Amma is there right? Take care!" she said as her voice had love, concern, care and affection.

My lips trembled, my hands shivered and with moist eyes, I said, "I love you Amma. Please don't ignore me, there is no one, I am alone. I will go mad soon." and gave the phone back to Puneet who locked his palm with mine indicating the strong bond we shared.

22
Revival

Spending quality time in the arms of Puneet, during the presence of Kerala nurses did create the needed effect on my aimless mind, forcing me to attempt a wholesome approach towards the best available in my hands; the job and the way I do the job!

Reunion with Amma and her arrival to help me rebuild myself were strong signals of changing times. Smitha had changed her number, and I did not have it, I had lost all connections with Smitha and her family, yet her thoughts ran in my innate self without disturbing the exterior.

When the thoughts of Smitha were made to rest like a river bed, and I started building the understanding of my professional side, it was exposed that the mid-term debacle was not an unfair act, and that I hardly knew what all was there to work for, which I never did. Recognizing the agony became the near term objective and regaining the lost glory formed a longer term objective.

"Mission Smitha" had successfully created an array of virtually stitched curtains, which I was removing one by one to comprehend the anguish and to enjoy the joke I was subjected to. As the brain picked up the logical track with Amma's brilliant counselling skills, it became clear that my peers, my colleagues and my boss, they all made fun of me, and that was not the real Rama!

My image had tarnished, experts would declare tarnish as an understatement, it was beyond recognition; as the Management Trainee stint studded with three Es, Extended, Embarrassing and Exasperating neared an end, it was time for me to move to the place of action and apply the mettle I had picked up during the training. But it was not only me; the entire company was knowledgeable of the fact of my failures in picking any mettle.

The resultant was the dismissal of attempts of my influx into any team, no one wanted me! But I told myself every morning before I set out for work, "It can't be worse than this. Go and face them, you want to resign as you can't be take this further, but, the resignation will only prove them right. It might sound stupid if you tell this to somebody, but you got to prove everyone wrong and show them that you have it in you to rub your ass off and deliver competitively. Stay on! And smile." I would pull the tie and make a knot.

During those days of self-realization, came a moment, when a satellite factory, situated remotely in Goa, was entering a trajectory of ruthless expansion. And they needed a goat, who could work like a donkey and remain loyal as a dog! Could they get anyone better than me? Many turned down the idea of moving to a place known more for fish and beer skills, rather than industrialization and opportunities. It was a clear case of suicide and a method of dumping your own career, as pundits in office said. And then my unusual, parallel side whispered in my head, "Rama, ask for this opportunity, tell your boss that you would like to go there and do the best, and will steer the ship and establish the systems. What if you don't know? You can any day learn. You are the stud. Go for it!" I was finding the lost confidence back.

And the stars who had only raped me without condoms for the last couple of years, turned on their head to shower their support; before I stepped up the ante to grab the opportunity, my boss asked me to join him for a drink after work. As mentioned earlier, times had changed and the evidence was, "Drink after work."

An eye to eye co-ordination and a little bend of a neck from the boss meant that the day was to be wrapped and the "Drink after work" to be solemnized! Boss denied me the freedom to pay, by taking out his wallet before me, and blocking my hands to deny complete freedom, and said, "One Signature bottle" (We went to one of the bars run by powerful Jaats and Gujjars of Haryana where you buy the bottle of your choice and then chose a table for yourself and then the sides will follow!)

"Bottle?" I cited astonishment, for my tryst with the hospital! But that was in vain, as my boss promoted my booze abilities, and said, "We will finish it off. Relax." and we walked into the bar flooded with alcohol loaded crowd of the north and the air was buzzing with smoke, abuses and loud laughter.

I found the perfect opportunity to show my interest when we began to drink, but I still looked for the perfect moment. I thought, "When the whisky is poured into the glass, I should ask then. No, probably asking when the ice cubes are put would be better. What about when we strike our glasses for cheers? The first sip of the drink could be better!" and my boss said, "Do you have cigarettes?" and I instantly took out the packet, unwrapped it and pushed one out for my boss to pull, and then lighted it up for him, and my boss asked, "Do you know your extended training stint is over and it is the time to move?"

"Yes sir" I said curiously.

"And I don't know about others, but personally I have seen you working hard in the past couple of months." Boss made a background to inform me about something.

"How do you say that?" I looked for the long lost appreciation, once more!

"Want to hear good things about you? Is it?" he said and smiled. I blushed.

"No, no sir!" I said.

"The reports what you send out these days and the grip you have developed on your numbers are quite satisfactory and no one seems to complain about them." Boss began to open the secret box.

The first dose of satisfaction spread on my head, and I smiled for finer details. Boss said, "They are looking for someone to take care of factory costing in the Goa factory and I proposed your name."

I did not react to show that was the expectation, rather I displayed surprise, and said, "Goa? But I heard that there is no team there and everything needs to be started from the scratch, will I be able to manage?"

Boss said, "Do you think that you will not be able to manage? I have told them that you will be able to handle it properly, and now don't let me down." he gave the necessary boost, called motivation, with a personal flavour peculiar to north Indians, generally termed as "*Naak na Katwana*" which was actually not required in the remotest corner as this is what I waited for and I smiled to say, "Sure sir, when is the move planned?"

"Chill Rama, I know you are super excited to go out there and do your best given the past performances you have, however, please understand a few realities and that is the reason I asked you to come for a drink today." the discussion became serious, but I was tough to be up for any seriousness, any hell, but no more anguish!

Boss continued, "First of all, don't expect anything fancy out there, it might be in Goa, but it is far from the picture of Goa you might be carrying in your head, it is somewhere in the middle of a jungle. And, there will be no one reporting to you, you will be reporting to the Factory Finance Manager. There are clear chances of you working for 14 to 15 hours every day as you will be required to do at least three men's job. Also, you will be expected to establish strong systems due to the expansion which is being planned so that the future is stabilized. This will bring in lot of pressure and you might even want to resign at times. But let me tell you that the amount of learning you have there, especially when you do trial and error, is way too satisfactory."

"I understand everything sir, but I fail to understand how come I have been selected when there are so many talented and experienced people out there." I was curious.

"This position was offered to quite a few, but they turned it down for some reasons, the reasons could be the challenges and the difficulties which I told you about." my boss justified the rejections.

Considering that as a life time opportunity, all the more when the doors of Goa were widely opened for me to get into the application of everything I was going to learn. I landed in Goa in November as scheduled, breathed a new air of relief and a belief that the garbage was getting disposed in the value chain unlike Gurgaon! Getting rid of the "Scrap" tag was the foremost objective and proving my previous boss right was parallel to the foremost!

Forgetting that I was living in a holiday destination, it began to turn out into a leave less experience with the profession, where I deliberately threw myself into work deleting Saturdays and Sundays from my calendar!

My first leave in Goa came exactly after two months of sixteen incessant hours a day, the only reason being that I was setting up a home and it required a big round of shopping, which included the furniture, the home appliances and kitchen equipment!

The drop in the fuel bills, booze bills, food bills and most importantly the air fares had helped me revive the savings' base without suffocating myself and multiple employers. With the calculations perfectly done, quotations arranged and a decent rented apartment in place, I was entering into a phase of disciplined livelihood, away from the misery I chose to live with. I wanted to make a strong statement to the past, and bid good bye forever.

And ironically, just an evening before my first leave, while I surfed Facebook, I happened to be at Smitha's wall for some reason (and that happened every day, so there was nothing ironical about it, it was just to arouse interest!) but she had unfriended me long back! I messaged her, "Hi, how are you? It has been ages we heard from each other. Have got transferred to Goa and now I am moving into an apartment and have left the Chummery. I just wanted to tell you that I am setting up a home here. It feels great to save enough money to do so. How about you? What are you up to these days? Still in that flat with Cecilia? And yes, my parents are moving to Goa with me!" I felt that last statement was a nail in the coffin. Whose coffin anyway?

Smitha was not expected to reply and she fulfilled the expectation, and I went on to buy everything mentioned above, and was well on course in becoming a good boy who would get up on time in the morning, go to office on time, and would work very hard in the office, reach home on time to work out and finally go tc bed before 11!

Such phenomenal transformation was anticipated solely for the fact that my parents decided to move in with me for good leaving Raghav and Geeta alone to prosper, as they thought it was my turn to be blessed by their love, care and support.

A sound wall to lean against, the one who would take care of all, the underlying force for my very existence, the Mother was there to instil the confidence in me to not only take the mounting pressure at work, but to draw the best out of my stay in Goa. She would drive me to step out and explore Goa's beauty.

My savings continued to pile, as the entire spend was handled by Amma without depriving me of the leisure to spend. With getting accustomed to the job and the fancies around it, I began to find time to dig out the parties on Goan beaches with ease.

Though the turmoil of the personal life had settled down, it was still difficult on the professional scale where my boss would frown from morning till evening while making me feel absolutely useless by generating a negative feedback every time. His response from time to time would be "The management has a lot of expectations from you and you have a way to go to reach that mark." accompanied by *"Mazaa nahi aa raha tere kaam mein yaar!"*

At a time when my broad shoulders carried the burden of work of four men's ability, I wanted more appreciation before being put into the scanner straight away; I cursed myself for bringing this fate to myself. I often thought, "I have given the licence to my seniors to take my trip, it would take a stupendous effort from here on to change the image people have. They know they can give me any kind of feedback, and make me work any number of hours and I would not budge, purely for the fact that I needed it more than they did! But who gets this kind of hands on experience? If I am able to stick to this, forget about sustaining, I will be for sure a bundle of knowledge, quite indispensable from quite expendable as of now."

I began to take offs on Sundays, but the situation remained grey on the weekdays, where I continued to put in 16 to 17 hours of work daily, more importantly without complaining and most importantly while enjoying! Amma continued to tell me, "This is the age of your life where you have to work hard; it is ok that they make you slog, but they pay you well as well. So, keep doing it, be patient and things would be brighter." and I told myself, "And you chose this opportunity and it was already informed to you by your boss that you would be getting screwed up in Goa. Just do it!"

Amongst all the hardships, one thing continued to keep me going, and it was Amma's presence, she was the silent strength whose words of wisdom were to turn true. The efforts continued to pour in from me waiting for the luck to pour its share, and finally the day did come, when my work got the sizeable appreciation.

It was for the first time that after I joined Goa that my boss went on leave, giving me an opportunity to have a face-off with the factory management in the weekly meeting, where I realised in no time how my boss made me work long for different analysis and reports, which he used to steer brilliant logical discussions in such meetings. After these heroics, the only feedback he had for me was *"Mazaa nahi aaya"* when people went gaga on him during those meetings. I quickly understood that he would have never thought of saying that those analysis and reports were Rama's work and not his; to summarize, he took the credit of the hard work I did!

It is understandable that I worked at the behest of my boss, such reports were his brainchild, and however, telling me that I had a lot to catch up even when I had caught up a lot was insane, in fact slavish. And I had no clue that why he ate into my hard work, I was nowhere a competition to well established man like him. Some people are cheap, and you just can't help it!

My inputs during that meeting cleared the superficial doubt which people developed on my ability, due to the stories they would have heard about my credibility and the possible failure in clarifying such doubts by my boss. The first words of encouragement came from the factory manager, the respect commanding, and an ever smiling lady! She said, "Rama, I think you should attend the upcoming OMP exercise. Your inputs will be quite handy."

"OMP? What is that Mam?" I asked.

"Operational Master Plan. Prakash did not tell you about this?" Factory manager looked a bit miffed; seemed that something which I should have known was concealed from me!

"Oh! Yes, OMP. Right, I will attend, the abbreviation came as a surprise." I tried to protect my boss (Prakash) who considered me only as a doer and not a thinker. I could logically fit the happenings and make some sense out of it, that he would tell me only to make reports and would never tell me the reasons he would use those reports for. And I would blindly follow the mantra, "My boss is always right, he will always think well for and about me."

The day ensured that my outlook towards the job change, not whom should I do it for to how should I do it! I began to prepare reports without waiting for any prior go ahead from boss, directed those to the concerned, I began to participate in the discussions and issues voluntarily, I began to make myself visible at the place of action, I began to question my boss's authority on how I should work, I began to respect the timelines of the tasks, I began to don a thinking cap. Actually, I began to work finally! And people began to respect my position in the factory.

The long hours at work were getting reduced for my better understanding of the dynamics and I was quickly becoming a back bone to hold a pivotal position for the factory. Getting back to my witty self, I was becoming the "Wanted" in official parties, where I began to open up to crack jokes and flowed like a river where people would throng around me to listen to the nonsense I created.

The long hours ensured that I met people coming in different shifts in different departments, befriended them, learnt the operations from them, and began to trouble shoot. Not that those people reported to me, an effort to know people from various departments only appreciates the individual value; it was critical that I made solid relations with not only the senior staff in the factory, but also with the junior staff as the ground realities were known to them only! Such open relations not only ensured the smoothness with which I eased into the job, but also the respect I began to garner, for the first time probably while I worked!

And the nonsense ensured that I was approachable for one and all, my workstation became a highway inn, where people dropped in to lighten a bit, and boy I enjoyed that.

The one man army, the valiant sweats, the non-complaining attitude and a solid determination were the adjectives that studded my work and to prove that, I ensured that Goa factory became the first to go live on the SAP module (Systems used by the company to run daily transactions) up gradation by working seventy two hours at a stretch for it clashed with my other reporting and deliverables. Therefore, I received a well-deserved encouragement from the head office. However, to shake me out of my wits, my boss typed down a paragraph of appreciation for me in a mail circulated to everyone in the factory management and to concerned individuals at head office.

"Please note that ours is the first factory to go live on SAP 7.0 and it was ensured by commendable efforts from the Super Users of the factory. I would like to make a special mention of Rama, who engineered the entire upgradation in an effortless manner, without troubling the end users. He also confirmed that factory operations did not go long on Business Continuity Package, thereby ensuring no hindrance to regular operations. He has been chosen as the Star Performer for the current month."

It firmed the foothold I tried to make, and the applause continued to follow! And I wanted to ask my boss, *"Ab mazaa aa raha hai sir?"*

23
Return of 3S

"Twenty six is a good age to get married." Amma said during one of the long conversations that happened on Sundays.

"Who is getting married now?" I asked her acting ignorant of her intentions, which prevailed only to throw me at the mercy of some other lady before I moved ahead to choose some other "Smitha"

"Rajamani's son is getting married." Amma told me about one of the relatives from a set of relatives whom I hardly knew or wanted to know!

"Who is Rajamani? Is he related to Rajnikanth?" I was witty.

"Shut up! You should not make fun of those whom you don't know." Amma denied mockery. Appa like always was a silent witness.

"Exactly, I don't even know who Rajamani is, and you are telling me about his son? His son must be in US for sure. Right?" this was revolution, uncalled for.

Amma remained silent, for my unconditional love for those going to US, and said hesitantly, "Yes, he is in US. So what?"

"So what?" I repeated her last two words stressfully to make them magnum. I continued, "All the guys, especially Tam Brahms have one aim, and that is to go to US, and all the girls, have one aim, and that is to marry those who have gone to US. So, there is no surprise about Rajamani's son getting married. Even if he was twenty two, forget twenty six, he would have got married purely because he is in US. So, don't give me this nonsense of which age is the right age to get married."

Amma waggled in hopelessness and came to the point, "Whatever it might be and I don't care. You are twenty six right now, if we start hunting for a bride now, we will end up finding one by next year. We should not be delaying it now. I am going to float your profile online and with relatives. I hope you don't have an issue."

I thought intelligently, "Are you in any way giving me a choice? You have assumed that I don't have an issue and you will not stop even if I create an issue. You are getting bored in Goa and you find my matchmaking as the best way to wheel your time. Please go ahead, but remember that the acceptance lies in my hand. You will not hold my collar and make me sit next to the girl chosen by you."

Brilliant dishonesty came to my rescue again, and I said, "Ok. I am ready to marry. You can start." and Amma smiled leaving me to judge if it was actually the right time to get married. Due to Smitha's disaster, I had lost credibility on my choices and finding the right choice was the trickiest on earth.

I realised that even if Smitha was not there, tragedy with her had left a deep dent in my head towards women, that all they wanted from men was favours and they were not trustworthy. Subtle hints would throw me into a series of permutations and combinations to draw conclusion about females out of my past experience. Anyone resembling even an iota of Smitha or her mother's qualities would make me wary of them, without understanding that the qualities in women remained the same, only the degree varied. Therefore, moving on was just not becoming a reality.

At one point of time, I was enrolled with three portals promising a marriage in every twenty four seconds, but surprisingly, the huge list of women published by them could not woo me. The different relationship managers from all the portals tried their luck to seed the interest in me, but it simply did not work. It was not the failure of these portals, the issue ranged from Smitha's horrifying memories to my upbringing to my lifestyle, the last few hardly finding a match with Tamil Ladies.

My belief that Tam chicks were far from fashion and style was declared completely fit with girls turning up like ghosts in their profile pictures, where a nicely creased green dupatta would be draped around an ill fit, old styled yellow salwaar kameez. If this was not enough to scare the hell out of you, they would either wear rubber slippers or no slippers.

Above explained were the set of girls who either bothered to send an interest to me or those whom my family members bothered to send interests because their profile pictures were hidden. I never had qualms with the looks of a lady, but I always demanded someone highly presentable. For me, the most beautiful thing made by god was woman, and they should appreciate themselves.

There were other set of girls, other than "far from fashion" ladies whom my family sent requests incessantly, all of which were turned down. And the reason was my inability to get a foothold in US; these were the females who looked a point better than those mentioned above, and they assumed it to be a license to woo NRIs! Therefore, those who looked good thought they were beauty queens and wanted to go to US. My thought process was hitting the dust.

Another reason which killed the matchmaking attempt by Amma was my honesty with which I disclosed my disastrous relationship with Smitha to the few girls I spoke with and my straightforward attitude of telling them about my smoking and booze habits. I never understood that if the most sought after guys who resided in a shared rented apartment in US ever boozed or not! What were the girls thinking?

They probably thought that it was healthy and very nutritional to smoke and booze for Indians who stayed in US and it was highly rogue if it was done in India. It was frustrating to see the conditions conditional on the country of residence. Some profiles even said, "Willing to marry someone in US, the guy should be able to fund my higher studies there, dowry seekers please excuse!"

My retaliation to such profiles was mentioned on my matrimonial profile, "Those who are willing to stay in India should only apply." and my mother was bamboozled.

Amma often said, "You don't have to tell girls about your relationship with Smitha. This way, you will never be able to marry."

And my only response was, "I am sorry that I can't lie. I don't want to hide things. This will anyhow get disclosed when I marry the girl. I want each and every factor to be informed to the girls so that they can make informed choices instead of cribbing later on. If it works this way, then it is fine and if it does not, let the marriage go to hell."

The ceiling would come crashing on Amma's head and she would accuse Smitha profusely, "That girl will never be happy in her life; it is all because of her that you are like this today. She will never be able to marry anyone in her life because she destroyed you." and then she will speak to god, "Please god, please give some sense to my son on how the world works. He is such a fool; please find a good girl for him."

And I would think, "Why such hue and cry, animation and multiple parties involved in getting me married?"

And just when the marriage mania was reaching a saturation point, I got the call which would bring life to a full circle, taking me to the past and burying me in the new grave.

"Hi Bro!" this was the voice I knew, and the accent looked familiar.

"Hi! who is this?" I looked for a known answer.

"What the hell! You don't even have my number?" the complaint was authoritative.

"No, I am sorry!" I gave up instantly as I had better jobs in hand than to play hide and seek with a male.

"Can you tell me who you are or should I disconnect?" I offered to close the conversation and then came an expected yet an unanticipated answer.

"Bro, this is Ranjan! How are you?" and there was a well-deserved pause, because it made me think rapidly, "Why is he calling me up now? Oh yes, I never had issues with him, but I did have issues with his family. Exactly, even he had issues with his family; therefore, enemy's enemy is my friend. So, I should entertain him."

"Hi dude, I am fine. How are you? Where did you get the number from?" I slipped into a regular conversation while pondering over the reason of his call! If he did not speak to me all the while when I destroyed myself, where did the need arise now?

And Ranjan, as I knew, came to the point. Call him mean or not, I did not know, "I was planning to come to Goa. Guddu told me that you were in Goa...." and he was paused.

"Smitha still talks about me?" It brought an old faded smile on my face, and quickly I realized that Smitha could no longer bring smile on my face; and I switched to seriousness.

"Ok, whatever. So, you have plans to come to Goa." my switch very much evident which Ranjan read easily, "Bro, don't think that I am calling you only because I am coming to Goa and as far as your number is concerned, it is mentioned on your Facebook profile. That is about it. And you always had issues with Mama and Guddu, why are you dragging me into it? You know the say I have in the family, I was nowhere involved. Just that Guddu told me that you mailed her and that you have moved to Goa. I thought if we could meet when I am there. Rest is your choice."

Ranjan articulated well enough to alter the emotions I ran with, his last few statements reminiscent of the innocence I knew him for, and I caved, "Sure man, nothing of that sort, Let me know when you are here, we will for sure catch up." and Ranjan confirmed his itinerary, "I am there this weekend, Actually I had come to Hyderabad to meet Guddu, and you know what, I am working with HCL in Noida."

So, I became informative about the Smitha's family updates and more importantly that the drug carrier of the yore graduating to get a job with a 5 billion dollar enterprise! And I asked another unnecessary, not my business sort of question, "Is Smitha also coming along with you?"

Ranjan thought that my decision to catch up with him might change, he said, "No, she is not coming." and he was apparently true.

Ranjan's arrival in Goa worked up a task for me, that I took an off on Saturday to please my honoured guest by lying at home and office.

Hang on, but why was I doing that? Somewhere, in the distant corner of my idiot head, I believed that Smitha could still be a reality in my life, and was that the reason for me to entertain Ranjan. I could never figure that out, I stayed confused, yet I kept on buying beer for him.

With the nothing so special visit to Goa by Ranjan coming to an end, things came back to normal and I began to believe to have got fucked again as nothing happened which I longed for during Ranjan's stay at Goa. In fact, the chaos began to unwind, I wanted Smitha to be discussed, but I could not do that, and hence the life remained at zero.

Fucked and Screwed were synonymous for me, once I bit the dust again, I calculated the fancies of Ranjan which I paid for, and obviously could not draw enough courage to demand reimbursement. He was not related to me in anyway now. Yet, he enjoyed the tag of being the brother of my ex who dictated my life once.

However, Ranjan's visit was nothing short of the numerous visits I made to temples in my dreams, praying a miracle which would ensure Smitha's return into my life. And Ranjan's visit did turn out to be that miracle!

A new unknown number flashed on my screen, during the peak working hours of the maniac Monday. *In fact, every new number raised the heartbeats, because I began to expect them to be a call from the parents of the scary women on the Tamil matrimonial sites.*

But that number was a scorcher, I rushed to the conference room to answer it, "Hello!"

And then was the voice I lived for, the long awaited, the one which would let me skip a heartbeat, "Hi Rama!"

"Smitha?" I knew yet I confirmed and paused for it was after a year I heard her speak. My hands began to shiver and my forehead began to ejaculate sweat.

"Yes, How are you?" she sounded fragile.

"Holy shit!" I could have responded better, but I had stopped acting. And Smitha vociferated that.

"What? What happened? I expected a better response!" Smitha sounded normal, as nothing ever happened between us. I chose to co-operate.

"Yeah, I am sorry!" I offered an apology. Certain things never changed, like I apologizing to Smitha. *Legacy continued.*

"So how are you doing? You just vanished somewhere?" Smitha's casualness was irritating. *Oh is it? What did you expect after you and your NRI dad threatened me off police and embassy?*

"What somewhere? And what vanished? I messaged you on FB that I was moving to Goa? Right? And you also informed Ranjan about that?" I knew logic in and out, but never practiced it. Smitha giggled like a nine year old.

"Yeah, I just called up to say thanks to have entertained my brother so selflessly." Smitha said.

It was murderous because I was already getting troubled by a few excel sheets which I had left to answer the call where Smitha spun my head. "That is ok!" I managed to say. *I was a fucking selfish loser a year ago, what happened now? The best way to please a lady is to please her brother.*

"What ok? I asked Ranjan not to speak to you after whatever happened. But he did not listen to me and called you up. And you were sweet enough to help him out." Smitha finally uttered "whatever happened" which meant that she complied with "all was not well between us" status! And I did not step back to say that.

"Good you realized that things are not the way they were between us. I thought you forgot that."

"God, I don't need your sarcasm." Smitha would never take any nonsense, if it was from me. If it was from Mama, it carried the stamp from Chanakya!

I thought, *"Ok, then take this."*

"My parents are hunting a bride for me, I will soon settle down with someone." this was uncalled for, as Smitha had lost interest in me long back and wasn't that supposed to be a "Thanks giving" call only? But I wished to sense something, that if that news made Smitha insecure.

"Ok, great! You will find someone of your taste, who suits you. I wasn't good enough for you." Smitha said. Girls do this and expect disagreement, they expect guys to tell them how fit they are for them, especially when the girl has no intention of stepping into the guy's life again; but, do they leave any opportunity of confusing them?

I was a proven idiot, growing from strength to strength, I did fall for what she said, "No, nothing of that sort. Don't undermine the value of what you were in my life; had you been not so good, I would have never gone so far to get you." I did two things; first, told Smitha about her unmatchable importance in my life she held and second, made her realize the circus I went through to get her.

She went into the silent mode; a famous pause was followed by an abrupt statement, "Ok, fine. Thanks and all the best with your search. Take care."

"Bye! You take care too." I said and she disconnected, but now I had her number. And did she expect me to call?

I was successful in troubling Smitha by telling her about the bride hunting activities and the effects were to reflect sooner or later, even when I did not know that it meant something to Smitha.

Just a day later after Smitha called, I got a call again from the same number, I again braked on the excel sheets I slept with, went to the conference room and said, "Hello!" sounding firmer than the previous day.

"Hi, I thought you would call. But you did not." Smitha complained, but why? Someone should have told her that one call on the previous day would not have helped me to recover from the threats her dad shot at me.

But I played the tricks which girls generally play, picking up the statements and digging on them in every angle. "But did you notice what you said yesterday? Thanks and all the best with the search. I thought you were fine with me moving on with somebody else. Then how I could have called you up again? It had to make sense, and obviously, I have to get over with you completely if I am planning to move on even in my distant dreams."

Smitha needed time to comprehend with what I said. She probably thought, "What is that Rama is trying to say? Is he moving or not? Is he waiting for me? Is it that he does not want to talk to me?"

I managed an evil smile, but looked for Smitha's presence on the other side, "Hello you there?"

"Hey Rama, was I so important for you in your life?" Smitha was melting. It took a break up, alcoholism, fight with Thomas and Ranjan's visit to Goa to make her understand the importance she held in my life. But I sent another one for her to melt.

"Not my life. I always thought it was our life!" I was in the middle of romance in the middle of the work loaded day. She probably had not much to do. But wait, why was I becoming extra nice to her? Wasn't I planning to marry at the right age?

"Oh Rama…" and it was an awkward moment. Smitha broke down. Quite understandable, imagining your ex having sex with somebody else has to freak you out. And who gets a donkey like me who would just do what it took to keep her happy? I am sure none of the flying NRIs whom her Mama chose for her would have agreed to get their life slaughtered with Smitha, for the amount of disturbance her Mama would bring to their lives. I wanted to touch that topic. I was acting like a scoundrel, relishing the pain Smitha went through. It was ok, I went through the same.

"Hey, don't cry. Tell me what happened? Your Mama must have chosen someone for you as well. She always talked about getting you married to some big shot settled abroad. And what about PhD?" it was a clear act of rubbing not only salt, but pepper as well on her wounds. My smile broadened now. Did I actually love Smitha? Or was it an ego trip?

"Nothing, I never thought that it would be so easy for you to move on. At the time when I am fighting my loneliness and filling the emptiness after you left, you are happily searching a bride for yourself." Smitha began to flex her rights as a woman. I thought, "Searching a bride is fine, what was happily searching? Did she see my expressions or did Ranjan give her wrong signals. Fuck you Ranjan!"

"But you haven't answered my question yet." I wanted to know her status.

"No, Mama did not search anybody till now. In fact, I could not move on. And you know PhD was never my cup of tea. So, after you left, things have not changed at all. I am still the same Smitha you left." Smitha began to admit her weaknesses. It was revelation. But I wanted to correct her, "Hang on, I did not leave you, it was your crazy decision to leave me." But such moments of realization from Smitha only commanded silence from me and I provided that.

"To be honest, I have not figured out yet that what kind of woman I want to settle with. I knew only one woman and it was you." I began to open up.

"Do you still love me?" Smitha ripped me apart, picked me with two hands and threw me into inferno.

"What sort of question is that? There is nothing possible between us, will Mama ever agree? There is no point. Cut this crap." I wanted to say yes, but I said something else.

"Leave that to me. Say yes or no." Smitha stepped into my shoes and was putting pressure on the pedal.

"Yes, of course, I do but whatever I did was crime. I should not have abused you. With what face, I will face you?" I opened the confession machine.

"That is ok" Smitha was merciful. *What was that? I expected you to confess your mistake as well!*

"Mama has been saying that I should marry the one whom I was in relationship with, she is finding it difficult to digest that I was in relationship with you and I am marrying somebody else." Smitha said.

What crap was that? She can't be so sensible, I think that the fact she told every relative about me is making it difficult for her to answer those curious relatives about my whereabouts. She was ranting about me being from IIM Ahmedabad chosen for Guddu; she fell in her own trap and now sending her daughter as an agent to fix things with me again so that she could save her face with relatives. But why don't they admit that instead of giving out false stories? However, it does not matter to me as long as I get Smitha. Was I myopic again?

But I was not hesitant to mention that I was not falling for any of the erstwhile conditions which Smitha chose to bestow me with. "But let me tell you one thing very clearly Smitha. I am not going to leave my parents, come what may, I am not going to follow Christianity, the wedding if at all happens, will happen in both rituals and I am not going to settle abroad. And you have to return the copy of the undertaking which I gave to you. Don't think that I don't love you, I do love you but I love myself and my family as well."

"I respect your point Rama. You are absolutely right at where you are. I would have done the same thing if I was at your place. Great, I feel so relaxed and happy today. We are back together. I will call you in the evening."

I looked out of the window, wondering if there was no glass, then I would have jumped out because Smitha's response was swirling. I had to confirm if it was not a dream, "Are you sure about this? Because I don't want a heartbreak again, you don't know what shit I have gone through. Do anything but don't betray me."

Smitha looked determined in her decision to come back into my life or I should say *"Take me back into her life"*

"Trust me and I will take care of the things this time around. But promise me that you will also not leave me. I will speak to Mama about this. Love you. Bye."

"Bye." I said and disconnected, without responding to her "Love you" intentionally. It was time to rebound.

The love began to blossom again; Smitha made it a point to call every morning before she set out for work and every evening after she returned from work. I began to wonder the existence of Thomas in her life; however, I enjoyed the importance I got.

With all the talking between Smitha and me, I realized that I had lost the physical inclination towards Smitha; I neither kissed her on the phone nor asked for it which Smitha pointed out extensively. My whole purpose was to not get involved so much before Mama's approval once again. So, I distanced myself, practiced self-restraint!

When the complaints of Smitha for not being the usual donkey of the past became excessive, I told her during one of the conversations, "Listen, I want to get as close to you as you want, but this time, I want a clean chit from your mother before I get involved, also, since I am on the phone with you in the evenings, Amma has sensed that there is something fishy going on."

"Sure, I will tell Mama that things are back on track with you, but what does your mother say?" Smitha said.

"My mother has been hunting brides for me, I had begun to show interest, but now I am back with you. So, I have stopped looking at girls' profiles, I reject them without even looking at them and clearly change the topic when Amma begins to discuss marriage. Plus, I am on the phone with you, so, she knows that something is wrong." I clarified.

"What do you want?" I waited for 23 chapters before I was asked this.

"I want to marry you, but I don't want to be in a soup again. I am again taking *panga* with my family without any visibility. Don't leave me in the middle again, because I don't want to miss on the good girls whom I have been rejecting for you." there was a sense of sarcasm for the last thing I said.

Smitha snubbed it under her laughter, and said, "Sure, I will speak to Mama soon, I am just looking for the right moment."

Smitha's soon came a bit sooner than expected and a number flashed on my phone on the same evening. *Was Smitha tensed that I would marry somebody else that she could not wait anymore to get that settled with Mama?* That number I could identify easily, as it had been my duty at one point of time to ring that number for getting insulted every day. Good, you are an intelligent reader to have guessed it rightly! It was Mama.

A sense of confidence, yet respect was there in my tone, "Hello Mama!"

"Hi *beta*!" Mama responded. *Please god; please give me poison, she is so kind.*

"How are you doing Mama?" I said.

"I am fine. How are you?" she said and without bothering to know how I was, she continued, "Smitha told me about you." and before I could ask her what was told to her, she anticipated the question and carried on to answer on her own, "She told me that both of you are back together and you want to marry her again."

Did Smitha tell her that I played host to Ranjan in Goa? Did Smitha tell her that she called me up and felt insecure after she got aware of my marriage plans?

And did I say that I wanted to marry her? Oh shit, Yes, I did when she asked me what I wanted. So, was I in a trap again?

But, I chose to just say yes to what Mama asked. I was surprised that Mama did not hint at any of the erstwhile conditions; she probably thought it was futile to ask me such things as she assumed that I was bound by them for my life.

I did not bother to ask her anything because I had no idea what Smitha told her. So, I entered into a closed ended question answer session with Mama. Of course, she asked questions and I answered them in yes, no, yeah, hmm and ok.

"So, it is good that things are fine again." Mama said.

"Yeah" I said. *I hope you are not crying when you are saying this.*

"I will speak to Papa and also convince him." Mama said.

"Yes" I said. *Please tell him that I did not chase your daughter, he might get me jailed.*

"We are planning to get her married by next Feb." Mama said.

"Ok" I said. *I am sure that you are not interested in my readiness.*

"Are you planning to move out of the country?" Mama asked.

"No" I said. *I have moved out from country liquor to high end whisky.*

"Ok, can you come to meet me so that we can talk it out again?" Mama asked.

"Hmm" I said and Mama jumped in, "What hmm? What are you thinking?"

And then I got a chance to say what I thought, "I have loads of work Mama, and I cannot come that far. Please let me know everything over the phone, but I can comment upon anything only if you commit to get her married off to me."

Since I made my thoughts very clear to Mama, she said, "*Beta*, we have known you for some time, I am ok with the marriage. But you should be ready by Feb." Mama said.

Mama did not tell me what "Readiness" meant. In the ecstasy of getting Smitha back and to avoid unnecessary problems, I did not bother to ask what "Readiness" was. Mama did not talk about any conditions and so did I.

"Yes, I will be ready by Feb. you don't worry." I said knowing the amount of disco I will be required to do to convince my parents. I was living others' life; first her parents and then my parents.

"Ok *beta*. Bye." and she disconnected.

Though things had normalized, yet there was an air of disturbance, which I could never sort out. I chose to live with it, and got into a thorough relationship mode with Smitha, when I began to make love with her over the phone. We sailed smooth for months, and marrying Smitha began to look real again, when we discussed love, future, and kids; far away from the topics like religion, savings, money, job abroad. We lived it; both of us excelled professionally and got our share of rewards.

Smitha had done exceedingly well to achieve her half yearly targets, and she, with a few others from her colleagues were chosen for a three days trip to Tashkent. And wasn't she excited!

I did not ask her about the colleagues whom she went with even when I wanted to. Basically, I wanted to know if Thomas was going or not, however, my want to keep the relationship stable had over powered the want to know about the passengers travelling abroad.

Smitha had to return by Sunday evening, and I expected her call after her arrival. She would tell me in her child like innocent voice how much she enjoyed being there, the pictures she clicked, the clothes she bought and the shopping she did keeping me specifically in her mind. All such thoughts egged me to wait eagerly, and I kept on waiting.

I had begun to let Smitha go instead of being finicky about every detailed issue, therefore continued to wait more. I thought women liked men who were patient, and I was becoming a patient. But that could not happen further, I called her up and she disconnected.

I continued to call her and she continued to disconnect leaving me in a state where I thought everything, I even flipped through news channels to see if any flight from Tashkent to Delhi had crashed. After repeated calls which extended till late night, Smitha bothered to message me, "Relax, I am fine, will call you once I reach Hyderabad, I am at home right now. Don't call now!"

The message sent a wave of contentment through my body, yet, my historical inquisitive nature forced me to send a message to her, "Weren't you supposed to catch a connecting flight to Hyderabad? Why did you take a halt at Delhi?"

"I thought to meet Mama on the way. Good night now. Bye and don't call. I will call you." Smitha sounded mighty suspicious.

But didn't Mama know that we were back and we wanted to marry each other and everything proceeded out of her approval. What was Smitha trying to do was out of my comprehension, but I decided to ignore the reasons behind her heavenly ideas.

The logical reason behind my night vigil to know Smitha's whereabouts was supported by Raghav's and Geeta's planned arrival to Goa the next morning, I had taken a leave for a week to entertain those who remained with me during the bad times. It meant that I lied to Mama about my mounting work pressure and my inability to meet her to discover again that how big a loser I was and to buy samosas for her relatives.

I was not worried as Smitha had confirmed that she would call me, more importantly the engrossment to entertain the brother and his wife had taken over my interest and we did not leave a second to enjoy every moment of togetherness. I also messaged about my inability to speak to Smitha freely as I was at the job of helping my family explore the best in their vacation.

Smitha called up incessantly all of a sudden, only for me to disconnect again and again, I did the same what she did to me, "Relax, I am with my family; I can't obviously speak to you as I don't want any mess. Please understand. I will call later."

Smitha messaged, and she breathed fire, "So, you are on leave and entertaining your family? Why did you lie to Mama that you could not meet her? I am seeing that you don't give me the same importance which you gave me earlier, if this is the way you want this to be, I will call it quits."

I don't know if I was wrong in lying to her mother, probably yes, probably no. I only knew that if I entertained her brother while lying to my family, how wrong was I in doing it the other way round.

Smitha did not rattle me up, but she did manage to shake me up, and I messaged her, "Look here; I can't get into a fight with you now. I will call once Raghav and Geeta leave."

And she signed off, "Whatever! I don't want to stand second in your life. Take care of your family. Bye!"

Ladies, please understand that if a man loves his parental family, it does not mean that he does not love you. There is no connection. Why do you go nuts?

I called her up after two days, once I was free from the guide's job; it was a matured lady at the other end. Petrified and I said, "Hello. Who is this?"

And I got the first jerk, "Once you spend excessive time with your family, you stop recognizing us."

It was Mama, back to her usual best. You could not keep her out of action for long, "Mama. How are you?" I smiled trying to mock what she said.

"Are you in Hyderabad?" I asked.

"Why? Do I need to ask you before coming to Hyderabad? Did you ask us before getting your parents with you?" Mama threw sarcasm, and I was in no mood to tolerate any more nonsense. However, she did not answer me if she was in Hyderabad or not.

"What is wrong with you? Why are you speaking like that?" I confronted.

"See Guddu told me that you have been avoiding her because your family was there." Mama said firmly. She anyway knew everything.

"No, nothing of that sort. I don't want to discuss such things. Can I speak to Smitha?" Smitha was no longer Guddu. Mama handed over the phone to Smitha.

"Hello!" Smitha gave her snooty tone.

"Hi, what has gone wrong with you? Why are you acting weird? And where are you?" I asked her three questions, quite sinful of me! I was getting reprimanded.

"Shut up! I am not answerable to you. I am in Delhi and just because I have been tolerating your rude and dry behaviour towards me, I can't get the drubbing from you in any case." Smitha spoke something drawn out of some nonsense cells driving her. But what was she doing in Delhi again? It had been only a week.

I disconnected without speaking anything further, it was practically impossible for me to accept this behaviour after the kind of response Smitha gave to me during the last three months of togetherness. She in fact approved every act of me, what went wrong then?

I called a day later, expecting the atmosphere to have cooled down.

However, Smitha had something else to complain about, "I have been thinking hard about everything. You were right that Mama would not agree for this."

"But she did agree if I am not wrong." I cross questioned.

"But she got pissed off the moment she came to know that you lied to her about having lot of work pressure and not able to meet her." she said.

"Who told her that I lied? If it was you, then you are stupid." I shot back.

"Shut up! Plus, she is also saying that you are not planning to settle abroad, therefore it is not worth marrying you." Did she just say "Worth"?

"What? What shit is that? I made everything clear to you and that is how we started again. Now where is the issue?" While I spoke, Smitha gave the phone to Mama who looked to have prepared a speech to be hurled at me leaving me absolutely dejected and marred.

"Listen Rama!" … She continued, "We thought of giving you another chance but you failed to grab it. You seem to have no interest to grow in your life, you are happy staying here without aiming big in your life. Our Guddu wants to settle abroad and you don't seem to have any plans of moving out. Plus, I think that you are not at all ready for the wedding in Feb which you know according to our standards will be a grand occasion. I don't think you are prepared financially for it, or you have done any savings. And with your looting family staying with you, I am sure you are not saving even a penny. I don't understand that why did you buy a car when we already have one *(she meant that fucked up Wagon R, she did not know that it had fallen flat on its face from the fly over! And who told her that my i10 had anything to do with them owning a car or not?).* Your family wants to enjoy on the money you earn. Guddu cannot stay with your family, she is scared. *(Scared of what? She has managed to stay with you for so many years; she should have overcome all her phobias by now.).* Your family is ok, but your mom is like a witch, did you see the way she reacted on the day of engagement!"……………………..

Buzzzzzzzzzzzzzzzzzzzzzzzzzz……My ears got heated up when my creator was addressed as witch by the bitch. I intervened in the loudest of sound, "SHUT UP! THANK YOUR STARS THAT WE ARE TALKING ON THE PHONE. YOU CAN'T EVEN IMAGINE WHAT I WOULD HAVE DONE TO YOU FOR SAYING THIS. GET LOST. BYE."

And I threw the phone on the floor in desperation to have not done anything when my mother was abused. And I screamed at the top of my voice, while I looked at the broken phone to take out the frustration volcanically.

24
Done to the Death

"Why are you packing? Where are you leaving? Why didn't you tell me before?" the multiple questions habit would never leave Amma. And I cooked up an answer looking at her still sleepy eyes!

"I am going to Palolem today." my eyes red due to lack of sleep; courtesy, last night's dialogue with Mama.

"But why so early? It is only 5." Amma asked while she popped her eyes out, fighting the ever so gripping sleep.

And I checked the wall clock, and said, "Yes, it is very far."

"We went to so many places in the last one week; you could have taken some rest today. Anyhow, what time do you plan to return?" Amma was caring, yet granted freedom.

"Pretty late in the night. You don't wait for me and sleep. Ok?" I said as I wore my floaters.

"Drive safe and take care, don't go far into the sea." She said.

"Bye." I said.

I looked at Amma in the rear view mirror while I drove, thinking that how my decision of venturing out so early made the sleep deprived lady gather all the energy.

"Which is the first flight from now to Delhi?" I inquired at Go-Air's counter.

I did not drive to the random beach I told Amma, in fact, I came straight to the airport. I was flying to Delhi; to do what, I did not know.

"We have at 8:30 sir." broad smile lady, with mascara on tiring eyes told me.

"Can I get a return ticket?" I asked.

"For how many persons sir?" lady asked, while her right index finger was ready pointing at the keyboard to enter the details the moment I utter them.

"Only one ticket, and return is today itself." I said giving her some information before she asked for it.

She smiled, (In fact she smiled for everything, I was hating it then for the series of thoughts running in my mind), and said, "Sure sir, the return flight is at 5.45 in the evening, will reach Goa by 8.15."

She did some swift activities on her computer screen, (As if I would change my mind), and said, "Thirteen thousand four hundred and twenty six sir" and she smiled again.

Credit card, swipe, tickets and I walked straight into the Airport. As I collected my boarding pass and waited at the lounge, I continued to think, "Why the hell Smitha behaved this way? What went wrong?"

I boarded the flight, and looked at the runway from the window as it ran to take off; fascinated by that sight, I thought further, "Was it planned? Is Mama responsible for it? Did they ever go to school to develop such cheap thoughts? Why the fuck did she ever come back? Am I really hurt? Is it the anguish? What am I going to tell her once I meet her?"

My limbs moved perfectly to reach out for the luggage, the bus, and the cab however, my mind just did not refrain from deadly thoughts, "I want her in my life, do I? Is it that I could not do without her? Is anybody so indispensable? What is bothering me? The fact she dumped me again or her mom abused my mom. Should I go and sort it by talking to her? Should I plead her to reconsider her decision? Fuck yourself, why do I have to plead? It will be full and final today; I'll teach her a lesson of her life. I will kill her."

The frustration began to conquer the brain, and then my expressions. Lack of sleep, bantering head, ambiguity of thoughts and a ferociousness of Amma getting abused was turning me into a killing machine. I imagined myself as Arnold of the Predator, on the hunt!

The cab drove me into the apartments and honked. The security guy came running to open the gate and I rolled the shield down to wave at the security guard, who showed his tobacco hit teeth, for I was the resident of the same flat two years ago.

The temperature began to rise as I paid for the cab, my heartbeat speeded as I looked up to see if someone was at the flat's balcony, I looked for the Wagon R at the parking which ensured their presence at home, I pressed the elevator button expecting Smitha to walk out of it, my head began to spin as elevator dropped me at the desired floor, my nostrils heated up, I gained strength and anger. I pressed the door bell and at that very second, I hated Smitha and her mother the most in the world.

Smitha opened the door and......................................

With all the might, force and power my shoulder could transport to my palm, I planted the strongest of slap I generated in my life on Smitha's face. She was grounded and then followed the murderous rage as I stepped into the flat.

As Smitha screamed in pain, Mama came running in. I had stepped inside the flat and closed the door. Mama shouted at me, "What the hell do you think of yourself?" and she raised her hand to slap me, which I confronted. I held her raised hand, looked straight into her eyes which dreaded with fear and I raised my hand, instead of slapping her, bought the alter down with a big heave which was right next to the door.

While I strengthened the grip on Mama's cucumber like wrist, she shouted at Smitha, "Get up, go and call Ranjan and then police." Smitha got up and ran to pick her mobile. *By the time either of the two arrived, my job would be over. Anyhow, what could Ranjan do? I was in no mood to spare anyone.*

I freed Mama's wrist, walked like a man possessed, who eased into killing; followed Smitha and snatched the phone from her and banged it on the wall which blew into pieces. *If you made me break my phone yesterday, how the fuck can you have yours safe?*

Smitha and Mama looked at each other, we stood like three vertices of triangle; I relished the fear for life in their eyes, and with that fear, Mama said "What are you doing? You will not be able to marry Guddu this way." fear had overtaken the force in her tone.

I nodded my head in hopelessness, and said, "Do I look like a complete idiot? Do you think that I will believe you? That if I stop this, you will get us married?" I sighed and looked at the ceiling, then looked down again, and continued, "Who is in any way hoping for a marriage with your daughter?"

The terror had engulfed them and they stood frozen holding each other's hands, wondering what was coming next. Mama was the epitome of foolishness, and she proved that again; she spoke again, while being at the receiving end, "Do you think that you will be able to get away by torturing us? We will inform police."

I had calmed down slightly by slapping Smitha, by breaking the alter and then her phone, but Mama tickled my angry bone again and in a rage I went into the kitchen, picked the kitchen knife and came out to walk fiercely straight to Mama who stepped back expecting murder. Smitha intervened and said, "Please Rama, what are you doing? You are going to kill her? She is a heart patient on a pacemaker, don't scare her."

Smitha had tears in her eyes, but they could not melt me as they used to. I held her neck and drew her close and said, "The very thought of your mom getting killed took you just seconds to go down on your knees and plead, Did you ever imagine that what I went through every time you and your fucking Mama took shots at my family?"

I loosened the grip on Smitha's neck, she was choking. I looked over her shoulder, pushed her aside and walked towards Mama again, she began to puff and said, "No, no, no…" she expected the murder was on her way. Smitha held my right elbow, and dragged me back. She even sent a couple of blows on my shoulder with her weak palms assuming that the knife would fall and shouted, "Please please please...."

When her plead became irritating, I kicked the centre table vehemently and blustered the glass into pieces which shone from the floor. At that site, Mama muttered courage and uttered, "Why are you doing this? What are you going to get?"

I looked at her, made a gesture of slapping her and then kept the knife on her lips, asking her to shut up. "Satisfaction", I answered her second question first.

And the first question required explanation, I held both mother and daughter by shoulders, dragged them to the bedroom, and said, "Sit here." which they had to obey. *People don't have choice in the middle of the murder as long as the murderer does not want to give one.*

"Why am I doing this?" repeating a question helps one to interpret in the way he wants to, and then the answer becomes the unleashed weapon.

I smiled, telling her that she was stupid to ask that question, as the answer was obvious, I said, "Have you thought that how much you have tortured me? My crime? That I loved your daughter. And I was made to pay such a heavy price for that. You almost snatched the breathe out of me till the time I was in a relationship with her. I ditched every one including myself, I destroyed myself, my career all to make this relationship prosper. She knows it." I pointed at Smitha.

I continued, my red eyes were teary, for the pressure released from all nozzles as I was speaking then, for the first time, my heart out, "You always said that since I proposed to your daughter, the responsibility lay on my head. Ask her, we were seeing each other for a year before she told you about me. And all the time you believed that your daughter was not speaking to me because of the creepy promise you made her do, for your info, she met me every month. And coming back to your smartness, which you thought I could never crack, I always knew that you had some story to tell her and some other story for me. For example, when did I tell you that I slept with her and therefore, I consider her as my wife?" I looked sideways and hung my head down.

Mama listened cautiously, "If you always wanted that I should not be marrying her, you should have told that on my face in a dignified manner, I would have respected your call and walked out or would have acted to gain your confidence. Albeit, you resorted to cheap tactics;

Conversion, giving me unreasonable targets, savings, twenty five lakhs wedding, abusing my parents and when I gave in for everything, the drama you created on the engagement day was unreasonable. Plus, how could you abuse my family every time on my face? Just because I loved your daughter, you thought you had the license to make me dance to your tunes?"

"But..." Mama could not listen for long, she had to intervene.

"SHUT UP", I shouted.

"What but? And your family always used me as a servant, making me travel here and there and asking me to do other household chores. And If I could not, you made ruckus out of it. I had self-respect as an individual which you never recognized. Not your fault, I never recognized and gave you the license. And yes, get this thing straight into your empty head" I pressed her forehead with my left index finger.

"It was Ranjan who came to Goa. Do you know that? It was your daughter who called me and told me that you were not able to digest that she goes on sleeping with me and then marry somebody else. I had walked out of her life when Papa threatened me of police, jail and embassy. Screw you people, I deserved better than police, ask yourself. I thought of living a dignified life, before this bitch called up and showed her eagerness to marry me." I looked at Smitha.

"I fell into the trap again, but made clear that I was not ready for any conditions, but where the hell did everything come from now? Chuck it, I don't care ANYMORE." The last word had pain, determination and authority.

I paused, and looked at Smitha, "If at all you want to marry anyone, stop listening to your mother, if she keeps on interfering the way she did with us, you will have a bull shit life." and I threw the knife.

The disposal of knife made the duo believe that it was over and they could restart, "Who the hell are you tell her that what she should do and what not?"

I gave a plain look to her mother and picked the knife again, she froze, "I am what I am. But what are you? How the fuck you have such cheap thoughts in your head? You teach civics in school and you promote conversion, I think you have sewage water running in your body which is called blood." my conscience smiled at this comparison. I threw the knife forcefully and it toppled thrice on the floor to vanish somewhere under the bed.

"You don't deserve her, you are unlucky not to have Guddu in your life." Mama said decisively.

"Yes, I am unlucky, I am good for nothing, You can get her married to some NRI bastard whom she can shower with her luck and fuck. I am useless, unfortunate, and will not go anywhere in my life. Happy now? DO I NEED TO degrade myself further to please you more?" I signed off.

I picked my bag and walked out of the house and crossed Ranjan at the apartments gate, he tried to stop me, but I did not pay attention. He would have witnessed the damage to his home and the fear of his mom and sister. A message dropped in my phone; I made an effort to read through the broken screen. It was Ranjan, "You should have done this earlier and you would have been in peace. All the best for your life and stay in touch with me at least."

"GOOD LUCK", I replied.

25

Smitha Speaks After a Year

Hi everybody, this is Smitha, finally getting a chance to tell my side of the story. I know that you people hate me by now; all thanks to Rama's literary skills in defaming me! He might have believed that I only hated him, used him and then disposed him. True? Is it? May be or may not be. I am here to confess, rest is for you to decide.

You know it has been almost a year that he did what I hated him the most for; violence! You know that he slapped me and how he threatened me and my mother; he never bothered to call up after that, even I did not draw enough interest in calling him. Plus, he has moved on, I have seen his pictures with his new girl on FB. Therefore, I did not want to disturb his mental balance which is rare in his case.

So, you know what I hated him for and now you will know what I respected him for. Shocking it was that he called up yesterday; do you guys remember Dipti? Dipti Ahuja, the plastic smile chick who joined with him. Yes, attention drawing girl was in Goa last week, and Rama had gone to meet her.

People have a peculiar habit of not warning people on time, for they don't want to be interfering.

Rama said, "Hi Smitha, how are you?" I could not help but sport a smile on my face. I loved him at one point of time; honestly, it was good to hear him. He was the one who would die for me.

"Hey Rama, I am doing good. How are you?" I responded nicely.

"I know I should not have called you, but wanted to inform you about something. You need to be careful." He said, I thought his new girl had kept him really happy as he sounded peaceful. One girl took his peace, the other was restoring it.

"Yes, please. What is it?" I asked.

"I met Dipti, Dipti Ahuja. Remember her?" he confirmed.

"Yes, the one who joined with you?" I said.

"Ok. she had come to Goa. We were just talking about what is happening in our lives. I told her that I broke up with you and things could not materialize." he said and paused. I loved that pause, it showed that he still cherished those moments. And then he lied for that pause.

"Sorry, was drinking water." He did not want me to believe that he missed me, at times though!

"It's ok. Then what did she say?" I asked.

"She said that Vikas told her that you had been seeing some guy from your workplace and had been two timing with me. Since Vikas was not in touch with me, he told Ahuja so that she could warn me." Rama told the reason, was he going to discuss Thomas again? (Vikas is our batch mate who joined with me like Ahuja did with Rama, he was one

amongst those whom Rama hated from the core, Piyush types! He was a good friend of Dipti.)

"What?" I cited astonishment. "Then why didn't she warn you?"

"She said that I was so madly in love with you that she did not want any trouble by bringing this to my notice, she thought that time would tell me." he said.

"Wow, what a lame excuse!" I said.

"She needed Masala to discuss. See, I might have been an idiot to quarrel with you about Thomas, but the fact is that you were just good friends, I misread that. But the problem is that people like Vikas are spreading wrong things about you, which might not be good for you. The whole point is that if you are getting married and someone wants to do a background check on you and this Vikas bastard is ranting about your imaginative affair with Thomas, it just might not be good for you. So, you be careful. My job was to inform you. Two timing, that is the last thing expected from you. Bull shit." he spoke in length and gosh, what transformation! He was balanced now.

"Bye." he said abruptly.

"Thanks, I will take care." I did not know why I wanted the conversation to drag.

"It's ok. Bye!" he said again, the ever loyal Rama did not want his new chick to know that he spoke to me at length. Hence, he disconnected.

He still cared for me, even if he fought with me over Thomas, he could not digest that people spread rumours about me. The ever protective Rama, do I miss him?

It was last Sunday; I was making love with Thomas. Yes, the first confession is that I was dating Thomas and Vikas was true and did not cook up a story. Vikas cared for Rama and so did Dipti; it was only me who did not.

The relationship with Thomas had become slightly awkward for some months, he had changed the job and therefore, we could not meet frequently. Since I was treated by Rama like loyalty, my expectations were obviously higher and comparisons happened without fail. No man likes comparison.

Thomas would not meet me over week days, and would pick me up only on Friday night, and will only do, think and talk sex over the weekend. I enjoyed it initially, but resisted it later on. I knew that if it was Rama, he would ensure that I get dropped for work every morning and then picked up in the evening followed by dinner. I missed the importance. I called for it, so I lived with it.

I also came to know about Thomas dropping his female colleagues late at night and his flirtatious nature towards them. He even went out with them for lunches, I did not like it. I understand what Rama went through when I did it with Thomas.

Rama had begun to play in my mind a lot, he treated me like queen, and I had to tell this to Thomas clearly. So, the last Sunday, when Thomas was making love, (Oops, When he was having sex with me. It was Rama who made love with me) I said, "Thomas, I think we should get married now. This excessive sex will only make me mad."

Thomas did not pay attention and continued to fiddle with my bottom. I remember that how Rama would listen to me patiently whenever I objected during love making, but this guy only knew how to suck into me. I felt dejected, and I said, "Will you listen to me? Or is it only sex running in your mind? I also came to know that you have been dropping ladies late in the night and getting flirty with them at work. Do you get that?"

Thomas got up and said "What?" he never liked to be instructed or told something unlike Rama and I did not know why I accepted that behaviour.

"When are we marrying? I cannot do this forever, I will tell my Mama about you and I don't like that you get close with other girls." I told him.

"Listen, I will work it out. We will see what to do." He said trying to calm me down.

"I have been listening to the same shit for almost a year now." I raised my voice with Thomas, trying to be authoritative for the first time, which I did quite often with Rama and he accepted every damn thing.

Thomas did not like that, and said, for my shock, "I cannot marry you." and got up to wear his trousers.

I was nakedly frozen and my soul was shattered, "What? Why?" I lost temper.

"You are such a bitch! You ditched Rama for me who loved you crazily. What is the guarantee that you will not do the same with me?" he made pure sense for himself.

I persisted to look at him, trying to come to terms with what was happening, he said, "Even though he beat me, he did it for you. He loved you and you just dumped him like that. You are a slut and you can't be blabbering about me getting flirty with other women. Didn't you do the same with Rama?" he was taking my lessons on self-realization. Yes, I was a bitch, a slut.

"How dare you do like that? You cannot do this to me, I will teach you a lesson." I said even when I did not know what I was going to do to him. He knew that I was only speaking without saying anything.

He lit up a cigarette and said, "Fuck off and get lost!" and threw my bra on my face. I dressed silently, left his place and I have not spoken to him after that.

And yesterday, Rama called up. Life has its own ways of loving you and hating you; it does come a full circle. Poor Rama thinks that it was his screwed up luck that he could not be with me, he thinks that my mother is solely responsible for whatever happened, and my mother was at the knife point for the crimes I committed. What was I? A slimy bitch?

The day later I called up Rama during office hours, as he would be away from his girl.

"Hi, you gave Vikas your piece of your mind. Did you?" he still focussed on the Vikas's issue.

"Hmm" I said.

"What?" he said.

"You know what? Vikas is right." I said and waited for some emotion to generate.

"What? Come again, I did not get you." he said. I am sure he would have had a weird expression on his face.

"I said that whatever Vikas told Dipti about Thomas and me is true." I said that in one breath, thinking that what would Rama go through again.

He, as anticipated, disconnected the call, and after five minutes, called back, "Are you sure?" he was trying to recoup from the aftermath of mind blasting truth.

"Yes, in fact, I had some confessions to make." I was going to offer some more facts to Rama.

"Confession? What happened? All fine?" he sounded unfazed by what I told him, but he was pretending.

"I two timed with you Rama." I said in the lowest of voice.

"Ok. So, why are you telling this to me now? There is nothing between us. I called you up to tell you about Vikas because I thought it was important. It's ok. You will anyhow marry Thomas now? Easy at your place because he is a Christian, should be rich I guess." he tried mocking the conditions imposed on him. He had all the rights to do and say what he wanted, but why was he unmoved?

"No, I broke up with Thomas." I said with disappointment, yet contended.

"You broke up with him as well?" he said.

"But what is that you want to confess? Its ok, I am sure you moved on with him after the engagement was called off." he said. And just

when Rama's generosity was going over board, he behaved because his brain cells got activated.

"But why did you come back after Ranjan's visit to Goa?" the curiosity levels rose. I wanted that to happen as it would give me a platform to confess.

"You have been very nice Rama, I am not saying this because I want you to come back to me, and I know you won't but I wanted you to know a few facts. I can't live with those sins throughout my life; you were the biggest victim of whatever I did. I am your culprit. Let me just tell you." I said.

"Ok" he said, sounding sincere to know how he was screwed up.

"You know the first time you hit me because I took some time to get down from the car..." I began and he cut me short.

"Correction, I have hit you twice, and both the time for abusing my mother. Got that? I did not hit you because you took time to get down from the car." he said.

"Yes, you are correct. I narrated that story to Thomas the next day and he gave some advice and we became good friends. He was someone whom I could trust for his decent approach. Plus, I drifted away from you after you hit me." I said.

"Drifted? I never felt so." he said and I smiled.

"Then I went out with Thomas one day to one of the pubs here, I drank vodka and I puked and he took me to his home and I guess I was falling all over the place before I slept with him." I said.

"Hmmm" he said, his voice turning bleak.

"Remember you had called up that morning and I told you Cecilia was knocking on the toilet door? It was not Cecilia, it was Thomas." I said.

"Fuck, I wanted to ask you that but ignored." he said and showed disappointment.

"And it was not Mama who used to put conditions, I used to go and tell her the problems I faced with you, the issues I anticipated if I married you, that would turn into conditions and you always thought she was the mastermind." I said.

"What problems? Did you not want to marry me?" he asked.

"I wanted to but I began to like Thomas's company better than you, probably because he was physically present there. I am sorry." I said.

"You could have told me that. Why did you make me go through all the crap? Conversion, money savings and what not." he asked logical questions.

"I was scared. Scared of Mama as well, she would have killed me had I told her that I am dropping Rama and choosing somebody else. That is pure characterlessness." I said.

"So" he said.

"I wanted to bring you down in front of my parents, make it practically tough for you to marry me, that is why those insane targets of twenty five lakh wedding. Actually, I used to tell Mama that I wanted a lavish wedding and Rama should bear the expense as well. She put conditions on my behest." I paused to drink water.

I continued, "I always thought that you would automatically give up and then after a while, I will get Thomas into the picture."

"What was the scene when I had beaten him up?" he asked.

"We had just begun dating each other then and he used to tell me to get it resolved with you and he would not intervene." I clarified.

"What the fuck!" he said.

"And then why did you get ready for engagement and that hell lot of shopping? What was that for? That was unnecessary drama. So many people put into trouble." he asked more, he wanted to know more.

"You never picked up hints I gave to you that it was not working out, and you were pushing for the engagement and I had to do that to make you believe. Otherwise, you wouldn't have listened to me." I said.

"So, I was the one who told Mama that how wrong Rama was in not picking us up from the hotel and I encouraged their decision of dropping the visit to your place." I said.

"So, it is true that you guys did not start for our place and those stories of cab driver being ignorant of the routes were all fake." he confirmed.

"Yes" I said.

"But your parents should have been more sensible before calling it off." he said.

"That I don't know." I said.

"Shit. I am such an idiot. Shit man!" he cried silently. I didn't know if the agony of getting duped or the news of Thomas was hurting him.

"Then why the hell you came back last year after Ranjan visited Goa?" he was a question bank, but he had the right to know.

"I had a huge fight with Thomas over something and I broke up with him. Mama was pressurizing for marriage, So, I thought I would come back to you. I tried my luck and it worked, you had not moved on." I said.

"So, you mean to say that you are trying the same trick again? Had I not moved on now, it would have been easy for you to come back to me because you had a break up again?" he cross questioned.

"No, I told you in the beginning itself, please don't think like that. If that was the case, I wouldn't have confessed." I said.

"Hmmm. Right, then why did you go mad after coming from Tashkent. Hang on hang on, let me guess this. Thomas went with you to Tashkent, and sparks flew again between you guys. You got drunk again and slept with him, and then you realized that being with Thomas was easy and better. Right? So, I was a make shift arrangement for your emotions, basically you needed a shoulder to cry on." he made me feel small and creepy.

"Yes" I said shamelessly.

"aah..fuck... shit.. I am such an idiot, loser! I am so so so stupid. I could sense everything, yet I stuck to the relationship. Why did you do this to me?" he felt hopeless, he felt cheap, he felt disgusted, he felt that loving me was the worst thing he did.

"But what went wrong now with Thomas?" he still cared for me, he wanted my relation to work out with Thomas at least, he could sense that I was a loner now.

"Last Sunday, we had a huge fight and he said that if I could cheat on you, then why not him. So, he can't marry a girl like me. That is it. Anyways, you take care. Your new girl is really cute. Name is also nice, Richa. You are Rama and she is Richa. Both Rs, this should click for you. Bye." I said.

"Listen, its ok, whatever has happened has happened. You don't have to feel sorry for me; this was probably written in my fate. But anytime, any moment, you need any support, count on me. Why don't you come to Goa? It will be a welcome respite for you. I'll take you to good places, I'll speak to Richa, and she won't mind." he offered assistance and this is what I respected him for, always there for those he cared for.

"Obviously, she will mind. You haven't learnt your lessons properly. And I have been to Goa and seen the places." I said.

"When?" he asked.

"Just few weeks before the fake engagement day." I said sadly.

"With Thomas?" he asked.

"Yes" I said.

He said, "Good bye!" and disconnected.